PINK LIPS AND FINGERTIPS

A Lifelong Dream and the Faith to Find It

RICK WEBER

Blessings,

R.W.

IS 49:15-16

To Austin,
my precious son and constant companion.

Dream big, buddy.
Let God be your guide,
and never stop believing.

CONTENTS

CHAPTER 1

A FOOTBALL-SIZED HEART AND A MIRACLE

"You've got yourselves a miracle here."

Coming from the surgeon who performed the world's first successful human heart-lung transplant, those words took on a powerful aura, almost as if they had been spoken by God and piped through the speakers in the waiting room outside the Intensive Care Unit at Stanford Medical Center.

To the family and friends of Jeri Paholek, Dr. Bruce Reitz didn't seem to be the kind of guy who casually dispensed the word *miracle*. Although they knew he cared deeply for his patients, his approach was very professional. He was soft-spoken in his delivery and somewhat guarded in what he said. Theatrics were not his *modus operandi*. A miracle was indeed a miracle.

"Praise God," Carolyn said.

She raised her clasped hands to her forehead, closed her eyes for a moment and calmed her racing heart. Her hopeful, please-tell-me-something-good expression had turned into a serene smile.

"Yes," Junny said. "That's what we've been waiting to hear."

Junny gently put his arm around Carolyn's shoulder and pulled her close. After 38 years as husband and wife—and 35 as father and mother to Jeri—nothing needed to be said.

Junny knew Carolyn was chasing away that nagging fear with faith that Jeri would survive, if for no other reason than she always had survived. Carolyn wouldn't exhibit any demonstrative emotion, wouldn't say, "I'm so scared. Please hold me." There was no allowance for that. It was nothing but a positive attitude. *Believe. Pray. Fight. Win.*

Carolyn knew he was already pondering the next step in this wildly fluctuating story—what needed to be done now?—and that somehow he would lighten the mood, because that's what he always did.

Dr. Reitz saw the relief. The 15 sets of eyes that had been riveted on him were now relaxed. The prognosis had been given, the questions answered. With his latest State of Jeri briefing concluded, he turned and walked down the hall.

In an adjacent office, he dictated the operation report:

"NAME: Paholek, Jerami. DATE: 09/26/2003. FINDINGS: On opening the thoracic cavity, there was a large amount of blood in the left pleural cavity and minimal amounts in the right pleural cavity. PROCEDURE: The bleeding points were identified and dealt with with diathermy. The left and right thoracic cavities were thoroughly evacuated of all clot, and thorough inspection of all raw surfaces performed. Following thorough wash out of all 3 chest drains, and irrigation of the closed surfaces and mediastinal cavity, the lungs were then re-expanded fully to resolve areas of atelectasis. The patient was then returned to the North ICU in a much improved hemodynamic situation."

What were the odds that he would be able to write this kind of report? Or be able to stand in the waiting room and deliver that kind of news to sleep-deprived family and friends hanging by a thread, always anticipating his presidential entrance but never sure what it would mean?

Who gets a set of heart and lungs within eight hours of the failure of the first set of donor organs? Some patients were waiting a year or more to get their organs. Or never getting them at all—15 people were dying each day due to the shortage of all types of transplantable organs, and a new name was being added to the transplant waiting list every 18 minutes.

Kept alive by an Extra Corporeal Membrane Oxygenation (ECMO) machine—which literally was a temporary artificial lung and heart for Jeri—and given 24 hours to live without another transplant, she gets her second set of organs in less than a day? Dr. Reitz had been doing this for 22 years—ever since he made history in 1981, when he and Dr. Norman Shumway successfully transplanted a heart and lungs in 45-year-old advertising executive Mary Gohlke—and he had never seen two sets of matching organs in such a short period of time.

Forty-one hours earlier, Jeri had been a terminally ill patient who had been waiting only two months at Stanford for a heart-lung transplant—at 35, one of the oldest living Americans with primary pulmonary hypertension who had never had a transplant. Dr. Reitz had said that her chances of living this long without it had been less than 5%. She had been told that without it, she probably had a week to live. She kept it to herself, never telling her family, preferring not to add to the burden they were already feeling.

And deep inside her soul, maybe she believed that her renowned transplant team simply had it wrong. Her surgeons were looking at it from a clinical perspective, and she was looking at it from a God perspective. She knew her body was rapidly breaking down, but she had heard that kind of dire prognosis many times before.

Born with common ventricle—a rare disease in which the septum is entirely absent and the two ventricles merge to form a single chamber—she underwent surgery as a 17-month-old toddler, and nearly died. Common ventricle produced primary pulmonary hypertension (or Eisenmenger syndrome), a rare lung condition that would gradually destroy her organs. After that, she passed all the significant milestones that she wasn't expected to experience—her first day at school, Girl Scouts, her first date, high-school graduation, college graduation, marriage, all the way to being an adoptive mother in her 30s.

Her dire medical condition was full of twists and turns. Trips to a hospital emergency room for ventricular tachycardia were potentially serious—otherwise she wouldn't be going—but not quite to the extent that ER personnel might have thought.

She'd invariably be checked by doctors who did not know her and her story. They'd measure her oxygen saturation, see that it had registered at a dangerously low level and recoil in horror. *Code Blue! This woman is dying!*

"I'm fine," Jeri would say, reassuring them between gasps. "Really, I'm fine."

They'd look at Jeri's family members or friends, who would nod in agreement. "You don't know," her husband, Daryl, would say. "This is how she lives. She lives like this *every* day."

Back in 1995, Jeri had been listening to the radio and heard "Wonder" by Natalie Merchant, and said, "I think this song's for me." The lyrics describe how doctors have come from far and wide to stand in disbelief over the bed of a patient: *They say I must be one of the wonders of God's own creation, and as far as they see they can offer no explanation.*

How true with Jeri: They could not explain why she was getting off the examination table and walking out of the hospital after what she had come in for.

"We recommend that you don't walk," they'd say sternly.

"I was just at Six Flags AstroWorld yesterday," she'd say with a cute smirk.

They would have been even more shocked if she had told them everything, especially the part where she stood in the roller coaster line for 30 minutes, then walked right past the sign that read, "DO NOT go on this ride if you have a heart condition." Hey, at least she wore the lap bars and shoulder harness at all times.

She didn't have a death wish. It was quite the opposite—she wanted to live a long life to glorify God by leading others to Jesus Christ, and she wanted to experience all of the milestones in the life of her son, Brady. She just refused to be defined by her condition. And she refused to acknowledge that it was beating her, forcing her into submission, stealing her dreams.

She rebuffed suggestions from doctors that she should be in a wheelchair with an oxygen cylinder, and suggestions from friends that she should apply for a handicapped parking license. She couldn't walk a city block without getting a ride on Daryl's back or stopping to fill her lungs with air and let her heartbeat settle down, but as she viewed it, neither the wheelchair nor the license was designed for people like her. And she didn't want to be pegged as handicapped. No labels for Jeri. She didn't label people, nor did she want to be labeled.

So this 5-foot, 95-pound woman would pop open the trunk of her car, single-handedly wrestle with Brady's massive 38-pound Grayco stroller until she had it set up with him in it, push it into the mall and then prowl the aisles in search of a bargain.

She lived every day as a gift. She didn't worry about the things most people worry about. When her friends or family would phone her, she'd invariably be playing with Brady or watching him draw, enraptured by the way he filled in his circles, totally engrossed in the moment. It seemed to them that she was never vacuuming the carpet or dusting.

She was good to everyone, regardless of their status in life. She allowed God to love through her. She helped lonely people feel welcomed, appreciated, special. They were drawn magnetically to her and her distinctive laugh—a throaty, raspy concoction created by her weakened, oxygen-deprived lungs.

If it was true that life was an empty canvas, how would she fill it? With the bold strokes and brilliant colors of Picasso? Or with the precision and realism of Vermeer? She chose the bold strokes and brilliant colors.

In the years leading up to her transplants, she became increasingly bolder.

She was a borderline busybody, but because she did it with such compassion, she was allowed to get into everybody's business. Her thinking was, *I've found something, and you're nuts if you don't get into it.* She wasn't a classic evangelist witnessing on the street, but she wasn't afraid to approach anybody.

Jeri had a naivety, an innocence about how worldly things happened. She believed in humanity, that everybody had a soft side and any rough behavior they exhibited was just temporary, that all they needed was a dose of compassion and somebody to love. Even if people were dark, mean, cruel, selfish, it was just a matter of opportunity.

She believed in miracles—in physical healing, for sure, but even more so in the kind of miracles in which people were radically changed.

She used to tell her brother, Jayme, that if he was unhappy with anything in his life, he needed to just ask God to change it. This intrigued him because for so many years, she watched people pray for her tissue to be regenerated or for her heart to start working normally—specific things that never happened. And yet she believed. And not just believed, but believed strongly, unwaveringly.

She noticed that a lot of people were emotionally affected by what they saw around them—a Down syndrome kid with no friends, a homeless man, a person contemplating suicide, a family torn apart by divorce—but did nothing about it. *Enough talk*, she'd think. *I'm going to create some action here.*

And so it was that she wrote to Timothy McVeigh after he was sentenced to death for his role in the bombing of the Alfred P. Murrah Federal Building in Oklahoma City that killed 168 people.

Sure, he appeared to have hardened his heart: He had written, "If I'm going to hell, I'm gonna have a lot of company." But maybe he hadn't heard the gospel explained in a way that would reach him. Maybe he needed to hear about forgiveness, salvation and eternal life. Why was everybody so quick to write him off? Why weren't more people praying that he would receive Christ?

Then there was the time she drove to a downtown Houston courthouse to counsel an incarcerated 17-year-old girl appearing before a judge in a bid to have an abortion.

She believed strongly in the sanctity of life. Wasn't anybody going to fight for that baby's right to live? Maybe that girl had encountered nothing but condemnation and ridicule. Maybe she thought she had no other options. Jeri was prepared to tell that girl that she'd adopt the baby.

And then there was September 11, 2001, the day America came to a standstill in the aftermath of an incomprehensible act of terrorism.

All around her, Jeri saw people sitting in stunned silence in front of their TVs. Each minute brought a new revelation and more intense heartache. But nobody was doing anything. Jeri imagined that there were a lot of people out there who were overcome with grief, sadness, even anger, but had no way to express it or were too embarrassed or afraid to express it.

And so she and Brian Smith, the youth pastor at Grace Fellowship United Methodist Church in the Houston suburb of Katy, went out to the busiest road in Katy and set up a stand with a sign that read, simply, NEED PRAYER?

She didn't just approach infamous inmates or leap into action after devastating national tragedies.

She prayed and witnessed to ordinary people in ordinary circumstances because she believed in the Great Commission. She wouldn't be able to enter a mission field in the 10/40 Window that contains the largest population of non-Christians in the world, but she could go out and "preach everywhere," wherever that was, as the disciples had done in Mark 16:20 in response to Jesus' call. It was why Liz Jok, a friend and fellow Grace Fellowship member, called her a "modern-day female Paul."

Jeri participated in a "play group" consisting of mothers and children from the Cinco Ranch area of Katy, and they met regularly. One was Jewish. A few weren't attending any church. For some of them, thriving in their upscale enclave, materialism occupied the forefront.

It would have been much easier to stay within the confines of Grace Fellowship, but she considered her group to be a ministry, and she took it seriously. Things sometimes got catty, and sometimes they challenged Jeri's beliefs, but she never gave up on them.

She never gave up on anything.

Never gave up on people. And never gave up on herself.

In her small group at church, she let it be known in 2002 that one of her greatest desires was to have normal tone in her extremities. Because her blood was deficient in oxygen, her skin and mucous membranes had a bluish tinge—it was most obvious in her fingertips, toes and lips. "Please pray for pink lips and fingertips," she'd say. And they would.

She didn't want "pink lips and fingertips" because she was embarrassed. It was because pink always had been her favorite color—she'd frequently be seen in a pink top, khaki capris and flip-flops.

One day late in 2002, she was shopping with Lisa Leggett, a close friend and the wife of Grace Fellowship pastor Jim Leggett, at Town & Country Village in Houston. Browsing through Gap Body, they came across a perfume called "So Pink." They noticed it had the pleasing scents of grapefruit, jasmine, lily and orange, but they would have bought it even if it smelled like the dumpster outside of neighboring Escalante's, their favorite restaurant. It was all about Jeri. It was all about pink.

If she had pink extremities, then that meant her primary pulmonary hypertension had been reversed, that her extremities were getting the oxygen they needed. There was deep symbolism there.

The only way she could be pink would be to have a heart-lung transplant.

And so it was that she ended up at Stanford Medical Center.

And so it was that Dr. Reitz removed her damaged heart and said, "It's the biggest heart I've ever seen," perhaps not realizing that it was true figuratively as well as literally.

And so it was that she needed another set of heart and lungs, because the donor organs were not working.

And so it was that she received them, and the surgery worked, and Carolyn went into her room, gazed in awe at her exposed hand and whispered, "Jeri, you have pink lips and fingertips." When Jeri tried to rise from the bed, Carolyn said, "Honey, that's OK. You can see them later." And then Daryl whispered in her ear, "I love you. You'll be out soon." And he felt her squeezing his finger and could see her mouthing out the words, "I love you."

And so it was that there were complications with excessive bleeding and she had to have a third operation, and Dr. Reitz delivered the "miracle" quote that inspired elation.

This was a story that reached around the nation and even the world.

In Katy, one of Jeri's best friends, Katie Dolan, sat in front of her computer. She had been receiving regular updates from Jim Leggett and posting them on a CaringBridge Web site that had been created for Jeri by her brother-in-law, Taylor Delleney, and jump-started by the posts of her sister, Amy.

The news had been devastatingly bad: *Jeri's new lungs are working well. However, her new heart is not pumping on its own. Pray for her new heart, that it would start working.*

It had been miraculous: *They have found another set of organs for Jeri and are planning on operating at 10 p.m. CT.*

Then uplifting: *Praise God. Jeri is out of her second surgery and her new heart is BEATING ON ITS OWN. God, we praise you and thank you for getting Jeri through the night and ask for complete healing for Jeri today.*

Then troubling: *The doctors are going to operate to drain blood from Jeri's chest and to determine where it is coming from. The blood is not allowing her lungs to inflate completely. Jeri is still in critical condition. Pray for continued healing.*

Now Katie had more news. Great news. Her fingers moved slowly across the keys, tears of joy filling her eyes.

Jeri is out of surgery and everything went well. Her chest is free of blood and the bleeding has stopped. Our ongoing prayer is that her body would accept these organs as her own. That she continue to heal and be strengthened. After operating, the doctor came out of the OR and said, "You've got yourselves a miracle here." We knew that already! Thank you, God, for protecting Jeri.

She placed her cursor on ADD GUESTBOOK ENTRY and clicked once.

In the city of Miri on the island of Borneo in Malaysia, Josephine Kho sat in front of her computer, riveted to the updates. She didn't know Jeri. Hadn't even met her. But she was a friend of the Joks—they had met in 1994 and attended the SIB Church (Sidang Injil Borneo, or Borneo Evangelical Mission).

Josephine had been the first person to help Liz truly understand the Body of Christ—that we're all brothers and sisters in Christ. So when Josephine had interceded for Jeri, she hadn't been interceding for a stranger. She had been interceding for a sister.

Josephine had heard the call for prayer. She had seen those prayers answered in miraculous fashion. She had invested in this unfolding drama at Stanford. And now, 47 minutes after Katie's post, she felt compelled to reach out to Jeri from the other side of the earth.

Praise and glory to our God. Indeed He is awesome. Even reading the forwarded e-mails brings tears to my eyes. It's wonderful just to be in this BIG family of God. He is faithful. Will continue to pray for Jeri.

She placed her cursor on ADD GUESTBOOK ENTRY and clicked once.

In Katy, Deb Hubble sat in front of her computer. She didn't count herself among Jeri's closest friends, but Brady and her daughter, Claire, had gone to the same pre-school and were teammates in a YMCA T-Ball league. During practices and games over a period of months, Jeri shared with Deb her growing belief that a transplant was the only thing that could save her.

Deb had told people, "I don't believe you'll find someone like her ever again." Deb admired Jeri's heartfelt trust in God and her strength in keeping her life devoid of negativity, despite the trauma and hardship she had experienced.

Deb had read the posts. It appeared Jeri had come through, and she felt an overwhelming sense of relief. And now, 17 minutes after Josephine's post, she communicated to Jeri in the only way she could.

Your spiritual and physical journeys are an inspiration to us all. We all rush to our computers and answering machines upon return from anywhere, hoping to learn more good news about you. Tom and I and all the little "Hubsters" have been thinking and talking about you constantly. We all love you and can't wait to celebrate your return home.

She placed her cursor on ADD GUESTBOOK ENTRY and clicked once.

At Stanford, the epicenter of the news, they had no idea how this was impacting others—no idea that since the news had broken that donor organs were available, there had been 104 posts. Portland, Oregon . . . Calgary, Canada . . . Panama City, Florida . . . Kuala Lumpur, Malaysia . . . Baton Rouge, Louisiana.

All they knew was that this waiting game wasn't so bad now. Yes, after 35 years, her family had earned a doctorate in The Science of Waiting Rooms, but Dr. Reitz had created a buzz they had never before experienced during those interminable periods. Positive energy was carrying them now.

They reflected back on how far they had come in just 24 hours. How far Jeri had come. How far the Lord had brought them.

"This is the first day of the rest of her life," Carolyn said. "Maybe she'll have her own baby some day. Anything's possible, right? Running, exercising?"

"Running's a big deal for her," Jayme said. "She's always wanted to run and jog and train. And to be involved in Brady's sports with him."

"She looks great, doesn't she?" Carolyn said.

"Yeah," Jayme said, "there's a real sense of peace on her face."

Just after 6 p.m., their joy was shattered.

Jeri's kidneys were not functioning.

CHAPTER 2

AN APPARENTLY ORDINARY BIRTH

They called it The Land of the High Skies. If you stood on the outskirts of Snyder, Texas, in the table-top-flat desert farmland dotted with scrub mesquite, it seemed as if all you could see was sky. It opened up into an azure canopy, and, at night—unspoiled by the glare of bright lights—a canvas of constellations.

The hot, dry days occasionally were punctuated by sandstorms that left grit stuck between your teeth. Thunderstorms moved through, releasing a fresh scent that temporarily overpowered the stench of gas being burned off in the oilfields and the pungent smell of the cotton gin—which fell somewhere in between diesel fumes and a pile of burning leaves—as it worked round the clock to separate the cotton lint from the seeds.

The oil boom had cratered in 1951, but a decade and a half later, Scurry County was still the leading oil-producing county in Texas, inspiring the county seat's slogan, "Where The Cattle Grow and the Oil Flows."

Snyder had a population of about 10,000, but it had the feel of a town much smaller. If you received a parking ticket or were stopped by police, the news likely would beat you home.

For young adults, cruising was the core of existence, an activity that was equal parts strategy and science. They'd circle the courthouse square, honking incessantly at each other, then head south on the Big Spring Highway for two miles, trying to beat the stop light in a bid to reach the Highlander drive-in restaurant, where they'd park under the awning and wait for the car hop to come out and take the order. Or they'd stay on the main drag and head past the Canyon drive-in theater to Towle Memorial Park, where they'd do the one-mile loop around the duck pond and swimming pool, then head back to town.

On an unusually cool late October night in 1964, 22-year-old Junny Ivison found himself in a four-door '28 Buick at the stop light near the Highlander. A Thunderbird pulled up next to Junny's Al Capone car.

"You want to run that thing?" Junny said to the occupants, Linda Hayes and Carolyn Hall.

"Hey, take us ridin'!" Linda said.

When the light turned green, Junny pulled to the side of the road and the women piled in, Linda on the front bench and Carolyn in the rear, next to the passenger-side window that had no glass.

Junny had known Linda, the sister of his former classmate and buddy, Larry Hayes. It was through her that he met Carolyn the week before at a party at the house of his friend, Ronald Brewer. He was intrigued by Carolyn and wasn't at all intimidated by the fact that she was four years older.

After traversing the drag one time, Junny said, "Maybe we'd better let Carolyn in the middle, 'cause she's probably freezing." For the next few hours, the three of them—squeezed into a four-foot-wide bench—did the drag. When the women were ready to call it a night, Junny offered to drive Carolyn home, and she accepted.

With the spark ignited, they started dating.

They made for a very sharp couple. Junny had jet-black hair, hazel eyes and a 28-inch waist, and wore starched shirts and the black glasses made popular by Buddy Holly, who had grown up 87 miles away in Lubbock. Carolyn had dark brown hair with blond highlights—teased meticulously into a six-inch bouffant—along with hazel eyes and glasses with rectangular frames.

They'd go out to Jerry Hatfield's sweet shop, where Junny would hop up onto the ice-cream cooler with his guitar and sing "That'll Be the Day," "Peggy Sue" or other Holly classics. Or they'd go out to the field across from the airport and chase freakishly large jackrabbits with their car.

Or maybe they'd just cruise, tuning in to KOMA, a 50,000-watt powerhouse Oklahoma City radio station that featured an irresistible invitation every hour on the hour: "Stand by! For the Kissing Tone on K-O-M-A! When you hear the Kissing Tone, if you're a loyal KOMA listener, kiss . . . your . . . sweetheart!" Carolyn and Junny kissed on their second date. After that, they didn't need to be prompted by the Kissing Tone.

The romance blossomed more quickly than either could have imagined.

Junny loved her quiet, sweet, relaxed nature and the openness with which she expressed her feelings for him. And, of course, her spirituality—she sang in the choir at Colonial Hill Baptist Church. After the Sunday service, they'd hop in her white, four-door '63 Chevy and make the 70-mile drive to her grandparents' house in Stamford, where she had been born.

Carolyn was drawn to Junny's genuineness. He treated her with the ultimate respect. He didn't try to woo her with a lexicon of slick pickup lines—which was a very good thing, because she would have brushed him off the way she did the guys who tried them on her.

Carolyn's father loved Junny, even if he didn't eloquently express it. And Junny's mother adored Carolyn. One night after a late date, Junny took Carolyn home only to find that her mother had locked her out. Junny shrugged and took her to his parents' house.

"Mother," he said, eyeing her from just outside her bedroom door, "Carolyn got locked out of her house and she's goin' to spend the night with us."

"I'll scoot over," his mother said, "and she can just come on and get in bed."

Junny was a mechanic in an auto-repair shop and was preparing to head back to the University of Texas-Arlington. Carolyn was a receptionist at Humble Oil and had made plans to move to Midland, where it was relocating. Junny didn't want to lose her. It terrified him to think she might meet someone else, but he kept it to himself and didn't reveal his true feelings, obeying the macho male creed.

When the topic finally was broached, Carolyn decided to go with Junny to Arlington. They were engaged January 19, 1965, and moved to Arlington a week later. She landed a job in the personnel department at TXI Cement. He drove a yellow British-style double-decker bus at Six Flags Over Texas. All they really needed was each other's company—Carolyn would sit in the seat directly behind him and ride the bus for hours in the evenings, just to be close to him.

They were married March 26, 1965, in Snyder, with her Baptist minister, Miller Robinson, presiding over the service at his Methodist church.

Life was simple, and it was good. One weekend, Junny grabbed the mattress out of their Arlington apartment, rolled it up, stashed it in the back seat of her '63 Chevy and they drove to Turner Falls Park in the Arbuckle Mountains of south-central Oklahoma. They spent the night on that mattress, soon discovering that tarantulas were part of the bucolic park's ecosystem. When their terror had sufficiently subsided, they laughed uproariously. They loved to laugh. Laughter soothed the soul.

They had talked frequently about having a baby. She wanted children that had curly eyelashes like Junny's. He wasn't in a big rush, but Carolyn was feeling a sense of urgency as she approached 30.

Late in 1967, Carolyn missed a few days of work with what she thought was a nasty virus. Bowls of potato soup didn't ease the nausea that had gripped her body. She endured that feeling for weeks. Then, in January, she found out why: She was pregnant.

In March, they moved to a new apartment and made the nursery the focal point of everything in their lives, picking the colors, the cabinetry, the carpet. Junny, who was a receiving clerk at ARA Manufacturing—which made automobile air conditioning units—used the equipment to make Peanuts characters and the paint booth to give them a glossy finish.

Boy or girl? Their intuition told them it'd be a boy—they even felt comfortable enough to call it a "he"—but the sex really didn't matter. Carolyn just wanted a healthy baby—and she wanted it quickly. The nausea was wearing on her. After fainting one day at work, she was told by her doctor, Bryant Manning, that she was iron-deficient. "Eat a big steak," he told her. She meticulously approached her role as a future mother, never touching alcohol. The pregnancy was normal and the fetus seemed to be fine. That was the good news.

Carolyn was due on September 1, but her doctor had an idea: Why not induce labor on August 28? Then the child wouldn't have to wait an extra year to begin school. Great idea, but three days of inducing didn't get them any closer to delivery.

On September 1, they went to a furniture store and walked . . . and walked . . . and walked. At 4 a.m., she woke Junny. It was time.

Twelve hours later, appropriately on Labor Day, she delivered a 7-pound, 6-ounce girl at Arlington Memorial Hospital. Carolyn didn't remember any of the excruciating pain—only the sight of her daughter a few hours later when they brought her in.

The baby was dressed in a white shirt and wrapped in a blanket. She had an olive tint to her skin—not at all like any baby Carolyn had ever seen. She had brown eyes and dark hair, with Junny's hairline.

Her name was Jerami Ayn Ivison. She would be known as Jeri. Carolyn had wanted a unique name that that started with a J (after Junny) and ended with an "i" (something she had always liked). They liked Ann for a middle name, but decided to spell it after Russian-born novelist and screenwriter Ayn Rand because Carolyn had noticed Junny reading her classic, *The Fountainhead*, for a college course.

Could Carolyn adequately express to anyone—even Junny—how much in love she was with this baby? As a young girl, she turned her father's backyard storeroom into a playhouse. She played with dolls like most other girls, but she did it with undeterred passion and exquisite gentleness that her family had never seen. Her moments in that playhouse were pastel portraits. She was an imaginary mother with an extraordinary mothering instinct. No one was going to tell her that those rubber-bodied toys were just *dolls*.

Carolyn gazed at Jeri and felt a profound sense of love that she couldn't describe, didn't try to describe. Carolyn glowed. Not just because of Jeri, but because the nauseous curtain had been mercifully lifted. Her skin took on the sensation of renewal, of previously unimagined softness. She felt like a new person. A new person with a new baby.

With renewed energy, Carolyn poured her heart into caring for Jeri. Junny was impressed not only that Carolyn never seemed to tire, but that she loved every minute.

There was hardly a movement Jeri made that was not noticed and mentally stored away. Carolyn's attentiveness amazed Junny, and sometimes concerned him, but it wasn't like he was going to complain. Complain about *what? Too* much love?

In Ecclesiastes 3, Solomon wrote: *There is a time for everything, and a season for every activity under heaven. A time to be born and a time to die.* God had taken them into an incredible season. His perfect timing had delivered the perfect gift. How could they ever be thankful enough? A new life stretched out before them.

Of course, reality did hit Junny in the face once in awhile. The Playtex bottles with the plastic sac had to be prepared, which he'd do. The dirty diapers had to be changed, which he didn't do. His excuse was that he wouldn't be able to meet her exacting standards. Carolyn admitted that he probably was right.

At night when Carolyn would check on Jeri, she sometimes noticed a slight humming sound. Was she OK? Carolyn weighed all the positives—Jeri never had any difficulty breathing, her skin color was fabulous, she never had bouts of sustained crying and her mood was fabulous—and her concern gradually filtered away.

They noticed early on that it didn't take much to make Jeri laugh. Junny would entertain her with the same Gretsch guitar he had played for his friends and Carolyn, but he ditched the Buddy Holly songs in favor of folk and children's music for Jeri.

He'd put her in her infant seat in the living room and start out by singing, *There's a hole in the middle of the sea.* She'd smile. He'd add to the verse, singing, *There's a log in the hole in the middle of the sea.* She'd start to giggle and shake her hands. By the time he got to the last verse—*There's a flea on the wing on the fly on the frog on the bump on the log in the hole in the middle of the sea*—she'd be laughing and gyrating wildly.

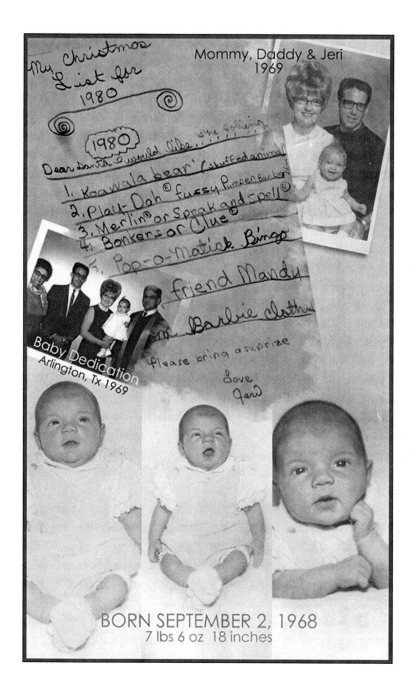

My Christmas List for 1980

Mommy, Daddy & Jeri
1969

(1980)

Dear Santa, I would like...the following

1. Koawala bear (stuffed animal)
2. Plaet-Doh® fuzzy Pumper Barber®
3. Merlin® or Speak and Spell®
4. Bonkers or Clue
5. Pop-o-Matick Bingo

6. friend Mandy

7. Barbie clothes

Please bring a suprize

Love
Jeri

Baby Dedication
Arlington, Tx 1969

BORN SEPTEMBER 2, 1968
7 lbs 6 oz 18 inches

27

Later that year, Junny's brothers, Allie and Deel, who owned a rapidly growing automotive business in the Oklahoma City suburb of Yukon, called to offer him a job. Carolyn and Junny decided to travel there to talk about the job and investigate the area. They had the right car for the trip: a brand new '68 Oldsmobile 98 two-door hardtop with a 425-cubic-inch Super Rocket V8.

On the way there, Jeri was playing with some plastic keys when the chain came apart. They heard a choking sound coming from the back seat. Carolyn was frantic, but Junny said, "Pull it out slowly so it won't cut her throat." Carolyn held Jeri's mouth open, found the end of the chain and gently pulled it out, her hands trembling.

When they arrived in Oklahoma City, they found themselves in the middle of a fierce sandstorm unlike anything they had ever seen. Junny pulled off Interstate 35 and wheeled his Oldsmobile 98 up to the pump at a Mobil station.

"Does the wind blow like this all the time?" he asked the attendant.

"Well, no sir," the attendant replied, "every once in awhile, it stops and blows the other way."

That was enough for them. Junny paid for the gas, put the 98 in gear and headed south on I-35. They never saw his brothers.

Back in Texas, Carolyn took a job as assistant manager of her parents' apartment complex, Midway Gardens, in Grand Prairie. She relished the opportunity because she wouldn't have to take a job that would require her to leave Jeri—her main task was to answer the phones.

When Jeri was about eight weeks old, Carolyn noticed while changing her diapers and holding her that her heart seemed to be beating abnormally hard and fast. At a checkup, she asked Dr. Manning about it and he said, "Baby's hearts beat fast." She did some research and learned that their heartbeats are almost twice as fast as those of adults.

On December 24, they took Jeri in for her shots. When one of Dr. Manning's associates checked her with a stethoscope, he discovered a heart murmur. Carolyn and Junny were concerned, but not panicked. Her brother, Mike Hall, had a heart murmur and grew out of it without any complications—something they attributed to God's healing power, something that could happen to Jeri. Besides, Dr. Manning didn't recommend any action be taken.

Jeri looked and acted like a normal baby over the months that followed in 1969. She had a happy disposition, seldom fussed or cried—even when she was dropped off at the church nursery. As long as she was around people, she was content.

They did notice something unusual: She never crawled. Jeri would sit on her bottom, dig in her heels and scoot wherever she wanted to go.

Her first words were, "Hah-ooh, hah-ooh." Carolyn and Junny had no idea what it meant, but Jeri found great significance in it, repeating it in every circumstance, waving to illustrate her point.

When she did learn to walk, she was taught not to get into things on the coffee table or end tables. She dutifully obeyed. Of course, she had a stimulating environment with parents who oversaw every stage of her development. Carolyn and Junny celebrated every milestone with joy.

In late December, Jeri started developing bronchitis. They put her in a hot shower and gave her steam treatments, but she was still struggling and her lips had turned blue. At 5 o'clock one morning in early January, they took her to Arlington Memorial Hospital. She was treated in an oxygen tent and admitted.

X-rays showed it had turned into pneumonia. Beyond that, there was concern that the heart murmur might be causing blood to flood the vessels in the lungs, resulting in her respiratory problems. Dr. Manning's associate recommended they take Jeri to Fort Worth pediatric cardiologist Andrew Megarity, so she was released and they took her straight to him.

When they met Dr. Megarity, they were struck by his warm, welcoming eyes and a deep, resonant voice that belied his 5-foot-8 stature. He seemed very knowledgeable. They felt they could trust him.

After Dr. Megarity did an EKG, he told them, "We need further tests. We need to do a cardiac catheterization."

When they took Jeri to Harris Hospital in mid-January 1970, the first thing they were asked to do was sign a medical waiver form that graphically spelled out the danger: She could die from this procedure, which was only being pioneered at that time. It would be the first of many catheterizations. And each time, Carolyn and Junny said a silent prayer before pushing the pen across the blank line at the bottom of the page. They would never get used to that feeling.

In the procedure, a thin tube (catheter) was inserted into an artery in Jeri's arm and guided to the chambers of her heart or into the coronary arteries. It was designed to measure the blood pressure within the heart and the amount of oxygen in the blood, in addition to taking pictures that offered clues about the pumping ability of the heart muscle.

After the catheterization, they waited a few days for the results. Dr. Megarity gathered them in his office and gave them the news they had dreaded: It was much worse than a heart murmur.

She had been living all her life with a ventricular septal defect (VSD) called common ventricle. Her septum was entirely absent, meaning the two ventricles came together to form a single chamber. Normally, the right ventricle sends all of its blood to the lungs to get oxygen, and the left ventricle sends all of its newly oxygenated blood to the body. But her two blood flows were being mixed.

It wasn't anything Carolyn had done or not done during her pregnancy. It was just a congenital defect that probably resulted from errors in the development of the embryo.

At some point, if she lived, Jeri would develop primary pulmonary hypertension (or Eisenmenger syndrome), a rare lung disorder in which the blood pressure in the pulmonary artery rises dramatically above normal levels. Dr. Megarity explained that the pulmonary artery is a blood vessel that carries oxygen-poor blood from the right ventricle to the lungs, where the blood picks up oxygen and moves to the heart's left side, where the left ventricle pumps it to the rest of the body through the aorta.

Hypertension meant an abnormally high blood pressure. Changes in the small blood vessels in the lungs would increase the resistance to blood flowing through them. The constricted vessels would cause her heart to work harder than normal to move enough blood through her lungs. In response to that, the right side of her heart would begin to enlarge.

The blood supply could begin to bypass the lungs altogether and go from the right side of the heart to the left side, and then out of the system. So the blood wouldn't be getting rid of carbon dioxide and picking up the oxygen it needed from the lungs, because the lungs were being bypassed. It would turn her extremities blue, stunt her growth, give her shortness of breath and gradually begin to kill her other organs.

Dr. Megarity then gave them the worst news of all: There was no known surgery or treatment to repair the problem. Medical science would have to catch up. In the meantime, they needed to perform major surgery to put a band on the pulmonary artery to slow the flow of blood and relieve the pressure, and also to close the patent ductus (which was supposed to have closed at birth).

Carolyn and Junny sat there, stunned and silent, gripped with the fear of losing her. Nothing in their lives had prepared them for this moment.

They knew that in the spiritual realm of their lives, there was only one thing they could do: Pray and turn Jeri over to God.

They turned to their church, First United Methodist in Arlington. It was as if Pastor Jack Payne had been put in their path for this moment. His son had suffered from a less severe heart ailment but had nearly died in ICU after the surgery. Pastor Jack took them into his arms, as did the entire congregation. Carolyn and Junny had harbored the perception that perhaps they were a simple, inelegant couple in a dynamic, upscale 800-member church, but they would never think that again.

They had many prayer warriors at work, but nobody was closer to their heart than Junny's sister, Oma James, and his mother, Adron Ivison.

Adron, who had been praying for Jeri since her birth from her home in Snyder, was committed to always living the Christian life, not just when it was convenient. She prayed regularly, seeking the quiet time in which she could hear God speak to her.

Oma felt that power. She believed it was an honor to serve God in the capacity that He called—that's what a servant's heart was all about. There was no time to think of it in any other way. The focus was on the target. And the target was victory. She knew there was no way she could comprehend everything that happens, but that victory was there for those who trusted Him and made Him the ultimate power in their lives—not an additive, but the source.

For her, that calling was intercessory prayer. She was well on her way to a glorious season of her life in which she would attend training sessions and seminars on intercessory prayer and serve as prayer leader and coordinator for many groups.

And so when Carolyn called with the news, Oma did what she would do on many occasions as Jeri's life unfolded. With her children at school and her husband at work, she would sit down at the kitchen table with one of her three Bibles. She would go to the Word and allow the Holy Spirit to give her the Scripture to pray for and believe, and then intercede until she felt like God had taken care of that. She would write the passages on a small notepad, send them to Carolyn and Junny and pray with them over the telephone.

"The Lord is giving us grace," Carolyn told him one night, "because I'm not freaking out."

There were moments of weakness. Not every day was filled with unwavering strength and courage. One day, Carolyn was pulling into their apartment complex, located next to a Wal-Mart. A thought went through her mind: *I want a professional portrait in case she doesn't survive.* So she dressed Jeri in one of her cutest outfits and took her to Wal-Mart's studio. As she enthusiastically coaxed Jeri to smile, Carolyn looked like a jubilant mother. But inside, her soul cried out, *God, please save her.*

Carolyn was pregnant with her second child.

And wondering if her first child would live to see the birth.

CHAPTER 3

WOULD SHE LIVE?

The morning of February 5, 1970, dawned just like any other. But Carolyn and Junny knew the day would turn out to be like no other.

It hadn't been a restful night for Carolyn. She was weakened by the same nausea that had plagued her during Jeri's pregnancy. She knew it would disappear when she delivered her second child in October. But what about the guilt she was carrying around like an anvil? When would that disappear?

She kept thinking, *What did I do to cause this?* The doctors hadn't said anything that contributed to her guilt. She knew the heart was completely formed in the fetus at eight weeks, so she hadn't done anything physically to cause Jeri's common ventricle. It was a congenital defect. Plain and simple.

She believed that one day, medical science would catch up and there would be a way to repair her heart, or that God would heal Jeri without the intervention of medical science. And yet she kept asking God, *Why couldn't it be me and not her?* Prayer warriors were at work, commanding Satan to stop his attack on her psyche.

Carolyn and Junny loaded Jeri into their 1962 Chevrolet station wagon—they recently had traded the 98 to his brother, Tommy, because they could no longer make the payments—and headed for Fort Worth Children's Hospital. Carolyn hoped they wouldn't pass any cemeteries—they unnerved her because of her fear that Jeri might not live much longer. The late-afternoon sun was fading fast. Maybe darkness would spare her from seeing any tombstones.

Junny knew she hadn't revealed to him all the thoughts churning inside. He didn't press her. What could possibly be the result other than unnecessary tension? He knew she left her burdens unexpressed because she didn't want to hurt those she loved, didn't want them to become mired in the same quagmire.

His gift was the ability to transform those serious, introspective times with tension-releasing chatter. If he had been blessed with enough hands to play his Gretsch guitar while driving, he would have done it. Instead, he made Carolyn and Jeri laugh most of the way to the hospital. The calm in the storm. That was Junny.

When they reached the hospital, they walked past the statue with the sign that read, WISH A CHILD WELL, and into the lobby, where they were indoctrinated into a community that would be a part of them for the rest of their lives. To kill time that night, they went to a playroom that was decorated in bright colors and fabulously stocked with games and toys. They pulled Jeri around in a wagon, delighting in her laughter. She acted as if nothing was wrong. But around them, they saw other children who appeared to be struggling with much more debilitating conditions. Some had outward deformities. Others appeared to be mentally impaired.

The next morning, hospital personnel came to get Jeri. They placed her in a baby bed with stainless-steel rails and, along with Carolyn and Junny, made the underground tunnel trip to neighboring Harris Hospital.

"Mommy will be right here," Carolyn said, caressing Jeri's cheek.

Flanked by a nurse on either side, Jeri lay in the bed, clutching Kitty—her favorite stuffed toy, a tiny kitten with lifelike white fur. As they rolled her away, she looked over her shoulder, smiling at

Carolyn and Junny. They choked back the tears, waving and smiling until she was out of view.

They looked at each other, thinking the same thing: *She's braver than we are. She's teaching us how to be courageous.* She was one young girl who never had to be reminded of the story of Joshua—how God spoke to him, telling him to be strong, and not terrified or discouraged, because God would be with him wherever he went; how God empowered him to lead the Israelites miraculously across the Jordan River; how they conquered Canaan and cleared out the wickedness.

Carolyn and Junny knew they were not great military leaders who were going to drive out evil nations. They didn't have to be. They just needed to rely on their faith that God would be with them wherever they went. They needed to be strong. Just like Jeri.

While they waited, Junny's thoughts drifted back to a pre-operation meeting earlier in the week with Clive Johnson, the surgeon recommended by Dr. Megarity. Dr. Johnson—who had thick, bushy eyebrows and a countenance that made him look like former Roy Rogers sidekick Gabby Hayes—seemingly downplayed the seriousness of the surgery. In his rich, rural Texas accent, he told them, "These kids come out of it with tubes attached to their body, and they're jumpin' up and down on the mattress."

Why did he say that? Junny thought. *To make us more relaxed?* Dr. Megarity was more of a realist, Dr. Johnson more of an optimist. Which approach was better? Confronting Jeri's mortality after just 17 months caused unanticipated pain, callously trampling the memories they had of a picture-perfect birth. But at the same time, they didn't want to sugar-coat the scenario. They were walking a tight rope.

In the operating room, Dr. Johnson started the incision near Jeri's breastbone and continued under her armpit and up to her shoulder blade. He inserted the band around the pulmonary artery, slowing down the pressure of the blood flow, and closed her up.

After three hours, he came out to meet Carolyn and Junny. The surgery, from a technical standpoint, had gone well. But she would be transferred to ICU to recover.

Hours passed before they could see her. When they finally were admitted, they couldn't have been prepared for what they saw: She was wrapped in bandages and a pink blanket, with a maze of tubes extending from her body to machines by her bed.

They were hit broadside by the reality: This was not the same deal as Carolyn's brother's heart murmur. It would not heal unobtrusively over time. They would see the scar and be reminded of her condition every day for as long as she lived.

"Mommy and daddy are here for you," Carolyn said, kissing her cheek and gently caressing her hand.

"We love you, Pill," Junny said. Pill was a nickname Junny's older brother, Allie, had given him when they were boys, and Junny had transferred that over to Jeri.

They were only allowed to visit with her briefly every four hours that first day. Carolyn and Junny camped in the waiting room, where they were given pillows and blankets.

The next morning, Junny went back to Climatic Air in downtown Dallas, where he worked in parts and shipping. It pained him to leave Carolyn and Jeri behind, but they were in increasingly troubling financial condition, and he couldn't miss much more time because he had no sick leave or benefits. Carolyn drew strength from a visit by Pastor Jack and his wife, who prayed with her.

Later that day, Dr. Megarity came out of Jeri's room after evaluating her and said, "Mrs. Ivison, she's not doing well." Her blood pressure had skyrocketed and her breathing was irregular.

Jeri continued to spiral downward. On the third day, Dr. Johnson said they were going to send her back to Fort Worth Children's Hospital so that "she can be with her parents." Carolyn and Junny took that to mean they were giving up on her, that medically her chances were not good, so the best option would be to give them 24 hours a day with Jeri for as long as she lived. Or maybe being with Carolyn and Junny would transform Jeri's condition.

The first day together was not what they had anticipated.

In the afternoon, Jeri started to experience discomfort. Her arms and legs began to stiffen, and her mouth oozed a white foam. Carolyn bolted from the room and ran down the hall, screaming, "Help! Help!"

A nurse rushed to the room. While Carolyn waited outside, the convulsions eased and Jeri stabilized. It was the most frightening thing Carolyn had ever seen—something she never wanted to see again.

Junny continued to leave during the day to work, but he would never truly leave Jeri. She was seared into his consciousness, tied to events that, on their own, had no significance. One day at the shipping dock, he heard a man yelling profanities. Turning around, Junny saw the man grab an apparently intoxicated lady by the back of her shirt, yelling at her to get up.

It cut a swath through his soul. Here was a woman who had wasted the healthy body she had been given. He had a young daughter in the hospital who could use a healthy body. Didn't this woman know what she had been entrusted with?

At night, he'd return to the hospital, with one of them sleeping in a recliner in the corner of the room and the other one standing over her bed or laying at the foot of the bed.

Carolyn would reach in between the bars around her bed, patting her gently. Perhaps the doctors didn't believe, but this little girl did. Carolyn looked into her eyes and saw a steely determination. She didn't look like she was ready to give up. Was it wishful thinking? Or was there something special going on?

She constantly told Jeri she loved her, and that she was going to be OK. Jeri's favorite nurse, Donna, had a special gift with comforting her. Carolyn could tell that Jeri trusted Donna implicitly.

One by one over the next few days, the tubes came out. When Jeri was allowed out of her bed, Carolyn would take her on wagon rides throughout the hospital floor.

On the ninth day, they walked out of Fort Worth Children's Hospital with their "miracle baby." That's what Pastor Jack had dubbed her during her stay there. Carolyn and Junny were overcome with thankfulness that their "miracle baby" had come out of it.

Standing on the sidewalk waiting for Junny to pull up in the station wagon, Carolyn took a deep breath and mouthed the words, *Thank you, God.* She hadn't breathed any fresh air in nine days. All of her senses were heightened, everything magnified almost incomprehensibly. She felt like she had emerged from a cave or stepped out of a black-and-white movie into Technicolor brilliance, kind of like Dorothy in Munchkinland after her house squashed the ruby-slippered Wicked Witch of the East.

They stopped at the wishing well and said a prayer of gratitude and thankfulness, asking God to watch over her as they took her home, and to put a veil of protection over her to safeguard her without the doctors' presence.

"She's going to be OK," Junny said. "She's one strong kid."

At home, Carolyn was even more protective than she had previously been. She'd follow Jeri around with a pillow, which she'd use to support Jeri.

Dr. Megarity and Dr. Johnson told them to guard against exposure to other sick children. A friend had told them, "There are two places you don't want to take her that people go to when they're sick: church and the grocery store."

Then there was her scar. Initially, they didn't want to look at it—especially the section under the left breastbone, where the drainage tubes had been inserted—and they were afraid to handle her for fear of tearing the black stitches. They had to be extremely careful not to allow the incision to get wet until the stitches were removed two weeks later.

Jeri had never been quick to fall asleep—she seemed to be enjoying her waking hours far too much to lapse into dreamland—but now they theorized that there was a medical reason: Her heart was beating far too fast to allow her to ease into a restful state.

Carolyn would stand over her bed, gently stroking her, singing to her and telling her stories. Carolyn was exhausted, with nausea every bit as intense with this pregnancy as with Jeri's. Still, she never wondered if she'd have enough energy to take care of two.

Jeri started taking Lanoxin, a cardiac glycoside that helps a weakened heart muscle to beat more strongly and helps to maintain a normal heart rhythm. There were added benefits: It would remove excess water from her body and would facilitate the distribution of the blood throughout the body, decreasing swelling in the feet and legs, easing breathing, and preventing tiredness and weakness. She would take it the rest of her life.

Lanoxin, a yellow liquid in a green bottle, didn't have a distinctive taste or smell, which certainly eased the process of administering it to her by a dropper.

Jeri's appetite fell far short of being prodigious. They struggled to find things she would eat, finally succeeding with mashed potatoes and gravy, macaroni and cheese, vegetables and ice cream. Still, the chubby, dimpled legs turned to frail-looking sticks, and her growth rate slowed.

Despite the seriousness of her ordeal, Jeri recovered very quickly — so quickly that Junny felt confident enough a few months after her surgery to regularly bounce her all over the bed.

He'd hold her under her arms, then let her hop, jump and fall on her back. Or he'd hold her arms and she'd climb up on his chest and flip onto the bed. Or he'd put her in a horizontal position, raise her up and let her fall onto the bed. She loved it. Carolyn hated it. She couldn't watch.

Dr. Megarity would check her every two weeks for the rest of the year, and would graciously take care of any of their needs or questions in between. Dr. Manning would see her every three months, plus her annual bronchitis-turns-into-pneumonia winter ritual. Dr. Manning would tell them at every visit, "Well, just keep on keepin' on." And so they did.

Carolyn and Junny were emotionally drained, but they continued to call on the Holy Spirit to fill them up, continued to summon the prayer warriors, continued to be lifted up by Pastor Jack and their church. The financial drain was a bit more problematic. It would require some creative solutions and the help of some angels.

Junny had set financial goals, and one of them was to be debt-free. It had been a nice idea, but now he realized that might never happen.

They were constantly forced to think about the money they didn't have.

One night, Jeri fell out of her wagon and onto the kitchen floor. Junny picked her up, cradled her and pronounced her nearly 100%.

"That sure is a big ol' knot on her forehead," he said, mentally calculating the expenses for an off-hours visit, "but I think she'll be OK."

"No, she won't," Carolyn said, "She could have a concussion. We're taking her to the ER."

In the months that followed, help came from Dale Steward, their banker at West Texas State Bank in Snyder. They'd run out of money, Junny would call Steward and explain his situation, and Steward would take care of the overdrawn checks.

Help came from Linda McClure, a Snyder friend of Carolyn's who knew another Snyder resident, Jack Lawrence, who arranged for them to receive benefits from the Texas Crippled Children's Services Program. The program helped children with chronic and debilitating conditions and was administered by the Texas Department of Health, Bureau of Crippled Children's Services. It would pay for a large portion of the office visits and medications until 1980, when Junny started working at Nucor Corporation and received benefits.

Help came from the apartment complexes that were springing up all over Arlington during a full-bore growth spurt. Well, maybe they weren't even aware that they were helping, but Carolyn and Junny felt blessed nonetheless.

Faced with units that needed to be filled, apartment managers clamored for customers, enticing them with deals that included no deposit and no rent for the first month. Carolyn and Junny would fulfill the six-month lease, then back a U-Haul into the nearest parking space and move their belongings to another apartment complex offering the same deal. They would move 17 times between 1965 and 1975, testing out life as calculated vagabonds of the Dallas/Fort Worth Metroplex.

One day, Junny's brother, Tommy, called. He had been made executor of their mother's estate and had a tempting offer: "Mom needs someone to take care of her. You'll never have to pay rent. We'll see to it that you inherit the home and properties. All you have to do is move your family to Snyder." Junny nixed that idea in the time it took Jeri's heart to go *thump-thump*. Leave Dr. Megarity and the medical professionals in one of the nation's largest metropolitan areas for Snyder? With a terminally ill child and another child on the way? He never even told Carolyn about the offer.

Carolyn and Junny never had any bitter feelings about their financial plight. They were too in love with Jeri. And too in love with the fetus inside of Carolyn.

At every checkup, Carolyn would press Dr. Manning about the fetus' health.

"What are the chances this baby will have a heart problem?" she'd ask.

"It probably won't have any problems," he'd say. "Jeri's problem wasn't hereditary. It was just a birth defect."

They had prepared a bedroom that Jeri would share with her new sibling, making bedspreads and toy box covers. The only thing left to do was wait. While they did that, they joked that they were hoping the baby would arrive on the weekend because the hospital's business office would be closed, stalling any attempt to collect money.

The baby did.

And the office was.

Jayme Alan Ivison arrived on October 4, but only after 24 hours of labor and a C-section administered because of a big head and possible breach position. He was 7 pounds, 4 ounces of jaundiced joy. It was difficult to tell who was happier that the pregnancy was over, Jayme or Carolyn.

Or Jeri, for that matter. She had expressed excitement about the prospects of having a sibling, even if it was a brother. She was a budding people-person who now had a full-time roommate. What could be better?

They never noticed any jealousy. She didn't fuss or throw tantrums because she was getting less attention. It was quite the opposite. She adored Jayme. When they'd bathe him, she'd sit there and gaze lovingly at him.

Carolyn and Junny appreciated the harmony, but even more than that, the unfolding beauty of Jayme's health. He ate well, slept well, had a happy disposition. His only idiosyncrasy was an aversion to doctors. He'd see the white coat and instinctively start to scream. It wasn't so bad. They imagined what life would be like if Jeri exhibited that phobia.

In the year that followed, Jeri's condition neither improved nor deteriorated.

Early in 1971, she added Lasix to her medication arsenal. Lasix, a "loop diuretic" with a point of action in the kidneys, would reduce the amount of fluid in Jeri's body—especially in the arteries and veins surround her lungs—allowing her heart and lungs to work better.

Shortly after that, she had her second catheterization—this one at All Saints Hospital in Fort Worth. The idea was to monitor her progress and measure the pressure to see if the pulmonary band was functioning properly.

The procedure revealed that the pressure in her lungs remained too high. That higher blood flow was causing the arteries to thicken and constrict down. Eventually, the lungs would suffer irretrievable damage. The band was working, but not effectively enough.

"How long does someone live like this?" Junny asked.

"We just have to take it one day at a time," Dr. Megarity said.

One day at a time? That was better than, "She has a week to live." But it seemed cliché and cryptic, and hardly inspired jubilation, because the implication was quite clear: Not only was a long life not in the cards, but Jeri might not ever appear in a kindergarten class photo.

From a medical standpoint, her heart and lungs could not function properly, never would function properly. The drugs would help, but the bottom line was that her organs would break down because of overwork.

When?

Dr. Megarity could not say exactly. Every child was different. But he would say this: A child with her condition was not likely to live beyond 12.

CHAPTER 4

THIS MUCH FAITH

In May 1974, Carolyn heard that faith healer Kathryn Kuhlman would be holding a healing service June 12 in Houston.

Carolyn was intrigued because she recently had read one of Kuhlman's books. Kuhlman had gained an audience with Pope Paul VI in the Vatican on October 11, 1972, at which he gave her a medallion and praised her for "doing an admirable job." Oral Roberts had invited her to give the baccalaureate address at his university in 1972 and had lauded her, saying "she represented the finest of the healing ministry of Jesus."

Carolyn also knew there was controversy about the legitimacy of Kuhlman's purported healings. Dr. William Nolen, a Minnesota surgeon who had been an usher at one of her services and had been granted access to talk to any of the ill, later wrote a book, *Healing: A Doctor in Search of a Miracle*, in which he maintained that he couldn't medically authenticate even one case of organic physical healing among the many that were claimed.

Carolyn understood the skepticism, but she believed that people could be healed, that Kuhlman didn't actually do it but was an instrument God used—perhaps in helping people to have enough faith for the healing to take place.

Her 34-year-old brother-in-law, Steve Nail, had terminal cancer—lung cancer had spread to his brain—and was planning on attending. He and his wife, Barbara, who lived near San Antonio, believed that he and Jeri could be healed. He hadn't always had that kind of faith, but he had grown close to the Lord during his illness and been baptized. He offered to fly them to Houston and pay for their hotel.

Junny wasn't a big believer in what happened at the celebrated, televised faith healings and wasn't in favor of a trip to see Kuhlman. They didn't argue about it. Carolyn just put it to him simply: "I want to do *anything* that might save Jeri."

Jeri didn't know why they were going. She didn't even know she had a terminal heart defect. Carolyn and Junny hadn't discussed it with her because they didn't want fear to infiltrate her soul and ravage her unrestrained joy of life. Although she knew she had undergone an operation, she never asked about the scar. She wore the same swimsuit as the other girls, and she wore it without embarrassment or shame.

On the morning of June 12, as Carolyn backed the car out of the driveway on the way to the airport, Junny stopped her with one last plea.

"Why are you doing this?" he said. "I don't understand."

"How could you not want this, too?" she said.

When they reached the Sam Houston Coliseum in downtown Houston, they met Steve, who gave them good news: He had saved seats for them within 10 rows of the stage. Carolyn was overwhelmed by the electricity generated by the crowd of over 12,000.

Kuhlman, then 67 and at the tail end of her healing ministry, was a striking figure, moving dramatically across the stage in a flowing white gown with gold trim as she spoke in crescendo tones. When she asked all those who wanted to be healed to come to the front of the platform, Carolyn, Jeri, Steve and Barbara moved forward.

Carolyn had expected Kuhlman to lay her hands on people—and hopefully Jeri—but she didn't do that, instead praying and then extending her hands in front of her in a gesture indicating that the sick would be "slain in the spirit" and fall to the floor before the Lord. Some did that.

Others got up out of their wheelchairs. Believing she had seen instantaneous healing, Carolyn wept with happiness.

As they walked out of the arena, Carolyn thought, *Had it happened? How will we know?* Neither Jeri nor Steve was crippled or had a disorder that could be discernibly healed. Only time would tell.

And time was not kind to either of them. Steve's cancer progressively worsened, and he died less than two months later. Jeri's heart still had the distinctive, loud thumping sounds that characterized her defect. Carolyn and Junny could hear them and feel them every time they held her.

Carolyn knew that some faith healers maintained that the sick absolutely had to believe they had been healed even if the symptoms and outward signs remained. She also knew that many people ended up suffering gut-wrenching heartache when the healing didn't happen.

She didn't have that heartache, but she was disappointed and couldn't help questioning herself: *Was there something I did or didn't do that prevented the healing?* Judy Marfell, her friend and prayer warrior, would tell her much later: "Maybe she was healed—just not completely. Maybe her condition would be even worse without that service."

Carolyn continued to occasionally watch the healing services on TV, never once concluding they weren't legitimate. Her faith, and Junny's, remained strong. Anytime they struggled, they'd rely on their support network.

Over and over, Adron told them, "The doctors are wrong. God tells me she's going to live a good, long life."

Carolyn and Junny noticed that she had even more difficulty in falling asleep. She seemed to be afraid of the darkness that settled in when the lights were turned off. Had she already processed everything that happened? Was she afraid that she might not wake up the next morning?

They kept a nightlight in her room—a nursery lamp with a white shade and pink-and-blue lamp, with a blue-roofed birdhouse at the base of the lamp and a hole in front that allowed a ray of light to come out of the birdhouse. Later, they'd leave the bathroom light on and partially close the door so there would not be complete darkness in her room—a practice they'd continue everywhere. Some of their relatives weren't thrilled with the idea, but Carolyn and Junny didn't budge. They would do anything to make her more comfortable and less afraid. They didn't expect understanding from those who hadn't been where they'd been and experienced what they'd experienced.

They were a family of five now. Amy Ayn Ivison had been born April 15. They were still struggling financially—Amy's first car ride, on the way home from Arlington Memorial Hospital, came in a beat-up tan Chevrolet with a crumpled fender that Junny's high school friend had given them—but they never lacked happiness.

Even though Carolyn didn't have a spare moment for introspection or solace, she loved it. She was an attentive, selfless mother who derived her joy from seeing her kids' joy. If there were four pieces of pie left, she put them on plates and watched Junny and the kids chow them down. It amazed her that so many of her friends would go out every chance they got, leaving their babies behind. It would take an emergency—or a special occasion like New Year's Eve—to get her to do that. She didn't go to the movie theater with her friends. Didn't have the desire to.

She would never have consciously gravitated toward any one of the three kids, but she had an almost indescribably deep and profound connection with Jeri. It was almost as if they were part of the same person.

Socially and physically, with her own time and her own health, Carolyn's life would be defined by Jeri's life. Unknowingly and imperceptibly, she gave up her own life: *Now this will be my life— surviving this child.* There was no line-in-the-sand moment like there is when we choose a college or change our career. She just did what she knew she needed to do.

She unabashedly admitted she could be overprotective. But who would argue with that? Junny realized that she could *feel* when Jeri was going to be sick. That's the kind of power that connected them.

A similar power connected Jeri and Jayme. Carolyn and Junny proactively orchestrated its beginnings, taking advantage of their closeness in age and Jeri's medical needs. One of Jayme's earliest memories would be of sitting under the table in Dr. Megarity's office, catching the EKG tape as the machine spat it out. Everything Jeri did involved Jayme.

Jeri adored Jayme. She loved having him around—something he perceived very early on. It wouldn't be until he was 9 or 10 that she became perturbed by his antics—announcing his arrival in her room by passing gas, or picking up her stuffed animals and abusing them. No, for now, she doted on him and protected him, just like he would do later for her.

Virtually from the time that Jayme could stand on his own two feet, he had a plastic guitar in his hands, pretending he was his dad. By the time he was 5, he had become a guitar prodigy. Jeri would sit at his feet, enraptured by his playing. It was the equivalent of man playing for his girlfriend while she swooned over him.

Jayme accepted her admiration as a beautiful gift. Who wouldn't be glad to have it? Although he didn't find it particularly thrilling to have two sisters and no brothers—it made for some painfully long shopping trips—he did enjoy having somebody give him adoration that went far beyond anything he felt he deserved.

He graciously returned the love. One time, he went to Junny's weekly men's meeting at church, plugged in his amplifier and ripped his way through three songs. The men were astonished at his precocity. And they were especially touched when he ended his gig by saying, "Please pray for my sister."

Jeri's favorite song was a little blues-based gem they called "Honky Tonk"—a song by Ray Charles that actually is titled, "I'm Going Down to the River."

I'm goin' down to the river, jump overboard and drown. 'Cause my baby, she done left me. And I'm the loneliest man around.

It was the first song Jayme learned how to play. He had been in the garage while Junny taught the basics of the song to Carolyn's younger brother, Mike Hall. When Mike left, Jayme picked up the guitar and played a rudimentary version. He was off and running.

Music united the entire family. The kids especially loved music they could dance to. They'd put on an album by Herb Alpert and the Tijuana Brass and gyrate to a tune called "Tijuana Taxi"—which they referred to as "The Toot Song"—bending over and forcing their derrieres as high as they could and then pretending to fart right when the baritone sax kicked in. Jeri never told anyone until much later that her dream was to be a Broadway singer and dancer.

There were no video games, so kids had to be creative. Jeri and Jayme mastered that creativity thing. They devised an elaborate scenario involving their imaginary friends—John for Jayme, Martha for Jeri. It might have been a game to Carolyn and Junny, but it was serious business for Jeri and Jayme.

Junny might walk into the living room and head toward his favorite chair, but Jeri would forcefully intervene.

"You can't sit there!" she'd say dramatically. "Martha's sitting there!"

Sometimes Jayme would go to his parents with tears in his eyes, saying, "John's sad." And they'd have to summon up the requisite sympathy.

Junny, who worked in all phases of shipping and receiving for AMC, a company that manufactured automobile air conditioning units, would bring home huge boxes and make them houses to play in, cutting out windows and doors with a razor knife. They'd have tea parties inside, draw colorful pictures on the outside. They had an entire set of cardboard furniture adorned with cloth. Nothing was beyond their imagination.

Jeri largely determined the terms for the games. She rarely indulged in anything that was done a boy's way. Jayme didn't object. He knew selfishness was not the motive. Jeri had always known what she wanted. She never felt like she needed to do something to gain approval from somebody.

From a very early age, she had been empowered by bravely facing scary, mysterious machines and a phalanx of doctors who wanted to probe, photograph, examine, dissect and diagnose. That left her with a beautiful blend of confidence and self-assuredness that stopped well short of arrogance.

Her fragility worked in her favor when there were disputes in the house. She didn't take advantage of it, but if there were spankings to be administered, it very unlikely would happen to her. Their idea of discipline had been turned upside down when Dr. Megarity uttered the words, "common ventricle" and "We just have to take it one day at a time."

Jayme and Amy knew that Jeri had undergone some sort of operation—that was obvious from the purple scar that started out in her chest and veered across her ribs to the middle of her back. Jayme, fascinated by the stitched effect, had even traced it with his finger one time as they bathed together.

They didn't know Jeri had a serious heart condition. They just knew she was different, fragile, unique. She couldn't be treated the way other kids were treated. They couldn't be rough with her. They couldn't throw temper tantrums or engage in high-pitched arguments. And they *definitely* couldn't scare her.

One night, as Jayme and Jeri splashed around in the bathtub, Jeri pulled a green rubber block from the sudsy water, lifted it up and saw that a monstrous wolf spider was crawling toward her.

"Ahhhhhhhh!" Jayme screamed. He thought it was cool. He felt an adrenaline rush—until he noticed Jeri's face. It had turned to a ghastly white, and she clutched her chest. She staggered out of the bathtub and screamed for help.

Carolyn and Junny recognized it as ventricular tachycardia, an abnormally fast heart rhythm—120 to 250 beats per minute—that originated in the ventricle, caused faintness or dizziness, and could even be fatal if not treated.

They quickly found the nearest clothing—a few of Junny's T-shirts—and threw them on Jayme and Jeri, then grabbed Amy and headed for the ER. Jeri's heartbeat gradually settled down. It would be the first of many such trips.

Every two to three years, the family would make a trip to Houston so Jeri could undergo a catheterization at the Texas Children's Hospital Heart Center. The hospital had a growing reputation as one of the nation's premier medical facilities for children. It went beyond the expert doctors. The colors were bright and inviting, the mood dynamic and upbeat, the compassion in abundant supply. They kept the kids' minds on kid things, not on the reality that it was a critical-care unit.

Carolyn and Junny had first taken Jeri there on the recommendation of the landlord of their rental house in Crowley, 12 miles south

JERI, AMY, & JAYME
CHRISTMAS 1978
*the hypo-allergenic, plastic, white Christmas Tree

JAYME MOM JERI DAD AMY
JUNE 2000 • HOUSTON, TX

of Fort Worth. It made sense to Junny. Using his background as an auto mechanic, he figured that if a shop worked on nothing but transmissions, it should be pretty good at transmissions. So Texas Children's, with an entire floor devoted to children's hearts, should be pretty good at hearts.

On their first trip, they spent a lot of time in the waiting room and came to an inescapable conclusion: They weren't in this alone. Everybody in there had a child with a serious heart problem. They realized they weren't doomed. Although Jeri had a serious condition, others wouldn't walk out alive. Their parents would be using the hospital phone to arrange for the casket.

The trips were not without anxious moments.

One time, the hospital admitted Jeri into a room with a girl near Jeri's age. The girls were taken into the lab, Jeri first, then the other girl shortly after. When Jeri's roommate returned, Junny started pacing furiously. What had happened to Jeri? Another 30 minutes passed.

Finally, he bolted past the security door and into the lab.

"I'm Jerami's dad, and I want to know what's going on!" he said.

"We're doing a second catheterization," the doctor said.

"A second one?"

"Yes, we got a false reading from the first one. We went toward her lung and got the same readings and pressures as we had gotten in her heart. The catheter had done a U-turn and gone back into her heart. We knew those readings couldn't be possible because she couldn't live that way for even 24 hours, so we did another one."

The second one revealed that her heart hadn't enlarged, and everything was pretty much as it had been. They held her overnight to make sure there were no complications, especially clotting. That's the way all of them seemed to go. Carolyn and Junny would feel a cathartic release—until they had to come again and sign the waiver form that said Jeri could die during the procedure.

They knew that Jeri couldn't have felt comfortable during the procedure, but she didn't whine or complain. Carolyn and Junny more likely would be upset if the technician had to try three or four times to find the proper entry point for blood to be taken, or if the respiratory therapist had to continually pound on Jeri's back to loosen the congestion from her lungs.

Jeri's chatterbox tendencies ingratiated her with the doctors—much as they had with the judges at the 1973 Little Miss Fort Worth Pageant who had named her Miss Congeniality and placed a plastic crown on her thick brown hair.

Giggles and smiles. That's what people heard and saw. While she appeared frail—the chubby legs of her infancy gave way to toothpick shapes after her surgery—she didn't take on a sickly aura.

Jeri's terminal condition served as a powerfully unifying force to the family. The 263-mile trips to Houston weren't viewed as drudgery or shrouded in fear. The family would stay overnight and use the trip as a springboard to fun adventures. Maybe they'd go to Galveston and frolic on the beach. Or to the Battleship Texas, an historic ship that served in World Wars I and II and had found a resting place at the San Jacinto Battleground State Historic Site in Houston. On the way back, maybe they'd stop at Huntsville State Park, a 2,083-acre recreational area featuring a forest of loblolly and short-leaf pines encircling the 210-acre Lake Raven.

Back in Crowley, Jeri's life was similar to that of any normal child. She rode a bicycle, hopped on sheets of cardboard and surfed down the hill, scooted around in her Hot Wheels car along with Jayme and Amy, frolicked on the swings, merry-go-round and see-saw at the park and danced in a circle when Junny played Buddy Holly songs or "Jimmy Crack Corn" on his guitar. She swam, albeit awkwardly and with a reluctance to jump off the diving board—even if Junny waited for her in the water.

Although she would occasionally get winded, her activities were never limited. Dr. Megarity had told them she would be the best judge of what she should do. She would know her limits—how far she could go, and what would happen if she exceeded them.

When they attended carnivals or went to amusement parks such as Six Flags Over Texas, Junny would set her on his shoulder, wrap his arm around her legs and walk through the park, but that was primarily because he wanted to give her a rest—not because she asked for it. Her approach was daring and unafraid, riding the Tilt-a-Whirl and children's roller coasters.

No concessions were made for school—other than the decision to forego kindergarten, which was optional in the Fort Worth area at that time, in order to avoid potentially risky exposure to a measles outbreak.

She started out at Bess Race Elementary in 1975, then switched to Deer Creek Elementary halfway through first grade when Junny purchased the family's first house—three bedrooms, with then-trendy burnt-orange shag carpet and backyard swings—on the other side of Crowley.

Jeri, displaying qualities of leadership and extroversion, adapted quickly. Nobody ever had to ask what she was feeling. She just blurted it out. She could stroll into a group of strangers and emerge with friends. Pretty soon—before Carolyn and Junny knew what had happened—sleepovers had been arranged.

Unlike Jayme, who didn't like reading because he had trouble concentrating, Jeri voraciously attacked any book she could get her hands on. She took her studies seriously and seldom needed much help with her homework. Even when she missed time due to sickness or procedures, her grades didn't suffer.

Her teachers loved her and made sure they showed her how much. When she came down with pneumonia in fourth grade, her teacher made her a "Sunshine Box" with a gift for every day for a week, many of which were cat figurines.

On the final day of fifth grade, Deer Creek held its year-end games—a festive gathering that included various races and activities. Jeri, heartbroken that she hadn't won the broad jump, came to her parents with tears in her eyes.

"I wanted to win that *so* bad," she said.

"Jeri, you did your best," Carolyn said. "That's all you can do. At least you tried."

Carolyn turned to Junny and whispered, "Go get her a trophy."

Junny drove five miles to Burleson, where he found a trophy shop. He told the clerk his story. The clerk thought for a moment, then pointed to the top shelf at a small trophy with a lady holding a wreath: "I have this one here."

When Junny got back to the house, he presented the trophy to Jeri.

"You know, they misjudged the competition," he said. "They said you won. They wanted me to bring this home to you."

With a big smile, Jeri accepted the trophy and held it close to her chest.

It would be her last significant memory of Crowley.

Monumental change was on the way.

CHAPTER 5

TIME FOR A TALK

In August 1980, Junny received an unexpected phone call from his brother, Allie. There was an opening for a maintenance mechanic at Nucor Corporation's minimill in Jewett, 115 miles southeast of Dallas, where Allie was a foreman.

The mill had opened in 1974 with the purpose of supplying the nearby Grapeland joist plant with rods and angles, but also was gaining steel orders from outside the company. Capitalizing on the company's strategy of opening plants in rural areas ignored by other employers and offering high-paying jobs, Nucor experienced rapid growth in Jewett.

Carolyn and Junny were intrigued. Their financial struggles had weighed heavily on his psyche. He wanted his family to escape from the pressure of bills and have some wiggle room to enjoy life's simple pleasures. They had been praying their way through a financial maze, traveling infrequently, dining on a limited menu of low-cost meals such as chicken-fried hamburger patties and spaghetti, waiting for the chance to pay off a $3,200 loan that had defaulted. A savings account had been completely out of the equation.

His parts-management job in Crowley didn't offer much. No benefits. No raises. No hope for advancement. At Nucor, his salary would double, with the potential for a fourfold increase based on work-incentive bonuses tied to production.

Carolyn and Junny loved the idea of escaping the urban life. They had grown increasingly unsettled about the safety of their kids—a concern that was magnified when a girl was abducted on a nearby street.

But what about Jeri? How would a move impact her medical care? They called Dr. Megarity, who said one of the finest cardiologists he knew practiced less than an hour from Jewett. He also noted that a move to that area would carve 107 miles off the trip to Texas Children's, leaving them with a much more manageable 156 miles. And when they wanted to see or call Dr. Megarity, they could.

Junny took vacation time from his job so he and Carolyn could visit Fairfield, where Allie owned a house. It was 28 miles northeast of Jewett and was the only nearby town that had a hospital. They noticed a relaxed community with tree-lined streets and a quaint courthouse square. The school system was solid. They were sold. When Junny aced the interview and was offered the job, the only uncertainty was when they would move.

Junny gave two weeks' notice to his boss, who was not pleased. He was staring at thousands of parts awaiting a rigorous inventory.

"You can just leave now," he told Junny.

"OK," Junny said.

That might have been the easiest discussion he and Carolyn had regarding the move. The more difficult one involved Jeri, who was excitedly counting the days until her 12th birthday.

"We'll have a bigger house with a bigger bedroom for you," Carolyn said.

"I don't want to leave my friends," she said.

"Jeri, you'll make new friends before you know it. You're *so* good at that. Grandma will come visit, and you can visit her."

Carolyn remembered how she felt when her family prepared for a move. She thought her world would be ending. But she was shy and didn't have the gift of quickly ingratiating herself like Jeri did. Jeri could walk into a room and have a group of friends within minutes. Jeri would be fine.

On September 3, one day after Jeri's birthday, a 26-foot U-Haul truck sat in the driveway. Junny, impatient to get this life-changing adventure under way, gunned the engine. He and Carolyn had serious thoughts on their mind, but for their kids, play time beckoned. Jayme thought Amy could use an assist in riding her Big Wheels, so he gave her a push—a very forceful push. Amy, in panic mode, tried to stop the momentum by lowering her knees—leaving a chunk of skin from both knees on the sidewalk.

Then Jeri came out of the house hysterically screaming, "My hamster's dead!" They checked the hamster and found signs of life.

Carolyn was crying. Her mother was crying. Was this move a bad idea?

Things settled down and Jayme and their dog got into the truck with Junny, while Carolyn, Jeri, Amy and their cat piled into their '78 Ford Fairmont station wagon.

In Fairfield, they would be living in the Lakewood subdivision in a three-bedroom, 2,000-square-foot white-brick house Allie had vacated—the embodiment of small-town Americana. The property was shaded by almost 100 trees, including a massive backyard oak on which Junny hung a 20-inch-wide swing. He had a shop where he could tinker. The kids had enough area to race around on a go-kart. Junny also turned the garage into a game room so Jeri, Jayme and Amy would have a comfortable place where their friends could hang out. In Jeri's room, he ran a long car-hood spring from the ceiling and attached a wicker swing that became one of her favorite spots.

Best of all for Carolyn and Junny, they had peace of mind. The subdivision had one way in and out—nobody was on the streets who didn't either live there or was visiting someone.

Junny went to work at Nucor the day after they arrived. He didn't get a day off for the next month. Not that it elicited even a meager complaint. They treated him like royalty.

He found he had brothers who wanted to share in every aspect of his life. One of them, Gary Helmpkamp, had a friend whose daughter had a less severe heart problem and had gotten married and raised children. When Junny told him what Dr. Megarity had said when Jeri was 3—that a child with her condition might not live past 12—Gary said, "Ah, Junny, she's going to marry, have kids, grow old and live a long life."

The children enrolled in the school system and immediately flourished. Later, Carolyn and Junny would overhear one of their friends saying, "Those Ivison kids, they're geniuses."

Fairfield (pop. 3,580) was a place where everybody seemed to know each other. Allie had married into the Ward family, with a history that dated back to the Civil War. Many in town were kin to each other. It was the kind of place that kids returned to after college. It was a place where every child had his or her own identity, where reputations went along with you wherever you went. That's why Junny moved his family there—to build their own reputation.

At Fairfield Intermediate School, Jeri's reputation blossomed. At that age, good grades—and not necessarily good looks—earned popularity. Jeri got it. Junny did not ground the kids if they didn't get A's, but he did reward them if they did. That became an expensive proposition.

Many times Jeri would breeze through her homework and Carolyn would find her sitting in her wicker chair, watching TV. She became a huge fan of *Moonlighting*, and especially of Bruce Willis. The only thing better than watching a *Moonlighting* episode was the anticipation of the next one.

The Ivisons became very active in First United Methodist Church, with Jeri and Jayme, and later Amy, serving as acolytes.

When she was 14, she accepted Christ at a Baptist summer camp near Waco. She came back and told Jayme excitedly, "You *have* to go. It will change your life."

And he did. The very next year. And as she stood next to him, holding his hand, with the music softly playing and tears flowing, he could feel God tugging on his heart. He felt like she was leading him to something very good. He met with a youth minister who shared God's plan for his salvation by taking him down the Roman road. "You're saved," he told Jayme.

Later that night, everybody came out of the cabins and told their stories. Jayme found Jeri and said, "I got saved." She hugged him and cried in elation. As they stood by the chain-link fence that circled the softball field, she hollered at one of her friends to come over.

"My brother got saved tonight!" she said.

Later on, at the group sharing time, over 100 teens and their parents assembled. Traditionally, only a few teens—the very boldest—will step out of their comfort zone and speak. Of course, one of them was Jeri.

"Tonight's a great night because my brother got saved!" she cried.

She seemed even more thrilled about Jayme's acceptance of Christ at the same camp the following year than she was about her own. Jayme felt 10,000 feet tall. Here she was, putting a junior-high kid on a pedestal in front of all the tough senior-high boys.

Jeri sought God with all her heart in the years that followed. But by the time she was in 10th grade, she felt like First UMC was not feeding her spiritually. She felt like the church was cold and ritualistic. She did not see God at work there.

She started talking to Carolyn and Junny about attending First Baptist Church, where some of her very spiritual friends were being fed. The church had an active youth group that was led by a director who reached out energetically to the kids. Junny had some friends who told him they wouldn't let their children split off and go to another church, but he allowed her to spend a few weeks there to determine if it was the place for her.

"Is it special for you?" he asked.

"Yes, dad," she said. "I feel the Spirit there."

"Then go."

God became more and more real to Jeri, and she immersed herself in Bible study. Judy Daniel, a woman at First Baptist, made a plaque inscribed with Jeremiah 29:11: *"For I know the plans I have for you," declares the LORD, "plans to prosper you and not to harm you, plans to give you hope and a future."*

"This verse is for you," Judy told her, "because your name is Jeri."

In Fairfield, most of the students who didn't play sports—and that obviously included Jeri—joined the band. She started out as a baton twirler and clarinetist, then switched to the flag corps when she was in senior high.

Attacks of tachycardia became all too prevalent, most of them occurring after a night of marching. One night, she turned blue. On another occasion, they packed her in an ambulance and started toward Waco, but the tachycardia stopped before they got there. Sometimes the verapamil shots worked. Other times they had little effect.

Jeri never seemed worried that tachycardia might happen again. Part of that stemmed from a lifetime of trips to the hospital and the endless sequence of being probed, photographed, analyzed and ultimately sent home. And then part of it was simply her determination to do anything she wanted to do. She loved life her way.

That, however, was about to end.

Carolyn and Junny had never told Jeri the whole story. She had no idea she had common ventricle and primary pulmonary hypertension, no idea she had been staring down death for 17 years. She knew she had been taking medication for her heart, but she never asked what was wrong with it.

They had gone on their instinct of what was right at that time. They didn't want to cause Jeri undue stress or pain. Carolyn had been adamant that they couldn't let her know what was *really* happening. Carolyn believed the best and tried to ignore the worst—a posture that later would inspire her kids to call her a "fantasist."

But the picture had changed. Dr. Megarity had told them over the phone that she could no longer participate in the band. She was due for her yearly checkup in Fort Worth in August, just before the beginning of her senior year. Her day of reckoning had come. She had to be told.

To potentially soften the blow, they took Jayme along. He'd find a way to comfort her. He always did.

With Carolyn in the room, Dr. Megarity performed his examination of Jeri. Then he brought Junny into the room and asked Jeri to go to the waiting room.

Dr. Megarity brought out the hand-drawn heart sketches they had seen so many times. Their minds flashed back to those days when they'd be feeling so much tension about the results, and he'd

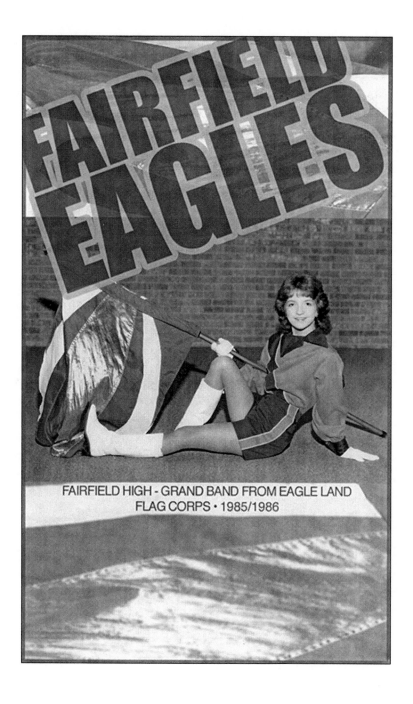

FAIRFIELD HIGH - GRAND BAND FROM EAGLE LAND
FLAG CORPS · 1985/1986

quell it by saying, "Well, her heart looks the same as it did the last time. This is good news."

He didn't say that this time.

He told them that her heart had worn out her lungs, which were now super-thin. Her heart had been pumping in its own weird way and at its own weakened effort, but her lungs had been overworked. The surgically inserted band was relieving some of the pressure, but not nearly enough. She had the lungs of an 80-year-old.

"This is life-threatening for her," he said.

"When do we tell her?" Carolyn said, fighting back the tears.

"Now. We need to tell her now."

Carolyn and Junny brought her in. Dr. Megarity explained the nuances of common ventricle and primary pulmonary hypertension. He told her exactly what he had told Carolyn and Junny about the danger. He said she wouldn't be able to participate in the band.

Jeri's eyes started welling up. And then she exploded in anger. He had told her things she didn't want to hear. She felt her entire world crashing down on her.

"How long do I have to live?"

"I've seen a few of these cases. One lived to be just 9. You're already well past that. Probably your late twenties, based on what we know and the medical treatment that is available now."

Dr. Megarity always had been able to assuage all the fears with his kind manner and reassuring voice. Not now. As they left the office and got into their car, Jeri freaked out. *It'll be a miracle if this doesn't induce tachycardia,* Carolyn thought.

Somewhere on Highway 287, Junny broke the silence.

"Jeri," he said, "you were not supposed to live past 12. You have done so well, and now you're 17. And as time goes by, they'll discover new things. God has blessed you with this life, and with great doctors who have helped get you to this point."

"What's going to happen to me, dad?"

Carolyn interjected, "Just because the doctor says that doesn't mean it's going to turn out that way. They don't know everything. God is in control. The doctors aren't."

"Why didn't you tell me?" Jeri cried.

"What good would it have done?" Carolyn said. "I didn't want you to worry."

Jayme—who normally would be cracking jokes and entertaining everybody—instead offered reassuring wisdom. Jeri said nothing, wearing a blank stare. After what seemed like half an hour, she burrowed her face into the corner of the back seat and fell asleep.

When they arrived in Fairfield, she went directly to her room. After 15 minutes, she left the house and went two doors down to visit Helen Kay Wood, one of her more spiritual friends. She came back after an hour, hopped on her bike and aggressively pedaled away, her eyes burning with intensity, her hair flying wildly, as if to defiantly say, *I'm capable of doing anything I want to!*

"Think we ought to go get her?" Carolyn asked.

"Well, no," Junny said. "Maybe she just needs to go do her thing."

They didn't know whether their approach had been right or wrong. But they knew she had lived a carefree, well-balanced childhood. She had faced a lifetime of needles, IV drips, scary-looking machines and objects glued all over her chest, and all of that had turned her into a brave, self-confident girl who knew how to deal with adults as well as children.

She would get through this. It was in her makeup.

But to further dampen Jeri's spirits, she later had to deal with the loss of Caroline Wilson, a 30-year-old woman from First Baptist who had befriended her. Caroline believed she would be healed from brain cancer, but it didn't happen—despite a healing service both of them had attended in nearby Corsicana.

Caroline's husband, John, had encouraged the relationship because he knew they could relate on a different plane: Both had terminal illnesses. Both thought of dying. When either of them felt pain and uncertainty, the other knew exactly what to say. They had a way of relating that no one else in their small town had.

One of Carolyn's friends from church told her that she saw Jeri one day walking in the cemetery near Caroline's gravestone. Jeri's psyche was being cut to its core by a double-edged sword. She wasn't just mourning the loss of Caroline. She was painfully examining her own mortality.

She held her true feelings inside, struggling for over a year with the painful questions she had for God: *Why me? Why would you choose to give me this rare condition? What have I done to deserve it?* She experienced times of desperation when she felt like she was dying and there was nothing she could do about it. She would never tell anyone that she felt Satan attacking her, telling her this mountain was too big for even God to move.

She knew one thing for sure: Others were praying passionately for her.

Carolyn regularly watched the *700 Club* and sent in prayer requests. One time, she heard Pat Robertson say, "Right now, there's someone with a heart defect. And as we speak, it's been healed." And she'd say, "He's talking about Jeri." And she'd claim that for Jeri.

She also took Jeri to San Antonio to visit a prayer-warrior friend of Carolyn's sister, Barbara, from Cornerstone Church. Carolyn didn't know anything about the woman or what she practiced, but she trusted the woman because she was so eager to see Jeri healed.

The woman requested that Carolyn and Barbara wait outside while she conducted the healing service.

Carolyn and Barbara had never been close, but in the time they spent together outside that room, they talked intimately. Carolyn, sobbing, shared her fears that Jeri would die. Barbara comforted her, and for the first time truly knew what they had been living with.

When it was over, the woman claimed Jeri was healed. Jeri's fingernails were still blue, but Carolyn tried not to let that cause unbelief. She asked the woman if Jeri should continue to take her medications, and was told that was up to her.

Carolyn continued to give Jeri her medications. As the days went by, they didn't notice anything different in Jeri.

Once her senior year started, her mood seemed to brighten. She had people with whom she could share her fears and uncertainties. Jeri represented a rare species. She was part of all the cliques: the jocks, the nerds, the intellectuals. She had almost as many black friends as white.

She looked different, for sure. She didn't have Down syndrome or a missing limb, but if she ever ran briefly, she appeared somewhat unorthodox. She endured some insensitive comments that are typical in the teen set.

She was as much the unpopular kid as the popular kid. She knew boys didn't look at her as a "knockout," and therefore were more interested in just being friends. She could identify with what it was like to be picked on, but she was accepted by and hung out with the people who made all of the rules. One time Jayme was walking the halls and he saw two usually rude, brutish football players run by, pick her up and carry her proudly on their shoulders.

Jeri was not embarrassed by her blue extremities or her physical inability to do the same things her classmates could do. She was one of them. She'd crack jokes, making everybody laugh.

Jayme was an introverted artist. His idea of a great night at the movies was to invite one person he could engage in a deep conversation. Not Jeri. She'd call up five friends and pile them into her maroon '87 Pontiac Grand Am. *Let's party!* Jeri would always want more people.

She thrived because she learned how to navigate relationships. She realized she had two choices: She could become embittered about the way society treated her. Or she could learn to laugh at herself and become a person who gave to relationships knowing she'd never get anything back.

She learned subliminally along the way that giving actually filled her up. That's true for everybody, but most of us are too selfish and wedded to our own agenda. She wanted to be with people because giving to others—listening to their problems, praying with them, helping them through their issues—distracted her from her own traumas. It gave her reasons to be active, to be *alive*.

She became special to her classmates because they got to be a part of this extraordinary life. It would be 2 a.m. The ambulance had taken her from the football field to the hospital. There would be 20 band members and their parents waiting to see what would happen.

The classmates would go into her room and see her immersed in this patchwork of wires, tubes and beepers. They'd ask, "What's the deal?" And she'd say, "They told me they were surprised I lived." That's pretty wild stuff for teenagers to talk about.

Jayme had classmates who had disabilities, but they walked the halls virtually unknown. They were recluses who had pulled back into their own issues. He'd watch in amazement as Jeri immersed herself in the yearbook staff and student government.

One of Jeri's friends was a girl Jayme was dating—and she went to the junior and senior proms with two different friends of Jayme's—which only served to bring her even closer to Jayme. After football games, Jayme's DJ service would handle the music at dances. Jeri would sit up on the stage with Jayme, and he'd just absorb her affection.

Even in the absence of the flag corps, she constantly pushed the envelope.

That fall, she played in the powder-puff football game. Helen Kay's boyfriend served as one of her coaches, and he watched over her, sending the most physically imposing girls to protect her. For comic relief, she had Jayme as a cheerleader.

Jeri's physical condition remained blissfully stable. Until March, when a sinus infection landed her in Fairfield Memorial Hospital. After two days, she started to have a series of frightening seizures.

Amy, sleeping at the foot of her bed in a cot, awakened to see Jeri in convulsions, foaming at the mouth. The nurses rushed in and hustled Amy out. Jeri would calm down for a minute, then have another even more intense seizure.

How much longer is her heart going to stand this? Carolyn thought.

Junny came back to her room one night to find Carolyn, Jayme and Amy on their knees praying in the hall outside her room. Carolyn had called their Methodist pastor, Bill Gandin, and Jeri's Baptist pastor, Tom Hiser. She thought Jeri wouldn't make it. Jeri had lapsed into a coma. They called Dr. Megarity in a panic.

"Let's get her to Fort Worth *now*," he said.

Carolyn hung up the phone and immediately was paralyzed by a horrifying vision: She was at Jeri's funeral.

Fairfield Hospital arranged for a chopper out of Tyler to airlift her to Fort Worth Children's Hospital, where Dr. Megarity met her and admitted her to ICU. They gave her a spinal tap and put her in a straitjacket restraint.

Carolyn and Junny spent the next two nights in the waiting room. Early on the second morning, they were awakened by the sound of her wailing. They washed their hands and were allowed to go into the room.

As Carolyn tickled her back and rubbed her, she blurted out, "Where am I?"

"You're in Fort Worth Children's Hospital."

"Is Dr. Megarity here?"

"Well, he's not here right now, but he has been."

"Has he seen me?"

"Yes, he has."

Knowing that comforted Jeri. She knew she could always count on Dr. Megarity.

Jeri's room was near those of two others who appeared to be in even greater danger: one with a heart problem who was not expected to live, and whose parents were preparing to remove life support; and another, the son of a youth pastor, who had fallen out of a van and suffered brain damage.

The youth pastor's ministerial team held prayer services and invited Carolyn and Junny to attend. All three children miraculously lived.

Jeri underwent every test known to medicine in her 10-day stay in Fort Worth. The doctors ruled out a plethora of things—brain damage, meningitis, bug bites—but they never diagnosed the cause.

"God is in control," Jeri told Carolyn and Junny.

Before they left Fort Worth, Carolyn called the Dairy Queen in Fairfield and requested they put a message on their board.

When they got home, they drove past and saw the comforting words: WELCOME HOME, JERI.

That quelled the anxiety at Fairfield High School, where rumors had rapidly spread that Jeri had died.

The community rallied behind the family. Houston Power and Light, where the mother of one of Amy's friends worked, gave the family a check for $500. First Baptist handled their house payment for the month.

In June, Jeri stood on the stage and accepted her diploma.

She was very much alive. And dreaming of much bigger things.

CHAPTER 6

THE ONE

He didn't ride in gallantly on a white horse and majestically sweep her off her feet. But to a frail-looking girl with a terminal heart condition who had wondered when a man was going to truly look deep inside and see what she had to offer, it sure seemed like it.

Glenn Pearson was tall, handsome and a member of the Corps of Cadets at Texas A&M, the largest uniformed body of students in the nation outside the U.S. service academies and regarded as the guardians of the university's traditions.

He had finished his sophomore year at the end of May and was living in Fairfield with his grandparents, Bob and Billie Pearson, who were members at First UMC and acquaintances of Carolyn and Junny. His grandparents loved Jeri and thought she and Glenn might turn out to be famous friends. But they immediately clicked and became inseparable.

Carolyn and Junny liked him initially. They didn't mind his propensity to show up around meal time or to feel comfortable enough to stretch out on the sofa for a nap. They viewed that as pretty typical for a college student.

They were, however, a bit taken aback by his argumentative, know-it-all nature. He seemed to portray himself as the authoritative expert on everything. No matter what they had done, he had done something grander.

Junny got vibes of phoniness and the disturbing notion that Glenn felt he was superior to a mere blue-collar mechanic from rural west Texas. Glenn would sit at the kitchen table and charm Carolyn for hours, but he made the mistake of not courting Jeri's father.

On August 20, 1987, Jeri returned home from a date and excitedly showed off her engagement ring. Later that night, she opened her Traveler date book and scribbled, "Engaged! RING." Carolyn and Junny felt ecstatic for her. They knew she probably had been scared that no one would fall in love with her because of her terminal condition. Sure, it had been a fast courtship, but she seemed happy.

Jeri had decided earlier in the year to attend Stephen F. Austin State University along with Jayme's girlfriend, Tracie Harris. She decided to stick with the plan. Although the university was in Nacogdoches—135 miles from Glenn in College Station—she felt certain it would work.

By January, she had transferred to Blinn Junior College's campus in Bryan and applied to Texas A&M, just a few miles away.

Through an off-campus roommate search, Jeri hooked up with Suzanne Milligan and lived at Oakwood Apartments. They liked each other instantly, even though they had little in common. Jeri came from a small town, was in a graduating class of about 40 and loved country and western music. Suzanne came from Houston, was in a graduating class of about 400 and loved pop-rock music, especially anything by Erasure.

Suzanne noticed Jeri's discolored lips—despite Jeri's penchant for applying dark shades of lipstick to hide them—and also her fingertips. Still, Suzanne had no idea that anything was seriously wrong until Jeri told her a truncated version of the complicated and heartbreaking story. Jeri's attitude toward it—and her straightforward, positive description—impressed Suzanne. Jeri said rather matter-of-factly that one day she would need a transplant. There was no doom and gloom in her voice. She said she had always been a miracle and would continue to be one.

Jeri had a big influence on Suzanne. One time, Jeri stood in line for three days to buy tickets to a Garth Brooks concert. When Jeri found herself in the hospital two days before the concert, she told the doctors she would be checking out in time for Garth—regardless of what they said. She made good on her promise, and Suzanne had even been converted enough to C&W music that she went to that concert, and later allowed Jeri to teach her how to dance to C&W.

Like Jeri's parents, Suzanne remained a bit skeptical of Glenn. She felt Jeri had naively rushed into a relationship that really wasn't good for her because she was being dominated into doing things she didn't want to do. She wanted to see him more often than he wanted to or could, because as a young Corps member, he had a very regimented schedule and little freedom.

Suzanne also noticed that he had little patience with her. He tried to help her with her math class, but those sessions usually turned hostile. He was preparing to be an aerospace engineer and had this stuff down. Why couldn't she get it?

Nevertheless, she spent just as much time on the A&M campus as she did at Blinn, soaking up all of the Aggie traditions and trying to spend as much time as she could with Glenn—which turned out to be a rather expensive endeavor. Because she didn't have the required hang tag to park on campus, she parked with her flashers on and accepted her tickets—and dead batteries. Her '87 Pontiac Grand Am had a high-amp alternator that wasn't designed to charge a battery, which meant that Junny replaced her alternator on more than a few occasions.

In May 1988, during Jeri's final exams at Blinn, Glenn dropped a bomb. Claiming he wasn't ready to get married, he said they were finished. Jeri had recently mentioned to her parents that Glenn's heart seemed to be changing, but it still violently rocked her world. When Carolyn and Junny drove up to see her, they noticed a bumper sticker in the apartment parking lot near her car: I LOVE MY CORPS GUY. Jeri had torn it off her car and tossed it on the ground.

She somehow got through her exams, but when she returned to Fairfield, she plunged even further into the emotional abyss. She cried most of the day, stopping only to eat and talk briefly. He had been her first real boyfriend, a Christian with a solid career ahead of him. She had thought her life was set. Now it was in pieces.

Jeri talked with Glenn's grandmother, who suggested she see a psychiatrist in Waco who had a good reputation. After seeing Jeri, examining her medical history and talking with her doctors at Texas Children's, he recommended that she be admitted to Providence Health Center's psychiatric unit in Waco.

While that thought frightened Carolyn and Junny, it seemed to be the best move. While not suicidal, she was severely depressed and not responding to anything anybody said.

Carolyn stayed with Junny's niece in Waco and visited Jeri every day. As the week went on, she noticed Jeri emerging from her depression. Jeri still had not given up on Glenn—she wrote daily letters to Suzanne, describing how much she missed him—but she also realized that in the group sessions, she saw people in far worse shape than her, people with haunting addictions and radical cases of abuse and family dysfunction. Not only had she been able to realize her life was far from over, but she had started to counsel a man to help him eliminate his demons.

By the time her one-week stay ended, she had returned to Fairfield with a new college major—psychology. She wanted to understand mental processes and behavior so she could help people.

In the fall, she and Suzanne moved into quadruplex housing near campus.

To Suzanne's dismay, Glenn re-entered the picture. She couldn't tell Jeri exactly what she thought of him, for fear that it might damage their relationship if Jeri and Glenn got back together. But on many instances when she noticed that Jeri had disappeared, she went to Glenn's room, corralled Jeri and brought her back.

"Leave him alone," she'd tell Jeri. "It's over. You don't need him. You're fine."

One day, while Jeri was in Fairfield with her parents, Suzanne opened the mail to find an envelope with an A&M letterhead and Jeri's name on it. When she called Jeri with the news that she had been accepted, Jeri screamed in ecstasy.

While Jeri shopped in nearby Palestine with Carolyn and Amy, Junny and Jayme hurried out to a store and bought up everything maroon and Aggie-related, then decorated the game room. The centerpiece of the room was a sign that read, WELCOME HOME, AGGIE.

When Jeri found that Aggie shrine, she let out a piercing scream and set a personal record for the vertical leap. As she gazed at the sign, she glowed.

"You're the best!" she screamed. "I can't believe I'm an Aggie!"

In the spring of 1989, she went to A&M to start classes. She wanted to do this alone, with no emotional handoff from Carolyn and Junny. When she came back on the first weekend, she told Carolyn, "Mom, when I drove down University Drive and saw those buildings, I said, 'That's my school!'"

With gusto, she carved out her legacy at A&M over the next three years. She examined her life and what God had planned for her. She decided that God had chosen to make her unique, and she was going to make the most of her life, having a good time while she did it.

In her psyche, she viewed her heart condition as having an impact mostly on her mind more than her physical body. She didn't think there was anything she couldn't do.

Her parents bought her a bicycle, which she raced around campus—until she wrecked it twice and decided to go by foot. This might have worked at a small, private college, but at A&M's massive, sprawling campus, it proved to be quite a challenge.

When she made her regular visit at Texas Children's to see the renowned Dr. Charles Mullins—who had established the specialty of pediatric cardiology in the U.S. Army—he asked about the physical demands that college had been placing on her.

"Well, are you able to walk across campus?" he said.

"*Able?*" Jeri exclaimed. "Dr. Mullins, I walk *miles!*"

She didn't tell him that she hadn't been simply walking to class. She had gotten involved in doing the cut—the lumbering of trees in a forested area—for the traditional Bonfire. That had never been a place for female students—they hadn't even been allowed to go the cut site until 1979—and it definitely wasn't a job for a terminal heart patient, since she had little endurance for it. But she did it anyway, keeping it a secret from not just Dr. Mullins, but her parents.

Like many college students, she allowed the lure of increased freedom and the distractions of her new life to damage her faith walk. She didn't go to church in College Station and rarely even cracked her Bible while school was in session, although she attended some Baptist Student Union events. It was a lapse she would later regret.

In the spring of 1991, she started rooming in McFadden Hall with Jana Terry, whom she had met during the previous school year. They were a dynamic combination.

Jana served as president of McFadden, with Jeri on the Hall Council. When the administration threatened to turn McFadden into a dorm strictly for honors students—a segregated move that both of them felt would be against the spirit of the school—they fought back. Jeri strung pink SAVE MCFADDEN ribbons all over campus, including on the YMCA building that served as the housing office headquarters. Within a few months, the administration abandoned its effort.

They also poured their passion into what they would later come to realize were unhealthy pursuits. The previous fall, they had set a goal of spending every day, for as many consecutive days as they could, at the Dixie Chicken—a legendary hole-in-the-wall bar that claimed to serve the most beer per square foot of any bar in the U.S. and later would be named one of the "Top 20 Dive Bars in America." They got all the way to Thanksgiving—a streak of nearly 90 days.

Jeri always wanted to be around the fun. If some people were immersed in an interesting late-night conversation, that's where she would be.

But as roommates, Jana's nocturnal habits conflicted with Jeri's need to go to bed earlier so she could be fresh in the morning for her part-time job working with a professor in the psych department. Jeri felt her health was being measurably impacted. She lasted just one semester with Jana before saying, "I just don't think we should live together." Jana, a self-described "maniac," didn't take it personally.

Although Jeri seemed to her friends to be outwardly carefree, her best buddy—Jayme—was exposed to the undercurrent that nagged at her confidence.

One night, as he drifted to sleep in her dorm room, her halting voice cut through the silence and darkness.

"Jayme?"

"Yeah."

"Still awake?"

"Yeah."

"I don't want to die."

He could hear her sniffle and start to cry.

"It's all right to be scared," he said. "I'd be scared if I were you. I'd be afraid. You have to trust God. What's worrying going to help? You will just drive yourself crazy. Your life would be way more in danger if you drove to downtown Houston every day. The odds are higher of dying from a car accident than one day keeling over from this."

In that moment of Jeri's vulnerability, Jayme realized that college is the time when everybody faces their demons. It's the first time that their support system, as they knew it, is not readily available. He knew what no one else did—that she had fear. He started praying hard for healing.

After having been worried that she might never find another man who would accept her as she was, she ended up dating prolifically. One was a trainer on the football team who would carry her on his shoulders. Another was a rancher—Jeri fell for him and his cows so much that everything she bought had to have cows on it.

Another was Stan Bludau.

Stan wasn't The One. But he introduced her to him.

Daryl Paholek had been one of Stan's roommates in 1990 and had graduated that December with a degree in building construction. He was working at a Hi/LO Auto Supply store (now O'Reilly Auto Parts) in College Station, had accepted a position in Austin and was planning on moving in May 1991.

Daryl had met Jeri through Stan, who dated Jeri only a few times. Jeri had hardly even noticed Daryl because of his reticence. Daryl occasionally had seen Jeri on campus and exchanged a hug and brief small talk. After Stan stopped seeing her, it had never occurred to him to ask her out. It was nothing against Jeri. He wasn't really interested in dating *anybody*. He had a limited dating history and was shy and unassertive.

Jeri, however, was very interested and, of course, very assertive. On Wednesday night, April 3, she tracked down his phone number from a friend and left a message on his answering machine, asking him if he would be interested in meeting her and her friends the next night for some C&W dancing. She mentioned that she had heard of his dancing prowess.

Throughout high school, Daryl had been a devoted fan of the big "Hair Bands"—Ratt, Poison, KISS, Van Halen—but C&W forced its way into his heart in 1986 because that's all the manager of the Hi/LO would play all day. Daryl enjoyed dancing to Garth Brooks and George Strait. He didn't feel that he could be termed a prolific dancer, but who was he to argue with Jeri? He called her the next morning and agreed to meet her at Graham Central Station in nearby Bryan.

Daryl thought it was a date. He didn't know Jeri's real intention: She just wanted somebody to dance with.

When she arrived at Graham Central Station, she nearly went into shock: He was waiting for her just inside the door. She had expected he'd be inside doing his own thing. *How sweet*, she thought.

They danced up a storm. Daryl was entranced with her fun-loving nature, her positive attitude and her ability to blend in with his friends. She was entranced with his modesty and even-tempered demeanor—a dramatic contrast after dating Glenn. Much later that night, in the parking lot of Taco Bell, she accepted his invitation to go out the next night to the Hall of Fame, another dancing hangout.

Jeri left out a minor detail: Her parents would be there, too.

When Jeri and Daryl walked into the club, she introduced him to them. The thought of meeting her parents on the second date—and technically, perhaps even the *first* date—overwhelmed him. He sat there in his cowboy hat and boots, nervous, scared, not sure what to say. To him, the whole thing measured pretty high on the Awkward Scale.

Carolyn and Junny didn't see that. They saw a gentleman who seemed to really care about Jeri, who wasn't jaded about the dating process. Carolyn thought to herself, *Here's a guy who would take care of her.* And he scored huge points when Junny saw him walk Jeri to the passenger side of his blue Chevy pickup and open the door for her.

Jeri had some pretty special feelings, too—but she wasn't going to let Daryl know them. Not yet.

They saw each other every day over the last three weeks of Daryl's time in College Station. She saw his demeanor as a strong plus, but confided to Jana that it confused her.

"I don't know if he's really interested in me," Jeri said.

"What are you saying?" Jana said. "Because he's not attacking you? Maybe he's just a nice guy."

"Really?"

"Yes, really."

"I've never been with anyone like this."

"It's not so bad, is it?"

Jeri and Daryl realized they didn't have a lot of time invested in the relationship, but they wanted to continue it by making the two-hour commute between their apartments once Daryl left College Station. They agreed to try to see each other every weekend.

Daryl had been accustomed to being on his own and going out with his friends, but he couldn't deny his feelings for Jeri. She secretly thought it wouldn't work—not just because of the distance issue, but also their wildly varying personalities.

Their spiritual differences could have been a problem.

Although Daryl had grown up as a Catholic and attended Catholic school through eighth grade, he had never accepted Christ and viewed attending church as something he was compelled to do, not inspired to do. It was too ritualistic and tedious for him. Everything seemed to be tied up in works and deeds, not confessing that Jesus is Lord.

Jeri did not talk much with Daryl about her faith. He knew she had accepted Christ and attended church camps. That's about it. They didn't clash because their lifestyle was party-oriented and involved late nights.

He didn't regard her heart condition as an issue. Without being specific about it, she had told him that first night at Graham Central

Station that it would prevent her from all-out dancing. She showed him her discolored fingernails. He noticed that she would lose her breath easily.

It would be only over a period of nearly a year that he would come to learn all the details. His feelings were developing strongly, and he didn't want to know the seriousness.

She told him that doctors said she wouldn't be able to have a baby, that her condition wasn't treatable and that ultimately it would take her life, but she was proving the doctors wrong. He took that as a sign that maybe she was not as sick as she should be, that even if she wasn't progressing, she didn't appear to be regressing, and that she'd have many years left.

In Austin, Daryl immersed himself in play time more than finding a career-oriented job in his field that would provide adequately for a family. He became content at Hi/LO, managing the commercial parts delivery program. This started to strain their relationship. Seeing great potential in him that he didn't see himself, she pushed him to try harder.

In August, Jeri broke the ice by telling him she loved him. Daryl had fallen for this petite fireball but was reluctant to spill his soul. Now he could. They had made it through the test of living apart. It became obvious to both of them they would stay together.

In February 1992, Daryl was transferred to Dallas, where he would manage a Hi/LO location. On May 15, Jeri graduated from A&M, with a Bachelor of Arts in psychology and a minor in education. She took a student-teaching job in Richardson, near Dallas.

Marriage was discussed, mostly on Jeri's initiative. But how would Daryl make it official? Would he prepare a trail of rose petals from the front door of his apartment leading to a box with an engagement ring? Would he row her in a boat to the middle of White Rock Lake and, illuminated by a full moon, place the ring on her finger? Would he surprise her by taking her to a Texas Rangers game and popping the question on the scoreboard at The Ballpark in Arlington? No, he wouldn't.

Romance was not in his DNA. He thought the man just asked the question, devoid of histrionics. Here's how it went: They shopped for the ring together, he later bought it and then proposed to her one

August evening in his Dallas apartment. She said yes, she would love to be Mrs. Daryl Paholek.

Daryl did score some very critical points with Junny when he went to Fairfield with Jeri and humbly offered, "I'd like to marry your daughter." Junny's first thought: *Chivalry is not dead!*

"Sure, we'd love that," Junny said. "On that note, you will *always* need to keep her insured. She'll cost you more money in a week than you'll make in a year."

He laughed, but he knew Junny was dead serious.

Daryl appeared to be the answer to their prayers. They couldn't believe how good he was to her—so patient, so willing to serve. She had expressed some concern about his spirituality, but not enough to set off any alarms. They knew she could be difficult at times, and he showed uncommon humility in the midst of that. They could see her bringing out the best in him and inspiring him to career excellence.

And she was glowing.

CHAPTER 7

KOALA BEAR

With the wedding date set—May 1, 1993—Jeri poured her energy into planning *every* detail. Not because she knew Daryl wasn't interested in doing it (which was true), but because she felt positively giddy. She finished her semester of student teaching and moved to Fairfield to live with Carolyn and Junny.

She embarked on a seemingly endless search for some very specific fabric for the bridesmaids dresses: hot pink, turquoise and white floral patterns. Her dress turned out to be much easier. They went 20 miles south to Buffalo and instantly hit pay dirt at Parthena's. Her bouquet would be all-white lilies.

Daryl's parents, Bobby and Margaret, offered to pay half of the wedding expenses, freeing up Jeri and Daryl to hold nothing back. The 400-guest reception would feature round tables with white tablecloths, a champagne fountain and a barbecue meal. Jeri got everything she wanted except the Aggie War Hymn at the end of the wedding ceremony—the wedding coordinator at A&M United Methodist Church emphatically nixed that idea.

Jeri probed Daryl for his opinions, but like most guys, he proved to be frustrating because he didn't give her an answer—or the answer she wanted. He was a happy bystander. She was a stressed bride-to-be.

One month after the engagement, virtually everything was set. Think Jeri was excited about this day?

Meanwhile, early in 1993, Daryl accepted a job in Hi/LO's Houston construction department and rented an apartment in Pearland, about 17 miles southeast of downtown. He would coordinate old-store remodeling, merchandising and any construction work that needed to be done if the company bought or built new retail stores.

As the wedding day neared, Daryl was not consumed with any second-guessing or doubt about the step they were taking. His nervousness stemmed from the idea of standing up in a church full of people. Being a classic introvert, he operated best in a behind-the-scenes role. The last thing he wanted was to take center stage.

On May 1, with half a day to kill until the 3 p.m. ceremony, Daryl got up at about 6 a.m. and, along with his co-best men, Chris Janak and David Derkowski, easily carved a round of golf into his morning.

He arrived early at church for pictures. They went so smoothly that the men's portion of the wedding party had extra time. Daryl's nerves were on edge, so he and the men decided to walk two blocks to the Dixie Chicken. They were a bit out of place there—eight men in tuxes—but they didn't care, because the pitchers of Miller Lite were cold.

The detour went smoothly. Except for the fact that a few of the ushers didn't duck out of the Dixie when Daryl and the others did. As a result, they were late in arriving to usher some of the guests to their seats. Jeri found out right before the ceremony began, and she was not amused. She calmed down when she started hearing organist Ron Ollis belt out the opening of Bach's "Jesu, Joy of Man's Desiring."

As a smiling Jeri entered to Richard Wagner's "Wedding March," Junny choked back the tears and waited for her to take his arm. Carolyn was crying. After defying death more times than they could count, Jeri was about to become a bride. This was the transcendent day of her improbable life.

MAY 1, 1993
A&M UNITED METHODIST CHURCH
COLLEGE STATION, TX

the biggest smile ever

Mr & Mrs Paholek

BRIDAL PORTRAIT
SYSTEMS BUILDING • TEXAS A&M CAMPUS
COLLEGE STATION, TX
MARCH 1993

Even Daryl teared up. As she approached, he thought, *She's radiant. She's my beautiful, glowing bride.*

Jeri's pastor, Bill Gandin, gave the address, followed by Jayme's solo of "The One," a song he had penned with Jeri.

> *Now we stand before Him*
> *Both in God's hands*
> *I know He's put us together*
> *And that this day was something He planned*
> *I've spent my life praying for you*
> *Not knowing if I would find*
> *And now I stand and behold you*
> *A miracle right before my eyes*
> *And I'll give you my heart*
> *And I'll share all my days too*
> *For the rest of our lives*
> *I'll give you all my love*
> *For I know that in you I have found*
> *The one*
> *In times of sunshine*
> *Or caught in the rain of life*
> *I'll kneel beside you*
> *And pray through the pain*
> *And I will be beside you*
> *I'll stay beside you*
> *And I'll give you my heart*
> *And I'll share all my days too*
> *For the rest of our days*
> *I'll give you all my love*
> *For I know that in you I have found*
> *The one*

Daryl's priest, Monsignor Malinowski, read 1 Corinthians 13. After a prayer, Gandin offered the marriage vows, the rings were exchanged and the Lord's Prayer was recited in unison. Jayme sang Steven Curtis Chapman's "I Will Be Here," while Jeri and Daryl lit a unity candle. Gandin gave the benediction, Jeri and Daryl were presented as husband and wife and then the wedding party left the church to Felix Mendelssohn's recessional "Wedding March," played by Ollis.

The program contained a special note from Jeri and Daryl: "We would like to thank each and every one of you for being here to share this special day with us. Please pray for us for our continued growth in love and commitment to God and to each other. May God bless each of you. A very special thanks to our parents for all the love, support and guidance you've given us. We love you so much. Most of all, thanks be to God for this incredible blessing and His abundance of love."

Both sets of parents rode with the bride and groom in the limo to the reception, where the Dixie Chicken Detour was already gaining legendary status. Relief filled the reception hall. Their first dance as husband and wife was to Restless Heart's "Til I Loved You." The photographer took two humorous shots: one of Carolyn massaging her aching feet and another of Junny with his empty pockets outstretched and a bemused expression on his face.

As Jeri and Daryl disappeared into the limo to begin their five-day honeymoon, Carolyn was dogged by the nagging thought: *Is she going to be OK physically?*

She had no idea how prescient that would be.

Carolyn and Junny had expected to receive a phone call regaling them about the joy that had washed over Jeri and Daryl as newly-weds and the special times they were enjoying in San Antonio—the romantic strolls down the picturesque River Walk, the fascinating historical context of the Alamo.

But not *this* kind of a call. Not a call of desperation.

On the second day, Daryl called with the news that Jeri was experiencing intense abdominal pain. She couldn't even get out of bed and move around. They were heading back to Bryan—to St. Joseph Hospital's emergency room. Based on what Daryl had told Jeri's doctor, a cyst on her ovary likely had ruptured.

Although this probably had nothing to do with her heart, it was recommended that they go to St. Joseph's rather than to an emergency room in San Antonio, where doctors who weren't familiar with Jeri's radical medical history would likely think they made "the great discovery" about her heart and shockingly low oxygen-saturation levels. It would only complicate the treatment of her abdominal issue.

The two-hour drive to Bryan seemed like four. Even the slightest bump would exacerbate Jeri's pain. At the hospital, the on-call doctor said tests revealed a ruptured cyst on her ovary, likely caused by sexual activity—a pronouncement that Daryl would have preferred not be given in front of his new mother-in-law. Jeri spent two days there, with doctors monitoring her heart to make sure the medications were not causing complications.

In many ways, it served as the perfect indoctrination for Daryl into the complex medical life of his new bride. A ruined honeymoon? If he could patiently navigate his way through this minefield, that would bode well for their future. And he did. Much later, they'd be able to joke about the honeymoon that went ridiculously awry.

They checked out of the hospital and headed straight for their apartment in Pearland, where their wedding gifts awaited them.

When they had unwrapped all of the gifts and settled into their lifestyle, reality set in for Jeri. They loved the small-town atmosphere—a dramatic contrast from the chaos of Houston. But other than Daryl's aunt and uncle in nearby Friendswood, they knew nobody.

Jeri didn't have a job, so when Daryl worked, his people-person wife was home alone. Junny had once described Jeri as the kind of person who could get on an elevator on the ground floor and have a circle of friends by the time she reached her floor. But she had no elevator now—just a hauntingly quiet apartment.

A few times a month, they would drive to Fairfield and spend the weekend with Carolyn and Junny. Jeri would hang out primarily with Carolyn while Daryl watched TV by himself, napped or went with Junny to his backyard shop to help with oil changes or tune-ups.

Those weekends would be therapeutic for Jeri. Carolyn had been so nurturing through all the tough times, and Jeri had a difficult time letting go.

"The umbilical cord has never been cut," Daryl would joke, and both of them would laugh.

They didn't see Daryl's family as much. Both families got along beautifully, but Daryl felt tension on his side—especially from Margaret—because of all of the time he spent in Fairfield. He argued with his mom occasionally, explaining that they needed to do it at this time in their marriage. He wanted nothing more than Jeri's happiness. As long as Jeri was happy, he was happy.

After a year of marriage, Jeri landed a job as a risk analyst at Phibro Energy (now Valero), a trader of natural gas and electricity based in downtown Houston. It fit her personality perfectly. She'd sit on the 37th-floor trading floor, tracking the profit or loss of each deal, analyzing the market trends and how they affected Phibro's business. She fed off of the pressure, chaos and noise.

Unfortunately, the job didn't really end when the trading did. The job description unofficially included copious amounts of after-work partying—which manifested itself in what Jeri perceived to be a high rate of adultery and divorce in the department. Sometimes her boss would order a limo to take them to an upscale restaurant or a bar, with all expenses paid.

After a year or so, Jeri began to distance herself from that intoxicating lifestyle and get serious about finding a church family. It had been far too easy to backslide, without the accountability she had felt in her youth group at Fairfield.

The idea of church didn't particularly appeal to Daryl, who insisted that if they did find a church, it would have to be Catholic. She would have none of that. Nor did she appreciate the excuse he'd find to avoid going to any church: "I'm tired."

Jeri had grown up in a household where alcohol was not permitted, where even some TV shows that Jeri regarded as harmless were forbidden. She had seen the fruits of that strong family life and wanted it for her marriage. She wanted a base of solid rock, not sand.

They discovered that they had made a mistake by not fully hashing this out before their marriage. Both of them exhibited stubbornness that created tension they had trouble quelling.

She viewed this as a calling from God. If Daryl wouldn't fulfill the Bible's call for the head of the household to lead the way, then she would. Every week, she'd ask: "Where are we going to church this week?" That turned into a rallying cry that pretty much became an order: "We're going to church!"

Finding the right one proved to be almost as frustrating as convincing Daryl they needed one.

They visited Second Baptist for a while. They went to an Episcopal church in Pearland for about six months. They participated in First Baptist's Metro Bible Study—a Monday night supergroup with two hours of praise and worship, along with a lesson—for a year. None of them seemed to be The Place.

Part of the problem stemmed from Daryl's propensity to grade everything against Catholicism. Even though he didn't agree with many of the tenets of Catholicism, it served as the only thing he could use to compare these new experiences. In the back of his mind, he wondered, *Will my family and friends question me if I am not part of the Catholic Church?*

It struck Jeri that marriage did not seem to be as easy as others made it look. She hadn't realized all of the things that would change with the union of one man and one woman.

Her independent, do-her-own-thing-all-of-the-time nature had to be altered to take into account Daryl's desires and needs. Sharing the most basic things—the bedroom closet or the tube of toothpaste—seemed strange to her.

And the powder keg in virtually every marriage—money management—certainly threatened to explode their dreams.

Daryl's "Peaceful Phlegmatic" personality meant he was easygoing, took the path of least resistance and had administrative qualities. Jeri's "Popular Sanguine" personality cast her as a live-in-the-present woman—impulsive, inattentive to detail and disorganized.

Money management requires careful planning, discipline, forward thinking and organization—everything that Jeri's personality would not allow. She hadn't ever held a real job, hadn't been taught financial responsibility and had been bought many of the things she wanted by her parents.

"When it comes to money, that Daryl is just anal," Jeri used to joke. "He's just a thrifty nerd."

He had to teach her how to save—a move that she later would thank him for. They began to work toward goals together—first a new car, then a house.

The combination of their totally opposite personalities proved to be good most of the time. Jeri's vivacious nature brought Daryl out of his shell. Daryl's grounded nature gave Jeri a firm base from which to operate. Jeri called Daryl "Dare," short for Daryl. He called her "Baby."

To everyone who knew them, they seemed inseparable. Anytime they were seen together—whether on the couch, at the fireplace or the kitchen counter—they were snuggled up. Even at dinner, they sometimes shared a chair, like they were glued together.

Amy had noted this, saying, "You two are always snuggled up and hunched up together like a couple of koala bears. Jeri and Dare, Koala Bear!"

At other times, their opposite personalities clashed. Daryl wouldn't get excited when she did and wouldn't get down when she did. The chart of her emotions contained a collection of wildly fluctuating and jagged lines; for Daryl, nothing but a flat line.

Sometimes she loved his even-keel disposition and recognized it as a beneficial way to keep the stress level low. Other times it drove her crazy. They'd be engaged in a disagreement and she'd yell, "Just fight with me! I want you to yell at me! Say something!"

Her frustration level boiled over at times. She'd be so upset during an argument that she'd storm out, get in the car and drive until she had calmed down. Daryl tolerated that. For a while. Even though her attitude upon return was usually one of total calmness and forgiveness, he finally put his foot down: "That's the last time you're going to do that." And it was. She respected the fact that he drew a line in the sand.

Jeri spent most of her time cooking. Salads, cheesecakes and Cornish hens were her specialties. She even entertained the idea of attending culinary school, but nixed it when she determined she wasn't artistic enough.

Since Jeri tended to be extremely scattered—*A to-do list? Are you kidding?*—she couldn't be bothered to put household items back in their place. No problem for Daryl. He served her magnificently and without hesitation or complaint, doing most of the washing, drying, folding and vacuuming.

Carolyn and Junny saw how he dealt with Jeri and concluded that they could have searched the world over and not found a better husband. He took everything she dished out and still stood by her.

To Jeri, it seemed that her parents sometimes fawned excessively over him.

Carolyn would hear her snap at Daryl and admonish her: "Jeri, don't talk to Daryl like that."

"Oh, mom," she'd blurt out, "you think Daryl can do no wrong."

Jeri continued to encourage Daryl to gain confidence in his abilities. She told him he could do much better than Hi/LO and insisted that he send resumes to builders to take advantage of his degree.

By August 1995, it paid off. Pulte Homes hired him as a superintendent/builder and he happily put Hi/LO in the rear-view mirror. They started looking for a home in Cypress Mills, 28 miles northwest of downtown Houston, and found a subdivision and house they loved.

One weekend, they decided to investigate the Cinco Ranch area of Katy—25 miles west of downtown—because Pulte had a new neighborhood there. They knew nobody in Katy, but they loved the beautifully landscaped 7,600-acre master-planned community and the highly regarded Katy Independent School District. The house would cost $10,000 more than the one in Cypress Mills, but they felt God leading them in this direction.

Early the next year, they took one of their biggest steps as a couple when they attended a weekend Family Life Marriage Conference in Houston. Daryl wasn't thrilled about attending—it would mean a lot of touchy-feely expressions—but he knew it was important to Jeri, so it became important to him.

The purposes were many: to examine God's purpose in bringing them together; understand the role that hardship plays in making their marriage stronger; break free from past hurts; learn to recognize the strengths in their marriage that were disguising themselves as obstacles; and create a plan for a long-lasting marriage.

The conference featured a number of seminars interspersed with breakout periods where Jeri and Daryl were put in positions where they sometimes had to confront uncomfortable demons. They had a date night. Each wrote a love letter to the other.

Their most compelling takeaway? They realized the importance of keeping their marriage Christ-centered and finding a church where they could grow together and worship.

And so they ventured off into the fertile spiritual territory of Katy to find that church. They tried First Baptist, Kingsland Baptist, St. Peter's United Methodist. None seemed quite right.

CHAPTER 8

THE POWER OF PRAYER

The phone call came like a lightning bolt out of the sky in April 1996, jolting Jim Leggett out of his chair.

James Jackson, senior pastor at Chapelwood United Methodist Church in Houston, wanted to propose an idea that Jim didn't know had ever even been discussed. James said Chapelwood had saved money to help start a new church in Katy, a rapidly growing area where Chapelwood saw a need. Would it be OK if Chapelwood recommended Jim to the UMC bishop as the pastor who would plant this church?

Jim, a 30-year-old, self-described "engineer nerd" who had graduated from A&M with a chemical engineering degree, had been pastoring a two-point charge: Grace UMC in Hearne and Gause UMC in Gause, a pair of quaint towns about 25 miles northwest of College Station. He knew every member and had visited each one in their home. Jim and his wife, Lisa, felt a strong sense of contentment.

Living in Hearne, they could practically hear the Aggie roars coming from Kyle Field on fall Saturdays. On the other hand, the big excitement in Hearne centered around watching the cotton grow and waiting for squirrel-hunting season.

Jim and Lisa prayed for God's guidance and felt a call to go to Katy. A week later, Sam Duree, superintendent of the Northwest Houston District of the United Methodist Church, called and formally offered the invitation.

Jim immediately hopped in his car, drove to Katy and conducted a two-day prayer retreat. For hours, he drove the city streets, pouring out his heart: *Help, God. We have no idea how to plant a church from scratch. God, if you had some surrendered vessels through whom you could start a brand new church here, what would you want to do? What would be your vision, your mission?*

He scribbled in his journal the things he felt he heard God saying. They became some of the first mission vision statements of Grace Fellowship United Methodist Church.

Back in Hearne, he and Lisa called the 11 most prayerful people they knew in Texas and said, "Would you adopt us in prayer? Here's what God's calling us to do. If you'll commit to pray for us in this new church plant and if you'll commit when God leads to fast, then we'll commit every two weeks to send you a fresh list of what we need prayed for." And all 11 committed to that.

Jim and Lisa committed to a "prayer experiment," making prayer the major focus of the church plant, depending on God, plugging into the vine.

On June 9, 400 people from Chapelwood signed up and agreed to pray for the church plant every day for six straight months. Ninety-six agreed to take turns fasting for a 24-hour period over the next seven weeks.

Then 50 people from Chapelwood agreed to consider being a missionary by coming to an informational meeting. They cast a vision of what this new church might look like and then asked 22 of them to be on a start-up team.

But where would they worship? The Methodist Church had given Jim geographical boundaries inside which there were only two schools—and both already had church plants meeting in them. They could meet in a Municipal Utility District building that would seat 50, but their faith was much bigger than that.

One day, as he drove down Mason Road, he looked off to the side and saw what appeared to be Camelot in the distance. With the inspiring voices of singing angels seemingly filling his car, he gazed down the one-quarter-mile driveway, flanked on each side by a horse pasture, with a stately white mansion at the end.

Inside, he met with Toni, the programming coordinator for the Southwest Equestrian Center's mansion. She walked him around the mansion and into an upstairs ballroom that seated 500. *This is it, this is it!* he thought.

"Well, Toni, how much would it be to meet here?" he asked.

"$2,000," she said.

"$2,000 a year?"

"No, it would cost you $2,000 every time you met here."

"OK . . . OK."

But inside, he thought, *Are you crazy, lady? We don't have $2,000.*

He wrote the pray-ers and fasters with a request: "Pray us in to the Equestrian Center mansion."

A few weeks later, he went back to reserve a small room for their informational meeting. While Toni finished the paperwork, Jim saw her write in her calendar.

"Toni," he said, "would you mind looking into that calendar for me? Does anybody ever meet here on Sunday mornings?"

She flipped through an entire year and said, "Nobody ever meets here on Sunday mornings."

"Look," he said, "I can't give you $2,000 a week, but I could give you $250 a week. That's what the schools charge. I know that doesn't sound like a lot of money to you, but we would meet here 52 Sundays a year, so that's $13,000. If nobody's ever meeting here on Sunday mornings, then that's $13,000 of income you're not getting now."

"Well, let me go talk to the owner," she said.

She came back and said, "$500."

"$300," Jim countered.

She went back to the owner, then returned and said, "$325."

"We'll take it, we'll take it!"

The 22-person start-up team began meeting in July 1996. They met three times a week. They visited other start-up churches on Sundays to see what it looked like. They'd meet on Sunday nights to pray and worship. They fervently planned and prayed, one time ripping out the pages of a Yellow Book and praying by name for everyone in Katy.

Three weeks before the scheduled start, Jim called the Katy postmaster.

"We've got this mass-mailer brochure coming to the post office," he said. "It's about to go out. But before you guys send it out, could six of us come down to the post office and pray over it?"

Silence on the other end of the phone. Jim could envision the postmaster muting the call and screaming, "Crazy on line 2! Crazy on line 2!"

Breaking the awkward silence, the postmaster said, "Well, sure, nobody's ever asked that before. C'mon down."

So six of the team went to the post office, laid hands on the brochures, anointed them with oil and prayed, "Oh, God, would you make these brochures invisible to churched people. But God, when an unchurched person gets this in the mail, would you reach out and grab them and draw them to yourself and draw them to this or another life-giving church? Anoint these brochures."

All summer, they had been planning and praying for 250 for the first service. With two weeks to go, while praying during a jog, Jim didn't hear an audible voice, but in his spirit he could feel God saying, "Trust me for 600." And in his spirit back to God, he said, "God, I'd love to trust you for 600, but these people have been working hard all summer long, planning and praying for 250. I can't go tell them 600." Once again, he felt God saying, "Trust me for 600, trust me for 600."

So they figured out how many workers they would need to service the children's and youth ministries, then called up everybody they knew in greater Houston: "Don't leave your church, but will you come and help for the first three months?" By faith, they printed 600 bulletins.

At 6 a.m. on September 8, Jim unlocked the front door of the Equestrian Center mansion. He reached into his pocket, pulled out a small jar of oil, anointed the front door to chase out all of the demons from the party-happy place. He walked through every room, inviting the spirit of God to come and take up residence.

At 9 a.m., the prayer team showed up and walked through the ballroom, laying hands on and praying for every single chair. At 10, about 40 gathered in a circle, prayed together and then dispersed to their stations.

At 10:10, about 10 worshippers were in the ballroom. At 10:15, 20. At 10:20, 30. And then, at 10:22, a team member came running into the ballroom.

"Jim! Jim! Come here!"

He led Jim out onto the second-floor balcony overlooking the driveway. Jim couldn't believe his eyes. Was this the final scene in *Field of Dreams*? He saw a bumper-to-bumper string of cars backed up all the way onto Mason Road.

"Holy cow! We're going to have a church!" he said.

Jim turned out to be wrong. Grace Fellowship UMC didn't welcome 600 people for its first service. It welcomed 663.

And when all of them had gone, 22 start-up members sat in a daze, just amazed at what God had done.

"You know," Jim said, "prayer works."

*　　*　　*

On January 5, 1997, Jeri and Daryl turned out of their subdivision and headed north on Mason toward First Baptist. They never made it.

Two miles into their trip, as they approached the Equestrian Center, they saw a Grace Fellowship sign. Why hadn't they noticed it before? They had driven that stretch of road dozens of times in the past few months.

Daryl checked his watch. Grace Fellowship's first service would be starting in 15 minutes.

"Let's go try it," Jeri said, and Daryl agreed.

From the moment they entered the door, the whole thing had the feel of serendipity. Welcomed warmly by greeters, they settled into their seats. On stage, worship pastor A.J. Bass and the praise band belted out the kind of loud, passionate praise and worship music that Daryl usually disliked because he found that the emphasis frequently was on the performers and the performance—instead of God. Except that this had a different feel. The band was not the focal point. The worship was.

They loved Jim's style. He wasn't fire-and-brimstone preachy, nor did he fill them up with a prosperity doctrine that promised God's free-flowing favor and ignored the Bible's numerous references to the struggles that believers would have to endure. Jim preached straight from the Bible, offered eloquent anecdotes and stories, and challenged the congregation with ways to apply the message in their own lives.

When Jeri and Daryl left a service after visiting a church for the first time, they had always found things they didn't like. Not this time. Both agreed this would be where they would worship. It didn't hurt that Grace Fellowship was just in its infancy. They could get in on the ground floor and be a part of something special.

They didn't waste any time. Exactly four weeks later, they attended the Exploring Grace 101 class for those who wanted a primer on the church's beliefs, vision and membership process.

God, primarily through Jeri, had been working on Daryl for a few years. The time had come.

Feeling an irresistible tug on his heart toward the end of the class, he stared at the page in his booklet. He was being offered a chance to accept Christ. Many times at altar calls, he had felt compelled to get up, but he just couldn't seem to move his legs. His heart and his brain wouldn't line up.

How could he pass it up now? And so he silently read this prayer: *Lord Jesus, I want to know you personally. Thank you for dying on the cross for my sins. I open the door of my life and receive you as my Savior and Lord. Thank you for forgiving me of my sins and giving me eternal life. Take control of the throne of my life. Make me the kind of person you want me to be.*

Daryl could feel God speaking to him. He felt comforted, felt God's presence. He didn't show it outwardly, but Jeri could tell exactly what had just happened. She saw it in his eyes.

They had added a spiritual bond to their physical bond. They had a new church family, a new house, new friends—some pretty radical life-change units. They were moving into a different phase of their life together.

About half of the 663 who had shown up on September 8 became regular attendees. Jim's philosophy centered on the concept of making the church seem less intimidating and more welcoming by emphasizing small groups. The focus would be on people, particularly on families. People would minister to each other, essentially training leaders.

He hand-picked Jeri and Daryl out of that 101 class to be in the small group he and Lisa had formed in October 1996, meeting in the home of Garrett and Katie Dolan.

One day, Jim visited their house to drop off the lesson and the details of the group. Daryl couldn't have been more shocked. He had a vision of the church pastor being an untouchable, holier-than-thou figure who did not associate with the members at that level.

On March 2, Grace Fellowship was officially chaptered. Two days later, the church purchased one of the horse pastures—12½ acres in the front yard of the Equestrian Center.

That same week, Jeri and Daryl found themselves in the Dolans' den. Daryl—operating way out of his comfort zone—gutted it out. Jeri, of course, jumped right in.

As they sat in a circle on the floor, Jeri and Daryl introduced themselves. At one point, Jeri offered, "I'm not feeling very good." Lisa and Katie noticed her darkened lips and fingertips. Jeri did not go into detail about her condition, but over the next few months, the entire story came out.

Katie felt an eerily strong connection with Jeri. She and Garrett had moved to Katy in August, shortly after doctors had told them that their 4-year-old daughter, Emily—who hadn't been expected to survive the delivery and was born with disabilities and complex medical needs—was suffering from kidney failure.

Three weeks after Jim had given his first sermon at Grace Fellowship, the Dolans called him and asked him to come to their house to pray over Emily. She died that night. In the weeks that followed, the Dolans struggled with their faith in the midst of trying to understand why Emily would suffer so intensely, why her life would end so tragically short.

Katie had been immersed in nuances and protocol of the medical world for four long years. She could identify with everything Jeri had gone through, and Jeri could do the same for Katie. As Jeri continued to describe her condition, Katie realized that the scar Jeri had was almost identical to Emily's.

Everybody in the group came to understand that Jeri's petite stature belied her strength. She packed a powerful punch—not with a loud voice, but with strong opinions. By the world's standards, she was weak. But in her spirituality, she couldn't have been stronger.

Lisa and Jim found themselves drawn in by Jeri's beautiful mix of authenticity, boldness and faith. Jeri openly admitted her fear, but also said, "OK, I'm going to trust God." Lisa thought, *If you're not scared, it's easy to trust God. That's what makes her faith that much more incredible.*

She never dominated the group, nor did she serve as the group clown. She became a master at igniting discussion.

"Here's what I think about that," she'd say.

Or, "I don't understand the Scripture in light of . . . "

Or, "We need to pray about . . . "

In the years that followed, Jim—ever the "engineer nerd"—found himself making a mental chart, with Jeri's boldness and faith occupying the Y axis and trending up and up and up. Likewise, he could make the same chart with Daryl's spirituality.

In the beginning, Daryl barely opened his mouth in their small group. Virtually the only time he talked would be when they broke up into groups of three to share prayer requests and pray for each other, or when they shared their best and worst moments of the week—but only because he *had* to talk then. Still, he felt no pressure—just warmth and security.

Jeri and Daryl, ignited by the energy of the church and their desire to serve, found themselves working in the nursery together. They dealt primarily with six-month-old babies—Jeri called them "my angels"—pretty much one per adult worker for the morning. That's where Daryl changed his very first diaper.

He preferred working with the team that turned the Mansion's second-floor room into the church's sanctuary every Sunday morning. Along with up to seven other men, he'd arrive at 7 a.m., set up the stage and arrange the chairs.

Jeri had an idea for another area of service: the youth ministry. Jim had mentioned it, suggesting that they talk to youth pastor Brian Smith. Brian was looking for young couples, particularly those with no children because they would have fewer family obligations.

Daryl fought the idea—it would be another excursion out of his comfort zone—but when Brian asked them to lunch, they met with him and poured out their hearts about their love for children.

Jeri had determined that because she was doing just about anything she wanted to—including many things that astounded doctors—she could also carry a baby during pregnancy, and it wouldn't be as difficult or as dangerous as they said it would be. Her thought process was clear: *I have done everything else that many normal people do. I am sure I can do this.*

She began to pray about God's will for her. God revealed His plan, telling her that this was not about her—it was about another living person. She realized that even if she survived the delivery—a rather dubious notion according to her doctors, given her weakened heart and remarkably low lung capacity—her little baby might not be able to get the things it needed to survive along with her. God convicted her that if she got pregnant, it would be a selfish act. He gave her perfect peace that adoption would be the answer.

Brian saw the passion and realized that because they had no children, they could encourage the youth in the ministry while they waited to have their own.

And when Daryl found out Brian was a fellow Aggie, the deal was sealed.

From the very beginning, Brian noticed the fire in their eyes to build relationships with the kids.

When Jeri spoke to the entire group in the worship setting, she approached it as if it were the calling of her life. She openly addressed her medical condition. She wanted everyone to know why her physical appearance might seem a bit off. She shared her testimony about how God had given her an opportunity to live as long as He had, despite the commonly espoused medical opinion that common ventricle was a death sentence.

"Do not take anything for granted," she told them. "Appreciate every moment, every minute, every opportunity you have been given to grow and share Christ with others."

She went with them on retreats to Forest Glen in Huntsville (90 minutes north of Katy) and Frontier Camp in Grapeland (three hours north), both of which featured high-element activities. One involved climbing to the top of a telephone pole one rung at a time, putting your stomach on top of the pole and, without anything above to grab, getting to a standing position and then jumping off the top to a trapeze-like beam.

Too risky for Jeri in her condition, but not for the kids.

"If I could do that, I'd be up there in a second," she told them. She encouraged them to overcome their obstacles and motivated them.

The things she could do, she did with gung-ho fervor. They played games that involved mud or whipped cream or eggs, and she'd be right in the middle, screaming as loudly as they did and getting as messy as they did.

When the group went to Fredericksburg (3½ hours west of Katy) to climb Enchanted Rock—a 425-foot-high pink-granite exfoliation dome—she did it right along with them. She took frequent breaks and needed more time, but she did it.

She sang, laughed, cried and prayed with those kids. And they never forgot that.

Jeri couldn't get enough of the church. Her passion for prayer lined up perfectly with Jim's vision for the church.

Early in that first year, she sought out Dixie and Waldo Leggett, Jim's parents. Dixie had started a pre-service prayer session on Sunday mornings in the kitchen, adjacent to the ballroom where the services were held. Jeri wanted to be a part of it, so she met with a half-dozen others and covered Jim, the other pastors and the congregation in prayer.

Dixie didn't have to recruit Jeri to do anything related to the prayer ministry. Jeri just jumped right in.

Dixie had been spearheading a project involving weekly prayer requests submitted by the congregation every Sunday on yellow sheets that had been inserted into the bulletin. Dixie would type every single request exactly as it had been written, then mail them—later e-mailing them—to each member of a team that prayed for each request.

Jeri joined that team, and also the "Prayer Life" team Dixie had started. They'd meet on the first and third Tuesdays of every month for as long as they felt God leading them to—usually two to three hours—and prayed for the church, the pastors, the staff and any individual requests anybody had.

Jeri didn't make a big deal about her condition, but everybody knew about it and wanted to cover her in prayer.

"Don't pray for *me* all the time," she insisted. "Pray for everyone else."

Then she started her own team called "Praying Grace" that would pray specifically for the staff. The ministry was announced in the bulletin, but it didn't draw the response she had hoped for. Sometimes, she'd be the only one there at 9 a.m. on Thursday. Didn't matter. She remained faithful.

She then expanded that ministry, occasionally praying over them before their meetings—for their continued strength, for the tough decisions they had to make, for the role they wanted to play in the growth of the church, for their protection.

The staff considered it a huge gift. It provided encouragement and comfort, knowing that she would give of her time so lovingly to embrace them. They could see right into her heart.

Jeri lived Philippians 2: 3-4: *Do nothing out of selfish ambition or vain conceit, but in humility consider others better than your-selves. Each of you should look not only to your own interests, but also to the interests of others.*

She prayed for those who were praying for her. She had faith for people in difficult situations because she had to have that herself. Her condition gave her empathy and faith.

And yet she never tried to hide her fear about her condition. One Sunday morning after service, she asked Dixie to pray with her. She had an appointment the next day with her cardiologist at Texas

Children's, Dr. Ronald Grifka. She absolutely loved him, but sometimes the reality of those visits scared her.

"They're just going to tell me the same thing tomorrow—that I'm dying," she said.

Dixie admired that transparency. Despite her brave approach, she got scared sometimes, and she did not feel ashamed that anyone knew it. She knew what to do when she felt that fear: go to God and cast it on Him.

Dixie and Jeri grew very close. Dixie ultimately claimed a passage for Jeri, Psalm 91:14-16: *"Because he loves me," says the LORD, "I will rescue him; I will protect him, for he acknowledges my name. He will call upon me, and I will answer him; I will be with him in trouble, I will deliver him and honor him. With long life will I satisfy him and show him my salvation."*

They prayed it together before every prayer session. Except that Dixie would insert Jeri's name, so it went like this: *"Because Jeri loves me, I will rescue her . . . "* Jeri wrote a note in her Bible: "Dixie's verse for me."

Dixie was counting on a long life for Jeri.

CHAPTER 9

A BOY NAMED BRADY

The decision to go to New Life Children's Services was much easier than the decision to adopt. Jeri and Daryl felt like God made it for them.

In 1996, before they started attending Grace Fellowship, Jeri had gone to Metro Bible Study at First Baptist one night without Daryl. At the end of the night, she went to the altar to pray. A woman approached Jeri and introduced herself as Jenny. Jeri told her what was on her heart—that she was wrestling with the issue of adoption. Jenny, sensing the situation called for her to be totally vulnerable, told Jeri that she had placed a child for adoption through New Life. She recommended New Life as a compassionate and biblically based group that would treat everyone involved with respect.

New Life, located on the campus of Northwest Baptist Church in the Cypresswood area of northwest Houston, is a nonprofit organization that is more of a ministry than an adoption agency. When pregnant women walk in, New Life helps them with medical concerns and offers counseling on the issues involved in raising a baby—instead of pressuring them to give up their baby for adoption.

Once the woman decides on adoption, she would be given the option of viewing the profiles of prospective families. From there, it would be the woman's decision.

Early in 1997, Jeri and Daryl initiated the process. They had heard it could take up to six years from the time the paperwork is filed until the family receives the baby. They didn't want to wait that long, but they trusted God for the timing. In the meantime, Jeri quit her job so they could gauge how they would fare without her income.

They made their way through the requisite paperwork. The questions were penetrating and difficult: Would they consider taking the child of a woman who had abused alcohol before, during or after the pregnancy? What about drugs? They knew the more limiting their answers, the less chance they had of a successful adoption, so they wrote that the circumstances were not a concern.

They were also asked to make a video, which delighted outgoing Jeri but petrified introverted Daryl. They decided to take the video camera to their small group, where they filmed their friends talking about their desire and suitability for parenthood.

If there was a key element, it was the autobiography each one had to write. Jeri tackled hers head-on, penning a six-page letter that described her loving family life, her self-consciousness in high school, her high times at A&M, her courtship with Daryl, the early marriage difficulties and the role their Christianity played in drawing them closer. At the end of the letter, she openly described her heart defect and the way she had overcome the doubts it had created in her psyche. Describing the meeting she had with Jenny at the altar, she wrote, "Do you realize this whole thing is a real miracle from God? We do!"

In June, New Life accepted Jeri and Daryl into the program. There wasn't much communication after that, relegating them to playing an anxious and excruciating waiting game.

This did not resemble a normal pregnancy. At any minute, they could receive a call from New Life: *We have a birth mother who has selected you.* They had to have a nursery ready for a baby, and yet it could be years before they actually used it.

Jeri's primary concern was how the birth mother would view her heart condition: Would she eliminate Jeri because of the fear that she wouldn't be around long enough to raise the child? They did the only thing they could do—turn it over to God.

While they were waiting, Jayme and his wife, Stephanie, had their first child, Lauren. Jeri was thrilled, but it only served to heighten her sense of anticipation. She'd call New Life periodically and hang up the phone with an air of sadness.

In November, they started looking through baby books in an attempt to pick a name. For a boy, they decided to stay away from Daryl Jr., any member of either family or even any Aggie legend because they wanted him to have his own identity. Jeri saw the name Brady and immediately liked it.

Brady is Gaelic in origin and means "spirited." It had become increasingly popular—in 1993, it cracked the list of the top 200 boy names—but not too popular.

For a girl, they settled on Mia, which is Italian in origin and means "my."

On December 8, they received the long-awaited call from New Life. They had been chosen by a birth mother expecting a boy on December 19. She was 18-year-old Amber and was living with a foster family in church. No reason was given for why she chose Jeri and Daryl, but they later learned that Amber felt they would give the child undivided love because they had no other children. Amber's sense that Jeri wanted this baby so badly trumped any concern about her heart condition.

Jeri nearly jumped through the ceiling after getting off the phone. She already could picture this gift named Brady. The news obviously thrilled Daryl, but he reminded Jeri that Amber could change her mind within 48 hours of the delivery and keep the baby.

New Life said that could happen, and had happened. The adoptive parents get their hopes up. They vulnerably allow themselves to love a child they haven't seen. But they also have to know that the rug can be yanked from underneath their feet. It's a scary situation and can result in monumentally broken hearts.

December 19 arrived, but the baby didn't. *This is torture*, Jeri thought. Patience had never been Jeri's calling card, and now she was being asked to wait patiently for the miracle she would call her "sunshine baby." And yet she later would say that she had gotten "closer with God than ever before." She wore out her knees in prayerful worship.

New Life called on December 28 to say that doctors would be performing a C-section the next day because the delay jeopardized the health of Amber and the baby. A little more than nine months had passed since they started the process. It was almost as if it had been Jeri's pregnancy. She believed there was a reason why Amber's delivery had been 10 days late—God wanted to make sure she didn't spend Christmas alone.

The next day, at 11:20 p.m., he was born at Conroe Columbia Medical Center. New Life called to say that he had scored low on the Apgar test—which rates a baby's condition at birth through activity, pulse, grimace, appearance and respiration—because of breathing difficulties. He would be placed in the neonatal ICU unit.

Did they still want him?

Jeri never hesitated: "Of course!"

Amber had named him Brendan Michael, so Jeri and Daryl honored New Life's request by incorporating that into his given name: Brady Brendan Michael Paholek.

From behind the glass at the neonatal ICU unit on December 31, their first glimpse of him seemed rather incongruous: Mixed in with a handful of 1-pound babies struggling to survive was this 8-pound, 3-ounce, 21-inch giant with light-brown hair and blue eyes.

Two realities hit them: parenthood ("Oh, my gosh, we're parents! Are we ready for this?") and the 12 hours that remained until they could truly breathe easy.

Amber cried when she placed him in Jeri's arms. Jeri cried over how beautiful he looked as she fed him his bottle. Now she knew how Carolyn had felt when Jeri burst her way into the world 30 years ago. She hadn't carried Brady inside of her, but her love was unconditional and undeniable. She would devote her life to him, just as her mom had with her.

The deadline passed uneventfully. Brady spent New Year's Day in the hospital, foiling Daryl's plans for a father-son viewing of the Aggies' Cotton Bowl game against UCLA. On January 2, Amber signed the papers, checked out of the hospital and went directly to New Life for a scheduled meeting at which she would give Brady to Jeri and Daryl.

When they arrived in the room, the New Life counselor was chatting away, trying to break the tension. She knew exactly what was coming: A young woman, scared that she couldn't take care of her baby because she had no job and no support system, yet gripped by intense feelings of regret, was about to hand over her flesh and blood to a couple who were trying to contain their joy out of respect for the anguished mother.

Thirty minutes seemed like 30 hours to Jeri and Daryl, and three minutes to Amber.

"OK," the counselor said, "it's time."

Tears spilled down the cheeks of everybody—including Amber's boyfriend, who was not the birth father but had helped her through the pregnancy.

"I love you, Brendan," Amber said, kissing his cheek.

As Jeri held Brady in her arms, Amber and her boyfriend left the room. The counselor advised Jeri and Daryl to remain for at least another 30 minutes. If Amber somehow was able to see Jeri and Daryl put Brady in their car and drive away, it would only intensify her agony.

When Jeri and Daryl pulled their '93 Honda Accord into their driveway around 6 p.m., they hardly recognized the house. Balloons—each saying BABY BOY—hung all over the front of the house. An IT'S A BOY! sign was stuck in the grass. And occupying the entire width of the garage was a banner: TO GOD BE THE GLORY FOR THE THINGS HE HAS DONE.

From the second-floor balcony, Carolyn screamed, "They're here! They're here!"

When they walked in the front door, with Daryl carrying Brady, both sets of parents erupted in celebration.

After the party ended, neither Jeri nor Daryl could wind down. They worried about doing everything correctly. Their minds raced with the horror stories of parents' heartache over losing babies due to SIDS (Sudden Infant Death Syndrome), even though that primarily applies to infants between one month and one year old.

Daryl fell asleep, but Jeri—charged with adrenaline and anxiousness—kept checking Brady's crib to make sure he was OK. Finally, she just put him in bed with them. They alternated the feedings and diaper-changing. Brady slept the entire night without crying.

Although Amber had officially turned Brady over to them, they actually served as a foster home for six months until the court granted them full custody. They had to prove they were fit parents and also had to write to Amber every month for those six months. They poured energy into reading and digesting *Growing Kids God's Way*, a book New Life required of them.

Daryl would get up every morning at 5 o'clock and feed Brady before he went to work. Brady and Jeri would then sleep for another three hours.

"Good morning, sweet baby! I love you!" Jeri would say to him when he woke up.

Sometimes she'd sing "You Are My Sunshine," and he would look at her and smile. Jeri would wonder what he thought in those moments. She couldn't wait for the day when he actually would be able to tell her. She kissed him constantly—so much that she wondered, *Does he think I'm crazy? Or does it make him feel loved?*

In the afternoons, they'd go shopping, run errands or visit friends. In the hours before Daryl got back from work, Jeri would put on some music and sing and dance for him, sometimes read him a book or watch him play with toys.

Daryl would arrive home and greet him almost the same way as Jeri did in the morning, showering him with kisses. He'd tell him how much he loved him, sprinkle in some guy talk about sports and hold him on his chest while he napped.

Jeri and Daryl became prolific diaper-changers, but sometimes things didn't go exactly as planned. One time, at 2 a.m., both got up to change and feed him. Jeri removed his diaper and was preparing to lift him up to put the fresh diaper on him when she found herself in the line of fire—a diarrhea projectile blasted her in her hair. Daryl cleaned up the mess, she showered and both of them ultimately laughed.

On January 26, she wrote Brady a love letter in her journal:

I can hold you and snuggle with you and carry you in my arms all day. You are already growing too fast. You are up to 10 pounds now and already moving your head around so much. You are so handsome. I can't believe how beautiful you are! I can't believe you are finally here. I love you so much. I tell you that all of the time. The hardest thing for me right now is that I can't tell how you feel about me. I hope you love me. I hope you know how much I love you and how I want to take care of you and make you happy. You are so loved! Happy four-week birthday, sweet baby. I love you!

While Jeri continually wrote love letters to him, so did Amber. And Jeri saved all of them. She felt a bit uncomfortable reading all of Amber's expressions of love for the boy she was raising, but she also noticed deep sadness and tried to imagine the heartache. It only intensified her feelings of gratitude for the blessing God had given her. She honored Amber continually, sending her gifts on her birthday, Mother's Day and Christmas.

On March 9, Brady contracted a high fever and they took him to Texas Children's Hospital. All throughout the night, he'd whine and cry. Jeri's overriding wish was that they could trade places. *God, let me feel the pain.*

The staff took blood and urine samples and gave him a spinal tap, fearing spinal meningitis. Everything checked out OK. For the next three days, Brady needed an IV but gradually improved. Jeri never left his side.

Back at home, his growth seemed to be exponential. He'd blurt out goo-goo, ga-ga incessantly, hold toys in his hands, roll over on his side and even sleep on his stomach in his own bed in his own room. She called him "Mr. Happy and Content."

Having you in my life is truly like taking my heart out and letting it run around! she wrote in her journal. *Brady, I just want you to know how profoundly you have changed me. How deep my feelings go for you and how glorious every little thing you do is to me. God has created something more wonderful than I have ever seen or known, in you.*

I dream of our future. Of long talks and walks through museums and rainy days watching old movies and special dates where we go to the theater to see plays and musicals. But mostly I long for a hug and a kiss and a tiny Brady voice that says, "I love you, mommy!"

Brady's first word was "ball." He loved playing with any kind of ball they put in front of him.

By 15 months, he wore 18-to-24-month-old clothes and could run so fast that Jeri could barely catch him. They bought him a back-yard slide, where he'd climb and scream with joy. He loved watching *Teletubbies, Blue's Clues* and Elmo from *Sesame Street.*

Later in 1999, they met Amber for the required yearly visit. She told them something that day that gave them chills: Early in her pregnancy, before she ever heard of New Life, she had decided to have an abortion. On the night it was to happen, she found herself in her car, idling in front of the abortion clinic. In front of her, she saw a half-dozen people marching in protest of the clinic. They carried signs and were chanting loudly.

Amber didn't know what to do. She didn't feel she could raise this baby. But she also didn't want a nasty confrontation with these enthusiastic protesters. Tears streaming down her face, she slipped the gearshift into drive and pulled away.

She never went back. Her heart began to change, and her visit to New Life convinced her that she wanted this baby to find a home.

What if she had chosen a different time to visit the abortion clinic, a time when the prospect of a confrontation hadn't presented itself? Brady was even more of a miracle than they had thought.

Although they agreed on the way they wanted to raise Brady, they started having disagreements about the lifestyle they would have while doing it.

Daryl, who had taken a new job as superintendent/builder for Trendmaker Homes, woke up early and then had to spend much of his time in the sweltering southeast Texas humidity. By 10 p.m., he couldn't keep his eyes open.

Jeri, on the other hand, had an entirely different schedule. Because Brady was a sound sleeper, she could get all the rest she needed. On top of that, she had always been a night owl who had difficulty sleeping.

She wanted to watch TV in bed with the lights on, and Daryl didn't have a problem with that—he could fall asleep anywhere.

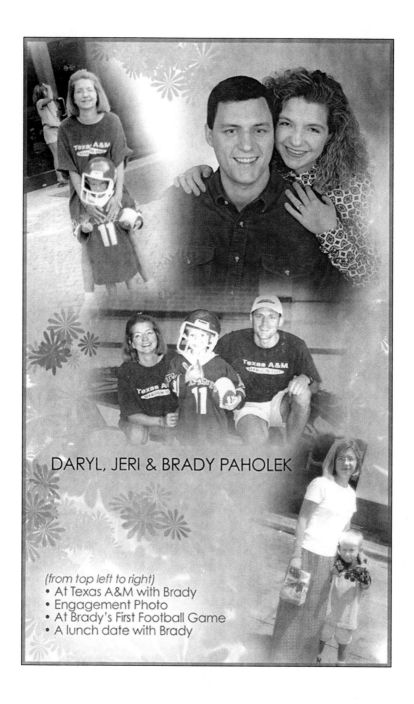

DARYL, JERI & BRADY PAHOLEK

(from top left to right)
• At Texas A&M with Brady
• Engagement Photo
• At Brady's First Football Game
• A lunch date with Brady

Except that Jeri wanted a conversationalist companion at all times. She didn't like being alone, and she felt alone when he had dozed off.

Virtually every night, after Daryl had fallen asleep, she'd elbow him and say, "Wake up! Wake up!" What did she want to talk about? Nothing in particular. She'd make something up. She could be very feisty when she was passionate about something.

Daryl felt like his energy level and job performance were suffering. After some of the arguments they had, she'd wait until he fell asleep and then get into her car, turn on some music and go for a drive to burn off the energy. The next morning, she'd tell Daryl about it, and that incited more arguments.

He didn't like the idea of her driving at 2 a.m., telling her he considered it a dangerous remedy to sleeplessness. Adding to the danger was her propensity for aggressive driving. Although he wasn't the only one to notice her heavy foot, she called him a "traffic nerd."

In a conversation with Lisa, she described what had been happening. Lisa told her that Jim couldn't get to sleep unless the room was dark and quiet, so she would turn off the TV and lights, even though she wanted to stay up another half-hour.

Jeri scoffed and said, "Pfft. Jim needs to get over that!" And they laughed.

Late nights were especially traumatic on the few nights when Daryl's job had taken him out of town. Before they adopted Brady, Katie fielded a few midnight calls from Jeri, wondering if she could spend the night.

She confided in Katie and Lisa that the nights were brutal for her and she had been seeing a counselor to help her deal with the anxiety. The days weren't so difficult because she buzzed around at break-neck speed, taking care of Brady and ministering to anyone she encountered. But when the light faded to dark and the noise to silence, the reality of her condition hit her hard. *Will I make it through the night?* Her mind raced.

None of us is guaranteed our next heartbeat. But for her, the danger lurked ominously close.

Most of Jeri's trips to the emergency room for tachycardia happened after 11 p.m. She'd go to Texas Children's, where they'd draw blood and administer an EKG but could never give a direct explanation for what caused the episode. Daryl speculated that her sleep anxiety had to be the trigger.

Jeri took a half-pill of lorazepam for anxiety, but she couldn't take any medication for insomnia because they conflicted with her heart medication.

They met with Jim once for counseling. They just had to work through it. Daryl tried to stay up as late as he could but not so late that he couldn't function the next day. Jeri tried to ease up on the elbows to the ribs, channeling her energy into journaling or writing letters.

Jeri believed that God had kept her alive so she and Daryl could raise this boy, teach him everything they knew and guide him to love God the way they loved Him. And yet she couldn't help but think that she might not be around to experience all of the monumental moments in his life, and worse yet, he might not remember her.

She didn't keep that fear to herself. In their small group, she would pour out her heart.

"Would y'all come to Brady's high-school graduation and sit in my stead if I'm not there? Would y'all come to Brady's wedding if I'm not there?"

"Jeri, cut that out!" somebody invariably would interject. "You're *going* to be there."

"I'm serious," she'd say. "Would you?"

And all of them would reassure her.

And then they would take it to God.

Jeri never directly shared her fear of dying with her parents. The conversations normally had a cryptic twinge, leaving Junny to wonder if Jeri was leaving out the deep-seated fears of her heart.

"Mom, do you think my lips are bluer than they were?" she'd ask.

"No, I don't think they're any worse."

On a few occasions, she told Carolyn, "You're just in denial."

Although her condition had been stable for a few years, phlebotomies became a yearly—and sometimes twice-a-year—necessity.

Jeri had polycythemia, an abnormal increase in the number of red blood cells produced by the bone marrow—causing her blood to thicken and increasing the risk for blood clots that could lead to a heart attack or stroke. In the phlebotomy, they would remove red blood cells from the blood—which could decrease iron levels in the body—and insert a blood product, using a five-inch-needle in each arm.

Daryl never got used to it. He'd have to leave the room before he passed out.

CHAPTER 10

THEY MUST KNOW NOW

At this point in her life, knowing what she knew about her diminishing time, she had reached an intersection with three potential paths.

She could flip the switch and turn off all of her fears. She could selfishly pursue the path of an adrenaline junkie, doing the things most people only dream about, regardless of the consequences. She could watch the sun rise over Machu Picchu, touch the white-marble majesty of the Taj Mahal, tandem-skydive from 14,000 feet.

She could become reclusive and careful, taking baby steps so she would never get hurt or exacerbate her condition, perhaps maximizing whatever time she had left with Daryl, Brady and her family.

Or she could tackle her fears head-on, relying even more on God and not her own strength as a person or her perseverance to keep on living a full life. She could take her Christian walk to an entirely different level. She could make sure *everybody* knew what she knew.

She chose the last path, reaching out even more than before, having a powerful impact on people she knew and total strangers who would later step back and marvel, *Who was that petite twister who worked her way into my life? She packs a Godly punch!*

It was why Junny would proudly tell people, "She's a participator, not a spectator."

*   *   *

Through her prayer sessions over the church's list of chronic-illness sufferers, Jeri became familiar with Jane Wiley's story.

Jane had been diagnosed with a convexity meningioma, a tumor that sits on the surface of the brain. Because it had wrapped around a main artery through which spinal fluid and blood flows, it had been deemed inoperable. If they had tried, there would be a 100% chance of paralysis or death.

Doctors suggested stereotactic radiosurgery, in which a helmet-like device is screwed into the patient's skull and three-dimensional, computer-aided planning software pinpoints the exact location of the tumor so it can be shot with high doses of radiation. It's known to be 95% effective in shrinking tumors. Jane, unfortunately, fell in the other 5%.

Anti-depressants and anti-anxiety medication didn't help. She would have to get used to the excruciating headaches and the risk of more seizures, perhaps even a stroke. At some point, the tumor could wrap itself entirely around the brain and end her life.

This would be enough of a burden for anyone to handle, but Jane had another one: Her father was dying of stomach cancer.

Jane got to the point where she didn't think she could go on. In August, after suffering a seizure in a parking garage and being locked in her car for five hours, she wondered if perhaps it would be better if her husband, Mark, and her sons didn't have to deal with her anymore. She viewed herself as a burden. *I'll take every pill I have. I'll fall asleep and that will be it. It will be peaceful. No blood.*

Jane had put on a clown face. She had tried to be strong and upbeat for everyone else, but inside she was dying. She had been seeing a therapist who could sense Jane was at the end of her rope. The therapist gave Mark her business card and said, "Call me anytime, 24/7."

On November 11, 1997, she received the call: Mark had found Jane behind the rocking chair in the corner of the living room, curled in a ball, shaking, crying, mumbling.

She had prepared the pills, but a terrifying thought popped into her head that she couldn't erase: *My boys will have to grow up knowing that their mom committed suicide. That would be a bigger burden for them than what I'm feeling.* Overwhelmed with the conflicting feelings, she collapsed and broke down.

The hardest thing Mark ever had to do was take Jane to Memorial Spring Shadows Glen, a psychiatric hospital in west Houston, and watch them take her away. She turned over everything, including her shoelaces, was overmedicated and spent all day in therapy every day for three weeks.

When she got out, she wasn't suicidal anymore. But things didn't get much better. She suffered a stroke early in 1998 because her spinal fluids weren't flowing. In September, her father finally succumbed to the cancer that had cost him 95% of his stomach.

Jane started receiving cards in the mail: *I'm praying for you. Jeri.* They were personal cards that made no mention of the church's prayer ministry. They seemingly were sent at random, but they always seemed to arrive at the time when Jane was at her lowest and needed them the most.

Jane wondered, *Who is this person?* At church, she asked someone to point out Jeri for her. When she first saw Jeri—pale, frail, with blue lips—she thought, *She looks like she needs encouragement.*

Jane started working with babies in the children's ministry. Brady was one of them. Jane saw Jeri every Sunday. It would be the beginning of a relationship both treasured.

Everybody wanted to talk to Jane about her illness, but she didn't necessarily want to. She wanted to talk about her heart, not her head. Jeri, of course, understood that. Jane knew the basics of Jeri's heart condition—the things everybody knew. They seldom talked about the specifics of each other's conditions. Instead, they'd talk about their passions at the church—a Bible study or a specific ministry—or their families.

"What can I pray for?" Jeri would ask.

"That my kids understand what mom is going through," Jane would say.

Jane wondered how Jeri could care so much about her when she was staring down death. Then Jane would feel guilty when Jeri went through a medical procedure and Jane had not done anything in return. Jeri didn't expect that. She did what she did because she wanted to.

Jane opened up to Jeri in a way she couldn't with anyone else. She knew Jeri understood.

Jeri gave her a feeling of profound self-worth and a belief that she meant something to somebody.

"God loves you," Jeri would say. "Even if you don't feel like you love yourself, somebody does. Think about that and praise Him and thank Him for what He has given you, instead of asking, 'Why me?' "

Jane finally got past the point where she asked, "Why me?" She would pray, "Father, I have you in my life. There are people out there who don't have you, and it would be so much worse if they were sick and didn't have you. Now use me for something. Show me what I can do."

*   *   *

In September 1999, Grace Fellowship held its annual Youth Roundup, a massive gathering of teens and their friends for games, fellowship and food.

In the end, they realized they had over-prepared: They had over 60 hamburgers and hot dogs. They would have to go to waste.

"No!" Jeri insisted. "This food has to glorify God in some way!"

Jeri and Brian called Katy Christian Ministries, but the director said the food could not be accepted because it had not been prepared in a certified kitchen. Other calls failed to produce a home for the food.

Jeri decided she would load up the food in her new Toyota Highlander and head east on I-10, looking for homeless people. Brian wouldn't let her go alone, so he hopped in and rode shotgun. She called Daryl, who didn't really like the idea. But what could he do? She wouldn't be deterred.

They found one homeless family. Jeri had a burning desire to do more than just feed them. She found it difficult to give them a meal and then disappear into the night, to go back to her comfortable home knowing that they had nothing. She had so many questions: Where will they go? What will they do? How will God provide for them on a regular basis?

But they continued down I-10, finding two men, both of whom appeared to be intoxicated. One of them, responding to her witness, began to share his faith back to her. Jeri shared the Lord's influence in her life, the importance of living life to the fullest, the ways God had blessed her and the ways she wanted to bless others. The man said God had given him art to share.

He walked away and returned a few minutes later with some paper and permanent markers. Placing the sheet of paper on the window crack, he began to animatedly draw a picture, getting so carried away that his lines were leaving the paper and registering on the interior door panel.

Brian could see Jeri's eyes widening. She knew exactly what he was doing, but she would not tell him to stop. She was simply happy that he could share something with them.

As she drove away, she turned to Brian and said, "Daryl is going to die! We got ink on our brand new car!"

Approaching midnight, they were unable to find a cleaning solution that would remove the marks, so she returned home and told Daryl that she considered serving to be more important than a car or any other material possession. She had resolved that this was part of her sacrifice. She wouldn't worry about a car when the man who inadvertently decorated it had no home.

And that wasn't all. They still had some leftover burgers and hot dogs, so Jeri and Brian went back the next night and ministered to more homeless people until everything was gone.

* * *

Like most people in America, Jeri followed the case of Timothy McVeigh, who on June 2, 1997, had been found guilty of 11 counts of murder and conspiracy and sentenced to death.

From his cell in Supermax, the federal prison in Florence, Colorado, he had penned "An Essay on Hypocrisy"—published by alternative magazine *Media Bypass* in June 1998—in which he maintained that the Oklahoma City bombing was "morally equivalent" to actions the U.S. military had taken against foreign governments. That didn't exactly engender any sympathy toward the fate that awaited him.

After he was transferred to the U.S. Penitentiary in Terre Haute, Indiana, to await his execution, he provided a detailed confession of the bombing to Lou Michel and Dan Herbeck, who early in 2001 would release *American Terrorist*, a chilling journey into the mind and heart of McVeigh.

McVeigh occasionally met with Father Ron Ashmore, the pastor of nearby St. Margaret Mary Catholic Church, who had been asked to head the prison ministry in the absence of a permanent Catholic chaplain. McVeigh had received the sacrament of confirmation at age 17, but according to Ashmore, became an agnostic before joining the Army three years later.

Michel and Herbeck told the story of how the Army recruits were required to either attend church service or scrub the barracks every Sunday morning. He chose to scrub the barracks—until he found out that nobody was monitoring church attendance, which inspired him to sign up for the service and then skip it to hang out in the fields or abandoned barracks. He'd arrogantly tell friends, "Science is my religion."

Jeri sensed that the attitude toward McVeigh was mostly one of condemnation. She understood that. It's difficult to drum up much sympathy for someone who characterized the 19 day-care-center child victims as nothing more than "collateral damage."

But, she wondered, wouldn't it be possible for him to confess his sins, repent and be saved? Isn't it natural for a felon to reach out to God during a period such as this? Hadn't there been thousands of genuine conversions that went far beyond the jailhouse variety that generated so much cynicism? Doesn't Christianity compel us to believe that God forgives any sin, regardless of how heinous? And if we truly believe in prayer, why aren't we doing it for him? Because we don't think he wants it?

Jeri felt that if she could just give him a hug and talk to him, she could break down all the walls. It would not be in her power, but in God's. Just a dream, though. There wouldn't be a hug, or even a trip to Indiana. So beyond praying, what could she do?

Jeri surmised that McVeigh had plenty of time on his hands, confined 23 hours a day to an 8-foot-by-10-foot cell. Talking to Jayme one day, she mentioned that she wanted to write a letter to him.

"Man, you should go for it," Jayme said. "Do it! Don't think about it! Go for it! If that's what you think you need to do, play your part."

And so she sat down and wrote to the man who had perpetrated the deadliest act of domestic terrorism in American history, laying out the road to hope: the idea that God's desire is to give him hope; that sin robs him of this life of hope; that Jesus cares for him; that he could receive hope through a personal commitment by repenting, believing Jesus died for his sins, confessing Jesus as his Lord and asking for forgiveness of sins and eternal life.

She gave him a prayer to say: *Jesus, I believe you are the Son of God, died on the cross for my sins and rose from the dead. I turn from my sins and invite you to become Savior and Lord of my life. Amen.*

Then she went to the post office, carrying a card on which she had written: U.S. Penitentiary, 4700 Bureau Road South, Terre Haute, IN 47802. She mailed the letter special delivery.

It's possible that McVeigh never even read the letter. It's possible that he read it and considered inviting Christ into his life. However, it's very unlikely that he actually did it—all the evidence points to a defiant man who went to his death believing what he had always believed.

In a letter to the *Buffalo News* published on June 10, 2001, he wrote that he was "sorry these people had to lose their lives," but pretty much ruled out any notion of an apology by clinging to the same rationalizations for the horrific crime. He also wrote that he was an agnostic and didn't believe in an afterlife, but if he discovered that it existed, he would "improvise, adapt and overcome"—his use of military jargon to illustrate that he viewed death as part of some sort of grand, demented adventure.

As his last statement, he submitted a handwritten copy of *Invictus* (Latin for "unconquerable"), the 1875 poem by William Ernest Henley: *I am the master of my fate. I am the captain of my soul.*

In the hours before his execution, McVeigh accepted last rites from a Catholic priest. What did it mean? Not a lot, according to Michel and Herbeck: "...To those who knew him, it seemed doubtful that McVeigh ever really apologized, or renounced the worldview he had clung to for so long. Again, we will never know."

On June 11, 2001, McVeigh said nothing before the lethal cocktail of sodium thiopental, pancuronium bromide and potassium chloride was administered. He was pronounced dead at 7:14 a.m. CDT.

"If you're looking for the absolute moment when Tim absolutely accepted Jesus without any positive doubt, you'd have to ask Tim," said Ashmore, who was on the prison grounds but did not administer last rites, "and Tim's not available. You'd have to ask God. That's not my judgment. That's not anybody's judgment. That's God's judgment. And only God can read his heart."

Concluded Larry Whicher, whose brother died in the bombing, "I don't think he gave himself to the Lord. I don't think he repented. Personally, I think he is in hell."

It broke Jeri's heart.

*   *   *

On the morning of September 11, Daryl called Jeri to say that a plane had flown into one of the World Trade Center towers.

Brady was watching Barney on PBS, and by the time Jeri could turn on the bedroom TV, the second tower had been attacked. *Is this a movie?* Jeri thought. Her insides churned.

Jeri took Brady to Grace Fellowship's day care, prayed for his safety and then headed to the Mansion to see if she could help in any way.

When she got there, she found all of the offices empty. Walking into the conference room, she found Brian, office manager Cindy Haas, discipleship pastor Jim Marshall, prayer leader Karen Coolidge and assistant to senior pastor Brenda Martin on their knees, weeping and praying.

Jeri's mind already had locked in on another mission. Hadn't Jim given a sermon earlier in the year that mentioned how prayer stations were being used effectively in New York City? What if they did the same thing in Katy right now?

"We've got to do something," Jeri said. "We have to help people know that God can still meet their needs."

Jeri and Brian went to the supply closet and grabbed two poster boards. On each one, they wrote, in large block letters, NEED PRAYER? Then they drove in Jeri's Highlander north on Mason Road, stopping just south of I-10 in a shopping center parking lot. They backed the vehicle up near the sidewalk facing the busiest road in Katy, opened the tailgate and sat down with the signs on their laps.

They didn't initially have many takers, mostly people who honked to acknowledge their signs, so they prayed for the passing cars and for people to see the signs and know God hadn't abandoned them.

One couple stopped. Shocked and in disbelief, they spoke in broken sentences. They just wanted to be heard and to hear from God. While Jeri held their hands, Brian prayed 2 Chronicles 7:14: *If my people, who are called by my name, will humble themselves and pray and seek my face and turn from their wicked ways, then will I hear from heaven and will forgive their sin and will heal their land.*

That passage is the basis for "If My People," a song A.J. and the praise band regularly used in worship. So Jeri and Brian sang that song and worshipped with this husband and wife.

Around 2 p.m., they changed locations to an intersection near Cinco Ranch High School, where many of the children of congregation members attended. A number of students recognized them and stopped to pray.

Even after the students dispersed, Jeri's day was not done. Before they had left the Mansion, Brenda asked Jeri if she would stop by the Krause Center, a Katy facility that provides help, healing and hope to troubled boys and girls between the ages of 11 and 17—one of them being Brenda's daughter. Brenda just wanted somebody to be available for the staff and kids on this terribly confusing day.

And so Jeri went. None of the staff knew who she was, but they were grateful that Jeri prayed for their protection and peace.

Brenda never forgot it.

* * *

Living out Philippians 2 (*Do nothing out of selfish ambition or vain conceit, but in humility consider others better than yourselves*), Jeri became a prominent prayer warrior at church, praying for those who were praying for her.

Near the end of the Sunday service, Jim would invite the congregation to come to the altar and pray. Jeri was one of the compassionate caregivers on the other side of the rail, along with Brenda and a few others. Seeing a woman cup her hands—indicating she wanted someone to pray with her—Jeri would gently kneel down and touch her arm, or perhaps cradle her in her arms.

It wouldn't have been surprising for a newcomer to the church to guess that one of those women had been given a death sentence— but it would have been a shock to learn that it was the one doing the cradling, not being cradled.

Not all of the moments were solemn. One Sunday, Brenda put her hand on top of the rail to brace herself while standing up, and the entire rail came off in her hands. Jeri, finishing her prayer with a congregation member, saw Brenda with the rail and a stunned expression, and couldn't help but burst out in laughter. She checked her laughter quickly so that no one would think she had been laughing at the previous prayer request.

Jeri and Brenda laughed at themselves a lot. Many times their humanness bumped squarely into the sacredness of their role. They found great relief in doing something so intimate with God and His people and then being able to laugh and not be so pious about themselves. Jeri was real. Brenda loved that about her.

Of course, Jeri did some pretty powerful intercessory praying right under her own roof. Nothing would give her as much joy as knowing that Brady had accepted Jesus Christ and been assured salvation.

She gave him his first memory verse, Deuteronomy 32:4: *God is the rock.* They made a poster together and put it in Brady's room.

On November 6, 2001, hours after Brady accepted Christ, she wrote in her journal:

God answered the many prayers I have prayed for your salvation. He answered that prayer in only 3½ years. I am so amazed by Him every day. God has been teaching me a lot about what He plans for you. I believe God has set you apart to be a Godly man who will minister to people in some way. I was reading 1 Samuel. I identify so much with Hannah. God is telling me that I am to set you apart. I prayed for you to be here and God answered my prayer. Now I want to do everything I can to grow you into a Godly young man. One crazy or wonderful thing is, I believe you already know God has a plan for you. You have to begun to have such a hunger and thirst for Jesus. You pray, sing and learn about Him whether I am with you or not. I truly believe you have a strong connection with God in some childlike way that I as an adult can't understand. But I wrote all of this to tell you that you are a new creation. You have Jesus in your heart. You prayed that prayer. Don't ever forget that.

*   *   *

On the morning of June 5, 2002, Jeri's eyes were drawn to a headline in the *Houston Chronicle:* "Teen in custody sues over abortion denial."

She read the article, which described how a 17-year-old girl in custody at Minola's Place of Texas, a residential treatment center in Houston, had sued because the facility had denied her release to get an abortion.

The girl had pleaded guilty to assault with family violence on May 1 and was scheduled to spend 60 days in a boot camp. After she learned there that she was pregnant, she was sent to Minola's to finish the term. On May 31, the day she was to have the abortion, State District Judge Ken Anderson denied her release, saying it was not in her "best interest."

A hearing would be held today at 1 p.m. at Bob Casey Federal Courthouse in downtown Houston before U.S. District Judge Venessa Gilmore.

The story disturbed Jeri on so many levels.

She passionately opposed abortion. She couldn't understand why God wouldn't allow her to have children, and yet other women could get pregnant without even trying and then casually choose to terminate their lives.

In addition, she and Daryl had been talking about adopting another child. Jeri had even written another letter to the prospective birth mother, offering, "When I think of adoption, my heart swells up. I want to cry. I am filled with love and wonderful feelings. I love adoption. I think it is a wonderful gift from God. We believe that God has a plan for each and every baby, even before they are born."

Holding the newspaper in her trembling hands, Jeri knew exactly what she had to do. She would go to the courthouse and talk to this girl. She would fight for this baby's life. She would even tell the girl that she would be willing to adopt the baby. She knew she would find a home for the baby, even if it wasn't hers. Impulsive? Sure, but she lived life fully engaged.

At the courthouse, her plan unraveled. She managed to find the girl and her attorney, Annette M. Lamoreaux, but Lamoreaux rebuffed her, refusing to even engage in a conversation. Judge Gilmore closed the hearing and decided that the attorneys could not reveal her ruling.

Only a female television reporter treated her with the decency she felt she deserved. The reporter sat on a bench outside the courtroom, comforting her and affirming her decision to be bold.

When the hearing ended, the 17-year-old girl was whisked away through a back exit. Jeri felt humiliated and distraught.

Later that night, she called Christi.

"Would you meet with me? I need to talk. And I'm probably going to be crying."

"Jeri, what's wrong? Is it your heart?"

"No, I'm OK. Just meet with me."

They met at Starbucks, but background noise disrupted their conversation, so they went to Christi's car and spent the next two hours there, crying, praying and commiserating.

* * *

"No! No! No!" Jeri cried. "This can't be!"

Jeri and Daryl had been relaxing in bed on November 10 when they heard the Channel 13 anchor say something that seemed incomprehensible: Amber had been murdered in her car early that morning in the Aldine area of Houston.

Jeri had been so certain that Amber would be a key part of Brady's life. But when she cried out to God, she could feel him saying, "You did not ask me when you made those plans. Those were *your* plans, not mine."

She could feel God telling her that she had not fully assumed the mantle of being Brady's true mother, that in her mind she had always been sharing him, that she needed to respect the birth family but realize that God had meant for her to be his mother.

Jeri cried throughout the night, asking God, "What do I do?"

"Be Brady's mommy, that's all. Just be Brady's mommy," she could hear Him say.

Jeri would describe it as perhaps the saddest week of her life. The grieving process took her by surprise. She'd be fine one day, then cry throughout the next.

Amber's family reached out to Jeri and Daryl, inviting them to the viewing. Jeri's worries about how they would react were unfounded, because they greeted them warmly, hugging and crying. They carefully pulled out pictures of Brady. Jeri noticed that they seemed to be treating them like they were gold. Jeri and Daryl felt honored and humbled.

Jeri wrote in her journal: *The hardest thing was seeing Amber in the casket. I don't want to remember her that way and I am going to try to forget that image. She was a sweet person. She loved others. She loved Brady so much. So much she gave him up. We love Amber. We always will.*

CHAPTER 11

CAN YOU PRAY FOR PINK?

On September 5, 2002, a tropical depression in the Gulf of Mexico was upgraded to Tropical Storm Fay, and it appeared to be heading straight for Galveston.

The next day, as the wind picked up to 60 mph, the National Hurricane Center issued a hurricane watch. Schools closed in Galveston and nearby High Island, and a voluntary evacuation was ordered. Although the hurricane watch was lifted, the storm surge went nearly five feet above the normal high tide. The wind kicked up massive whitecaps not normally seen on the serene Galveston beach.

Watching the reports on TV, Jeri started thinking about how much Brady would enjoy seeing those waves crashing in. The more she thought about it, the more she knew she just needed to do it. She would live for this day. She wouldn't be a disabled person who disconnected from life and became her disability.

So they piled into the Highlander and drove 80 miles to the island. As they crossed the Causeway, it became obvious that not too many people had the same idea. Lines of cars moved slowly in the northbound lanes heading off the island.

They found a toy store and Brady picked out a boat. And for that afternoon, they walked and talked. Brady played with his boat in the pools that formed along the beach. They'd go down to the area where the water was cascading in, and try to beat the waves to the seawall.

When they got home, they told everybody about their day. Jeri had no idea how deeply that drive-into-the-storm day would impact Brady later in his life.

As late summer faded into fall, Jeri faced another drive-into-the-storm event with far more serious consequences. Dr. Grifka and Katie would be key figures in unraveling the uncertainties.

Dr. Grifka first saw Jeri in 1994, when Dr. Mullins—who was gradually winding down a world-renowned career—started turning over some patients to other cardiologists at Texas Children's.

Jeri never even considered putting herself under the care of a normal cardiologist. She wanted to remain with a pediatric cardiologist because not a lot of adult cardiologists were comfortable with her problems. They had been trained to handle heart attacks and illnesses she didn't have. She was a grown-up with a kid's heart problem.

Jeri quickly became one of Dr. Grifka's favorite patients. He'd scan his appointment book early in the morning, and if he saw Jeri's name, he knew it would be a very good day. She was one of the brightest, most cheerful people—not just patients—he had ever known. She'd come by the office at Christmas and drop off cookies or give him birthday presents. They had a friendship that radically transcended a doctor-patient relationship.

That made the difficult tasks somewhat easier. Like reminding her that she wouldn't be able to endure a pregnancy. Or now, when he had to discuss the options for her eroding condition.

Jeri knew that with primary pulmonary hypertension, she had a progressive disorder. That meant it continued to get worse. The blood vessels in her lungs had become too constricted, which caused the heart to pump harder to overcome that. In response to that, the right side of her heart had begun to enlarge. That caused the valve between the right side and left side of the heart to open up. The blood supply had begun to bypass the lungs altogether and was going from the right side to the left side of the heart and then out into her system, so the blood was not getting rid of carbon dioxide and picking up the oxygen it needed from the lungs. Her organs gradually were being killed off.

That explained why her oxygen-saturation levels frequently dipped below 60% — compared to the 96-100% readings of normal people. (Dr. Grifka suspected that her levels were even less than 60%, because some machines are not accurate when the readings get below 65%. The only way to truly know would be to give a painful blood test in the artery, which they seldom did.)

That also explained why phlebotomies had become more frequent (and for Jeri, more frightening), her discoloration was even more dramatic and she was so fatigued she could not even climb a staircase without laboring greatly.

Just walking a block with Daryl had her gasping for air. If they weren't in a hurry, they'd stop and let her catch her breath. If they were walking with a group and moving at a good pace, she would have to stop and Daryl would give her a piggyback ride. Her friends understood and stopped to accommodate her breaks, but Jeri sometimes would get angry and frustrated because she didn't want to hold anyone back.

"Y'all are going to have to go without me," she'd say. "I'll get there when I get there."

She had to get more sleep at night and more rest during the day. This limited the things she was able to do. If she had never done them, it wouldn't have been a big transition for her. Because she had been dramatically more active than most patients with her condition, she had experienced a huge decrease in her quality of life.

There is no treatment for primary pulmonary hypertension other than a lung transplant. And with her heart being ravaged by the congenital defect, she was not a candidate for just a lung transplant. She had to have a heart-lung transplant.

Dr. Grifka had delayed serious talk of the transplant for three reasons: she had broken all the rules by surviving, so he had decided to just let her body do what it was going to do; when a patient gets a transplant, the only certainty is that the organs are not going to last as long as normal organs; and he wanted to allow time for scientists to come up with better medicines to keep the body from rejecting organs.

They had previously discussed the possibility of a transplant. Now it had become a necessity.

"It's not like a fuel injector, where they just pull one off the shelf and put it on," Dr. Grifka told Jeri. "They have to wait for a set of heart and lungs to become available. And when it is, it has to be the right blood type and everything has to match. Some people wait two to four years for an organ transplant. Many people die waiting for them."

This served as the biggest reality check she had had since 2001, when she suffered an attack of ventricular tachycardia, rushed to Texas Children's and was held two days for observation. It had been so serious that Jayme flew in from Florida. So serious that Jeri, during a vulnerable moment, suggested to Daryl that if she didn't make it, she wanted him to go on with his life and re-marry, instead of living in fear that someone might think he was failing to honor her memory. And she had a particular woman in mind—a member of the praise band.

"It's hard for me to think about re-marrying when I'm married to you," Daryl had said. "I can't get my mind to go there."

"It's OK," she had replied. "You and Brady will need somebody."

Now, with Dr. Grifka's transplant talk, she was thrust into a more acute state of concern. But she had no intention of fully committing to a transplant until she had invited God and her family and friends into the discussion.

When she mentioned it to Carolyn and Junny, they embraced it because they felt it would be her only way to survive. They still believed God would heal her, whether it was with the transplant or without it. One of Carolyn's high-school classmates, Harold Lloyd, had undergone a heart transplant two years earlier and appeared to be living a full, healthy life.

Daryl knew nothing about transplants, but he knew her suffering more intimately than anybody else. Dr. Grifka had told them that a fatal attack of ventricular tachycardia could happen anytime—while she was driving down the road or eating dinner. Daryl confided in

Jayme that his worst fear would be to wake up one morning and find her dead, having been in his normal deep sleep and unaware that his nocturnal wife was in distress.

He lived with this every day, walking alongside her. He would walk alongside her if she chose the transplant.

The next time her small group met, she mentioned her dilemma during best-and-worst time to start the night. They had no idea it had come to this point. Jim seemed more surprised than anybody. It sounded very radical to him.

In the next few weeks, they hashed it out during the small-group meetings. Their Bible study topic—faith—seemed to fall in line so perfectly with Jeri's new adventure.

She'd ask, "Is it more faith to trust God to heal me, or for me to do this heart-lung transplant? If God has given me a miracle by taking me this far without a heart-lung transplant, should I just keep trusting? Or is this transplant idea from God, and God has led these doctors to be able to do heart-lung transplants?"

The group wrestled mightily. Pros and cons were offered. Everybody carefully avoided choosing one side with conviction. They agreed that it came down to hearing the voice of God, rather than trying to choose a path. They agreed that God had led scientists to discover marvelous procedures. They didn't think that was outside God's will.

One week, Jeri mentioned that she ran into somebody at Katy Mills Mall who had had a heart-lung transplant. "What does that mean?" she asked. "Did God bring in my path a person who had been through this and was still living? Is God talking through that?" And the group was sure that's exactly what was happening.

The seriousness of Jeri's condition had become apparent to Jim earlier that year when some members of the small group spent a day at Schlitterbahn Waterpark Resort near San Antonio. They took turns giving her piggyback rides around the 65-acre park, and when it was Jim's turn, he heard something he had never heard in his life: *Yuhee, hah . . . Yuhee, hah . . . Yuhee, hah.* It was the labored breathing of a woman who couldn't go on much longer.

Holy cow! Jim thought. *This is what she lives with every moment.*

Experientially, that is when he really understood her condition. In terms of head knowledge, the understanding came in the weeks after Jeri first mentioned the transplant idea. It forced the group to ask more questions that would allow them to process it in their heads. When she told the group that she was having a bad day, each member would look at her fingertips and lips and think, *I don't think I've ever seen them that blue.*

Around this time, Jeri's relationship with Karen Coolidge entered a new and more beautiful phase. God had brought them together in the prayer ministry, and now they had a new focus: the transplant.

Karen loved Jeri's heart. She looked at Jeri and saw a woman who sought Jesus with everything she had, who loved talking to Him, being in His presence.

"Let's just find Him," she'd tell Karen. "Let's talk to Him. Let's be with Him."

And so they would go to a small room adjacent to the sanctuary, get down on their knees and bask in His presence.

One day late in 2002, Jeri seemed overwhelmed by the idea of a transplant when she met with Karen. She wanted to do what God wanted her to do. She did not take the decision lightly. But she wanted someone to come alongside her and help her with researching hospitals and the daunting insurance issues. And so they prayed for that.

That night, in the small group, Jeri climbed into Katie's lap and shared that she felt overwhelmed and didn't know how to move forward. As Jeri cried, Katie held her like she was one of her own daughters.

When the meeting ended at around 9, Katie went upstairs to her computer and punched in some key words: HEART-LUNG TRANSPLANT, HOSPITAL, SUCCESS RATES. The results tumbled out quickly, igniting her determination. The statistics, contacts and first steps were right there. She printed everything out. Within an hour, she had an impressive list of possibilities.

The Texas Heart Institute at St. Luke's Episcopal Hospital in Houston: For 13 consecutive years, it had been ranked among the top 10 heart centers in the country by *U.S. News and World Report,* with over 1,000 heart transplantations since 1982.

Vanderbilt Heart at Vanderbilt Medical Center in Nashville, Tennessee: The overall survival rate in its transplant program was more than one-third higher than the national average.

Stanford Medical Center in Palo Alto, California: The first successful transplantation of the lung was performed there by Dr. Reitz and his colleagues as a heart-lung transplant. Stanford had the longest continually active team performing lung transplantation. Stanford had a one-year survival rate of 85%, three-year rate of 75%, five-year rate of 50%, 10-year rate of 45% and 20-year rate of 25% — all well above the national rate. A handful of patients had lived over 20 years.

She called Jeri at 10:30 p.m. with the news. Jeri squealed in delight. The possibility of a new life stretched out before her.

The initial euphoria was tempered by two issues: Which hospital? And would insurance cover the procedure?

Daryl admitted to Jeri that even talking about it scared him a bit — not just the survival rate, which was at least 10% lower than for a heart transplant, but the idea that they would have to relocate and give up their church family and support network. The Texas Heart Institute offered the chance to stay home, but Stanford appeared to offer the best medical team. Trouble was, Stanford wasn't on the list of eligible destinations.

But when they found out in January that Daryl's insurance would cover the procedure at Stanford, they felt God opening the doors and offering clear direction.

Everybody knew pink was Jeri's favorite color. She wore it as much as she could without overdoing it. But now, she really started talking about pink in an entirely different way. The transplant opened up the possibility that her extremities finally could be pink. She wanted to be normal. Pink was normal.

She talked a lot about that. She'd hold her hands out in front of her — they were the closest and easiest part of her body she could see — and tell Daryl, "I want pink fingertips." Then she took it one step further. At the end of meetings, she'd say, "Please pray for pink lips and fingertips." And the group adopted that. It represented a very easy way to pray a very complicated prayer for her very complicated situation.

Once in awhile, she'd add pink toes to the mix. Some members of the group had commented on her beautiful feet. And the biblical symbol of that was her penchant for evangelism. She had been bold about sharing her faith. And the closer she got to a transplant, the bolder she got.

"I don't care what people think," she'd say. "Life's too short and they need Jesus."

Jeri and Christi prayed quite a bit together. They believed God was calling them into a ministry together. Jeri would use her story of her physically sick heart being replaced by a healthy one as an example of how God can transform our hearts. Christi would talk about how, even though she had a healthy physical heart, God had cleansed her of the pain she held in her spiritual heart after her attempts to reconcile with her alcoholic father were rejected.

When Jeri spoke in the small group, it never took on the tone of, "Have pity on me," or "Poor me, my life is so tough." She presented a very real portrait of her feelings—sometimes she'd say, "This sucks"—but she always found a way to praise God, regardless of her circumstances.

She continued to do that as she accelerated the discussions with Stanford. Before she could be invited out to Stanford for the testing process that would decide whether she was a candidate for a transplant, Dr. Grifka would have to send voluminous paperwork and Jeri would have to complete a psychosocial evaluation with a social worker.

Jeri harbored excitement and fear at the same time. Focusing became difficult. She found herself worrying about what might happen down the road, so she prayed that God would help her stay in the moment and focus on Jesus.

On January 13, the results of her blood work were not good. It had become too thick again. She would have to have another phlebotomy.

On January 27, the results of her kidney test were not good. She would have to retake the test and hope for better results to send to Stanford. She did that, and the results were the same: the protein level in her urine was very high and the creatinine level was off. Dr. Grifka didn't know exactly what Stanford was looking for. Perhaps her levels were not at all unusual for a heart-lung candidate.

A House of Prayer for All Nations
GRACE FELLOWSHIP UNITED METHODIST CHURCH

Lisa Leggett   Jeri Paholek   Katie Dolan
at Jeri & Daryl's "Small Group" Meeting

best friends
prayer warriors
life partners

On February 20, while Jeri and Daryl were at the bank, she received a call from Lisa Levin, the transplant coordinator at Stanford. She offered Jeri the chance to come out to be evaluated, and Jeri immediately chose the first opportunity: March 18-22. Dr. Grifka had offered a glowing endorsement of Jeri, not just as a transplant candidate but as a person. She cried tears of joy the rest of the day.

In an e-mail to her friends, she wrote: *I am excited! God can do this! There is nothing He can't do! I am ready to go for it!*

On February 25, Levin called again and said that Jeri had been "ruled in" for a transplant unless they saw an unexpected red flag during the visit. She told Jeri that 80% of the people who get to this point in the evaluation eventually go on the transplant list. That list was short at the moment—20, instead of the usual 40—and organs quickly were being found. Jeri would need to relocate immediately if she was put on the list.

She viewed the news as wonderful, but a day later the reality hit her. She looked again at the survival rates. *Do I really want to do this?* she thought. A few days later at church, Brandee Standley approached Jeri and placed over her shoulders a prayer shawl that she had knitted. Enveloped by the soft, comforting shawl and the sweet singing of the praise team—*Your love is extravagant*—Jeri felt at peace. She realized that God had brought her this far and would not abandon her.

Jeri, Daryl, Carolyn and Junny flew on March 18 to California and checked in at the Crowne Plaza Cabana. Two surprises awaited her: at the front desk, a charm-bracelet sand dollar that had been mailed from Jayme from his home in Florida; and on the TV screen in the corner of the lobby, a video from the kids in the church's youth ministry. As the kids poured out their hearts, saying they missed her, loved her and were praying for her, tears streamed down her cheeks.

The next day, she underwent blood work, X-rays and an EKG, followed by blood work, a bone scan and a pulmonary function test on Thursday and an ECHO scan and chest CT scan on Friday.

The tests showed that Jeri had: a "markedly enlarged" heart, with an upper-lobe diversion consistent with pulmonary venous hypertension; a large, almost completely calcified anterior medias-tinal structure that possibly represented a calcified old hematoma or old calcified graft material; an enlarged liver and spleen; and very prominent hepatic veins.

Jeri met with the surgical team and had all of her questions answered. Jeri felt like they regarded her as a special person and not just another patient.

They laid out the reality: The wait for donor organs could be long. Fewer than 50 heart-lung transplants were performed every year in the United States—probably the smallest number of organ transplants—because of the difficulty in getting both a heart and lung graft together. Those organs could go to two separate people instead of just one. A donor family could say, "We want them to go to this particular patient," but those situations were rare. In addition, organ-procurement groups frequently had difficulty in recovering lungs because they were compromised early from brain death.

Jeri learned that her new lungs would be organs never truly accepted by her body. She would be put on drugs for the rest of her life that would stop her immune system so that the organs would not be rejected—drugs that could damage her liver, kidneys, heart, bones and muscle, and possibly cause cancer. A biopsy of her lungs would be done every few months for a year, then once a year, to determine if the tissue showed any signs of rejection.

After the surgery, she would live in a campus apartment for 100 days—Brady could not live with her because of the fear of germs—and would report to the clinic each day. After 100 days, she could return to Texas, but it might be too dangerous to visit Brady at his elementary school or volunteer to work in an environment that included children.

"You'll be trading one set of problems for another," they told Jeri. "You're getting a foreign object in your body. If you survive, you'll have to take rejection medicine. The medicine you're taking now is nothing compared to that."

They presented three possibilities: She could be accepted and immediately put on the transplant list; they could determine she was too well and ask her to return in six months to be re-evaluated; or they could determine that she was too sick to make it through the surgery.

Jeri got the impression that the Stanford team regarded a transplant as an even more urgent matter than Dr. Grifka had. What she didn't know was that Dr. Ramona Doyle took a look at her discoloration and test results and privately told another team member, "I don't think she'll live long enough to have a transplant."

Daryl and Junny came out of the meetings cautiously optimistic. Jeri and Carolyn, meanwhile, were thrilled and upbeat.

They ended their stay with a car trip on the California coastline. Jeri's greatest desire was to go to the beach, so they picked up Oma and set off on a windy, 55-degree day. They drove through stands of tall timber until they reached Highway 1, where they headed north.

At Half Moon Bay, they got out and Junny, Carolyn and Daryl walked down to the water. Jeri paused to reflect on a rock at the top of a hill overlooking the bay. Jeri asked Oma to take a picture. Oma caught her in a rapturous expression: with a gigantic smile on her face and her arms raised high above her head, as if to say, "I feel free!"

On April 3, Levin called to say that Jeri had been accepted as a candidate. She would return to Stanford in three months. If she decided at that time that she wanted to be on the transplant list, she would need to move closer to Stanford so that she could be at the hospital within two hours of notification that donor organs had become available.

Stanford put Jeri in touch with a woman who had had a heart-lung transplant in 1994 at the age of 45 and was still very healthy. She also had several friends who didn't experience the same success—one died while having a lung biopsy, another from kidney failure, and she knew of others who didn't make it through the surgery.

Junny felt the surgery would be too risky based on the potential results, but he said he would support her decision. Jeri prayed that if it was God's will to have the transplant, He would give her a strong desire to do it.

Jeri endured some sleepless nights. She'd think she was ready to go ahead and do it, and then she'd read about post-transplant drug reactions or hear about a failed transplant, and she'd feel consumed by panic.

MARCH 23, 2003
HWY 1 - NEAR HALF MOON BAY

Jeri, Daryl, Mom, Dad, and Aunt Oma (Dad's sister)
had just finished 2 days of interviews & tests for
transplant candidacy at Stanford.

With this milesone, and the fact that it was Dad's
61st Birthday, a celebration-drive down HWY 1 was
in order. This photo, taken by Aunt Oma,
captured it all...the freedom of faith.

Notice the little black pager attached to her waist.
For everyone that day, this was a giant ocean of
possibilities for dreams to come true.

"I FEEL FREE"

I don't want to die, she wrote to Martha Russell, her Stanford social worker. *I'm an emotional wreck.*

Jeri e-mailed Amelia Rose Gonsiewski, a 21-year-old from Portland, Oregon, who had been near death when she underwent a transplant on May 23, 2002. Amelia admitted to Jeri that she was in a coma for three weeks after the surgery and the post-surgery drugs had some nasty side effects, but she highly recommended not only the procedure but the medical team at Stanford. She told Jeri that if she had a child waiting at home for her, she wouldn't hesitate to have the transplant. Amelia said she exercised six days a week, including a 90-minute hip-hop dance class.

Over the span of three days, they traded e-mails, and Amelia sensed that Jeri needed encouragement. So she wrote:

I did not think I was strong enough or stubborn enough to go through this, either. But you are. You will find that you have amazing reserves of strength that you will call upon. I just thought over and over, "I have too much to do still. I am not ready to die." You will be so amazed at what you can do. You will be great.

Around this time, Grace Fellowship's sermon series centered on the book of Joel, and the idea that while God is the omnipotent judge, He also is merciful and wants to bless those who trust Him. On April 6, Jim asked Jeri to give her testimony. Who better than Jeri to talk about trusting God?

She described how she had been trying to deal with the necessity of the transplant on her own strength. Then Katie walked with Jeri in the research.

"That was the point where I had to make a choice: Am I going to step out and do this scary thing or just forget it? I want you to be thinking about what in your life this is like. There are so many times God gives us an opportunity to step out in faith, whether it's marriage or a job. And it's so hard. And then God opens that door, and that's where God wants us to open our heart to Him and give totally to Him and take the first couple of steps. He has carried me for six months now on this journey with Stanford.

"I was very honest to God during this time. I said to Him, 'This sounds terrible. Why would I want to do this? Take out all my organs and put more in?' I've been real honest with Him: 'God, if you want me to do this, give me a strong desire to do this.' It's all very scary. I just have to give it to God every single minute. I can't let my brain go way down the road. I have to do it one step at a time and give it to God.

"I've had hundreds and hundreds of e-mails. There are four or five churches I know of that are praying for me: my mother's church, brother's church, sister's church. There are high-school groups praying for me, college sorority girls praying for me. I've gotten incredible letters in the mail from my mother-in-law's family, who I never had an emotional connection to, and they poured their heart out and sent me jewelry that meant a lot to them. People have left signs on my door and planted flowers in my yard.

"That's a tangible picture of how much God loves us. He loves us more than cards and gifts and e-mails. He just wants to be a part of everything in our lives. I think of that story in the Bible where Jesus takes the fish and loaves and He makes more to feed the people. And at the end, there is still a basket left over. That's how my life has been. I just have baskets of friends and love sitting around that God gave me. That's what He does. I just want to encourage you to be faithful."

On May 1, the National Day of Prayer, Jeri went to Grace Fellowship's sanctuary for what she thought would be a service for the nation and President Bush. Instead, the prayer focused on healing.

During the service, she felt called to approach the altar and ask for healing. But she didn't just pray silently for it. She said aloud, "Jesus, I want to be healed!" Many of her friends, including Karen, gathered around her and laid hands on her. Jeri closed her eyes and pictured the robe of Jesus. She pictured the scene in Mark 5:22-34 when the woman who had a seemingly incurable condition that had caused her to bleed for 12 years touched his robe and was healed.

As they prayed, Jeri reached her hand out in front of her body. A warm sensation came over her. She could feel the fabric of Jesus' robe in her fingertips. A smile overtook her face. *It's taken care of*, she thought.

In this holy moment, Jeri knew the answer. She knew God would heal her in any way He chose, and if He chose the surgery, that's how it would happen. A feeling of excitement came over her—excitement she never thought she'd feel about something this radical.

CHAPTER 12

WHAT HAPPENS IN VEGAS
DOESN'T STAY IN VEGAS

Now what?

After Jeri notified Stanford that she wanted to be put on the transplant list, the reality hit her: They had to move.

To keep their health-insurance benefits, Daryl needed to remain with his company. And God provided. Weyerhaeuser Co., which owned Trendmaker, had a subsidiary in Las Vegas, Pardee Homes. Jeri called Stanford and asked if Las Vegas would be a suitable place for her to live. Yes, she was told. A private medical plane could pick her up at McCarron International Airport and have her in Palo Alto in about 90 minutes.

Trendmaker's human resources department went to work. Daryl's perception, based on what he was being told, was that it was pretty cut-and-dried. But it didn't turn out like that. It dragged on for weeks.

By the end of May, Jeri had reached the point where she thought she would explode. She'd have days on which she didn't think she could handle the exhaustion. Then she'd snap out of it and feel great. The juxtaposition unnerved her.

She looked good: She wore a pair of cool new glasses Lisa picked out for her and a few new pink items in her wardrobe. In her pinkness, she was "ensconced," as George Costanza would say. And since she looked good, people thought, *She needs a transplant?*

Impatience ate at her.

"Let's get this show on the road," she'd say to God. "The move can't get here quickly enough for me. God, why are we waiting? I finally said yes. Now what are we waiting for? God, I trust you, but my brain wants to move before I go crazy. God, would you move? Show us what is next. Please."

Finally, Jeri—in her inimitable style—asserted herself, writing a letter to Pardee, Weyerhaeuser and Trendmaker executives. She explained her heart condition, saying Dr. Grifka felt she was "running out of time." She explained why it needed to be performed at Stanford, and why she didn't want to move to Stanford while Daryl remained in Texas. She felt she needed to address concerns about Daryl's commitment to work and his intentions behind the proposed move.

I want you to understand why we want this move. I didn't wake up one day and fall in love with the idea of moving to Las Vegas. . . . Daryl loves his job. He is a "golden retriever" type personality. He is loyal to the bone. He wants to do his best. I always laugh at him straightening out light switch screws. My word, who would notice those tiny things? . . .

I wish you could look at it as a person taking care of a mother with cancer or a wife with a difficult pregnancy or a child with a serious illness. People have stuff happen in their personal lives all the time. It doesn't mean that they want to rip some company off or take more than their share. . . .

I hope I have not offended anyone. I am the one in the family who gets stressed and has to do something about it. Daryl, as you know, is even-keeled. He is not an emotional person and he wants so much to not upset anyone. I hope you haven't minded hearing some of my emotion. Thanks for listening.

They didn't mind listening. In reality, much was going on behind the scenes, out of view from Jeri and Daryl. Clogged corporate arteries had to be navigated. Once that was done, in late May, the company notified Daryl that he had a job in Las Vegas. They marveled at how God continued to open doors.

With that worry out of the way, they headed excitedly—along with Katie, Garrett, Rob and Misti Matchett, and all of the children—to a one-week family camp at Pine Cove at Crier Creek, 50 miles west of Katy, from June 8-15.

The week featured family Bible study, speaker sessions, quiet time, recreational activities and evening worship. It couldn't have come at a better time, but physically, Jeri had continued to deteriorate. Her breathing had gotten more labored, her coughing more bothersome. Many times during the night, she would awaken disoriented, feeling like she would pass out. She had experienced this before, but now it had become more intense.

At one point, Katie suggested that she seek medical attention. Jeri pushed on. She wanted Brady to have indelible memories of the week.

Because the cabins were scattered around a 10-acre lake on a 700-acre deer reserve, Daryl had to drive her to Whitetail Lodge, where the meals were served, or to the next-door worship building. She didn't like that, but what choice did she have?

Others would notice her extremities and ask, "Are you OK?" She was very open: She told them she was a candidate for a heart-lung transplant, but always framed it in the context of, "Isn't it cool that I'm this way and I'm still able to be here?" Early in the week, associate director Sam Holm—who went by the camp name of Astare—became aware of her testimony and notified the staff. They prayed over Jeri and Daryl many times during the week—and long after they had left.

Jeri and Daryl had experienced so many incredible blessings that they were hardly surprised when they met a couple who had moved from Houston to the Las Vegas suburb of Henderson. The couple heard Jeri's story and offered to host Daryl when he went to Vegas June 26-28 to find a home to lease and meet with his new boss.

The blessings didn't end there. Astare also served as the worship leader—and it was in this role that he tangibly altered Jeri's life.

A few weeks earlier, a summer staff member had introduced him to a new song he had heard: "Blessed Be Your Name," written by Matt and Beth Redman in 2002. Astare and his staff would play it at camp this week for the first time. When Jeri heard Astare sing it, she felt the Holy Spirit working very clearly in her heart.

The lyrics—adapted from the book of Job—talked of praising God in the midst of abundance or in the despair of walking through the wilderness, being in the desert, suffering or feeling darkness closing in. *You give and take away. My heart will choose to say. Lord, blessed be your name.*

After a few nights, Katie said to Jeri, "That's so your song." And Jeri said, "I know. I thought the same thing."

Without knowing it, they had claimed the song—Jeri for herself, and Katie for her.

The next night, Katie asked one of the members of the worship team if he had the lyrics.

"Here," he said, pulling a wrinkled sheet from his backpack and handing it to Katie.

When they returned to Katy, Jeri immediately approached A.J. and asked him to add the song to the worship band's repertoire. A.J. didn't regularly accept song requests. Most of the time, he would say, "I will listen to that song and see if it fits in with what we do." And usually, it didn't.

But Jeri had unusual cachet. She had always been a tremendous encouragement to the worship team, had coined herself as A.J.'s second-biggest fan (after his wife, Angel) and always had blessed his heart with something she would say. Because she had been such an encourager and A.J. could sense God's anointing on her life, he just had to see how God might be working through her.

He added the song. They played it. And in the months that followed, it became the most meaningful song the church would ever sing.

When they returned from camp, Jeri immediately went to the ER. Her oxygen-saturation levels were as low as they had ever been. Tests showed no heart failure, but her blood was too low—the exact opposite of her usual problem. She was admitted to the hospital and given a boost of iron. After two days, she was released.

Jeri continued to battle problems with her biliruben (liver function), which was too high. Some days it came in at 3.0, and Stanford wanted it below 2.8. Something like that could jeopardize her ability to receive a transplant, so she carefully avoided salt and caffeine and made sure she drank a lot of water.

Daryl learned that his start date in Las Vegas would be August 4, so they placed their Katy home on the market and prayed for a quick sale. Jeri would leave July 9 for Stanford to undergo further testing, staying at her cousin Jana's two-bedroom condo in Fremont. On July 21, she would travel to Las Vegas and stay in a hotel with Carolyn and Brady. Daryl would wrap up all the details in Katy and then drive a rental truck to Las Vegas, arriving August 1.

Even in those frantic few weeks before she would leave, she never lost sight of the importance of her time with God, particularly her prayer sessions with Karen.

Jeri and Karen found themselves inextricably tied by parallel circumstances and time lines. Karen didn't face a monumental transplant, but she faced a monumental move to the other side of the earth at the same time as Jeri prepared for Las Vegas.

Karen's husband, Danny, worked for Unocal and had been offered a position managing the oil fields in Balikpapan, Indonesia, on the island of Borneo. The idea of uprooting her life and moving to Indonesia didn't thrill Karen, but she didn't want Danny to turn down a career opportunity. She wanted to go only if God wanted the family to go. Stepping outside of His will would mean loss of protection.

Jeri went face down on the carpet of the prayer room many times with Karen to discern God's will. In the process, He taught Karen so much, stripping her of her fear of taking three children and her husband into a Muslim nation. She was able to recognize fear for fear and pride for pride. She was able to recognize what she wanted versus what God wanted. As He took Karen through that, the same thing was happening in Jeri.

Karen and Danny had decided on May 3, a few days after Jeri's transplant decision, that they would accept the job in Indonesia.

And they would be leaving July 15—six days after Jeri would leave Katy.

"Isn't it amazing the way God weaved this together?" Karen asked Jeri.

It would have been impossible for anyone in Jeri's position to avoid thoughts of mortality. She had stared down death for her entire life, but now she realized that defiance, while admirable, had to give way to prudence. She owed it to her family to at least plan for the possibility that she might not survive the surgery.

After church on June 29, she cornered Jim in the hallway and told him she wanted to visit with him. They scheduled a meeting for July 2.

Jeri met Jim in his office. She told him she remained very optimistic about the transplant, but she wanted to be prepared. She wanted a memorial service where her life would be celebrated and people would not be overcome by sadness. She wanted it to be about God and not about her. Her demeanor communicated to him, *I'm not afraid.* She just wanted to have that face-to-face with her pastor and check that off her pre-surgery preparation list.

"Tell you what," Jim said. "I am honored to do this, but I'm going to put this in a folder and label it, 'Jeri Paholek, For The Year 2050.'"

She laughed heartily and said, "All right, I just want to let you know what I want for my funeral."

Jim tried to hide his feelings of awkwardness and nervousness. He had pre-planned a funeral only once in his life, and this represented the first time anybody had ever asked him to do it. He didn't want to picture Jeri's death—he couldn't imagine it any time soon—but he understood her feelings.

She listed her requests:

The service would be praise and worship.

There would be an invitation to receive Christ.

It would be real and true.

Jayme would speak and sing a song, if he felt up to it.

She would not be cremated.

Her burial spot would be near her parents' plot.

Jim suggested an outline for the memorial service: obituary, opening prayer, Scripture about heaven and eternal life, worship-music component, eulogy, time of open sharing and closing prayer. She liked those ideas. As worship songs, she chose "What a Good God," "Amazing Grace," "Blessed Be Your Name," "One of These Days" and "Legacy."

Jim, thinking of the rarity of this meeting, asked Jeri, "If you could talk to everybody at your service, what would you tell them?"

He furiously took notes as she started talking in a stream-of-consciousness flow.

"I'm gone, but I'm not afraid. Heaven is a wonderful place. Heaven is like when you walk into church and see your favorite friends, and the worship team's playing your favorite songs, and you hug your friends—Dixie, Karen, Christi, Lisa, Katie and everyone. Don't worry. I'm home with the person who loves me the most. It's all about Him. That's what we were made to do—love Him. Nothing else here can satisfy like Him. He's the point of life. He's very, very real. And what He says is very true. By choosing Him, you can live a more abundant and incredible life than you could ever imagine you could have.

"Tell Daryl and Brady and my family how much I love them. Tell my friends I love them more than they'll ever know. I have the best friends in the whole world. I want to ask all my friends to take care of Daryl and Brady. I ask some of you men to come alongside Daryl to help and encourage him. Brady, read my letters over and over and make Jesus your best friend."

Jim, stunned by the eloquence and beauty of what he had just heard, paused momentarily. Then they started talking about Scripture, and she listed her requests.

Psalm 34.

Phil 3:7-8: *But whatever was to my profit I now consider loss for the sake of Christ. What is more, I consider everything a loss compared to the surpassing greatness of knowing Christ Jesus my Lord, for whose sake I have lost all things.*

Phil 3:13-14: *Brothers, I do not consider myself yet to have taken hold of it. But one thing I do: Forgetting what is behind and straining toward what is ahead, I press on toward the goal to win the prize for which God has called me heavenward in Christ Jesus.*

Jim had read from John 11 during most memorial services, and she liked that suggestion.

Jeri's joyful determination registered with Jim. Instead of a sad funeral mode, she had an attitude straight out of Philippians 1:21: *For to me, to live is Christ and to die is gain.* Her message to Jim: "If I live, awesome. If I die, more awesome."

Jim's mind wandered to Daniel 3, where Shadrach, Meshach and Abednego refused to serve the god of King Nebuchadnezzar, saying, "If we are thrown into the blazing furnace, the God we serve is able to save us from it, and He will rescue us from your hand, O king. But even if He does not, we want you to know, O king, that we will not serve your gods or worship the image of gold you have set up." Jeri was saying, "My God is going to save me, but even if He doesn't, this is all good."

Jeri made it clear to Daryl that if she didn't make it, she wanted to be placed in a mausoleum—and not in the ground. Daryl figured she had seen too many TV shows where buried people were not really dead, and they came back to life inside their coffin six feet under. He'd give her a hard time.

"You're being ridiculous. When you're dead, you're dead. They know when you're dead, and you're not coming back to life."

She'd laugh.

"I know. But the thought of it scares me, and I don't want to do it."

As close as Carolyn and Jeri were, Carolyn didn't know everything churning inside Jeri's heart. After visiting Carolyn and Junny's house in Bryan for the final time before leaving Texas, Jeri walked out into the front yard, stood there and looked back.

"This is my last time to be here," she said.

"No, it's not, Jeri," Carolyn said. "The next time, you're going to get out of the car and run to the door. You'll have a new heart."

Carolyn had never gotten the idea that Jeri thought it might not work. In all of their meetings, they hadn't heard of many people who hadn't survived the transplant. It never crossed Carolyn's mind that she might not.

On July 3, Jeri wandered into Brenda's office, just as she had hundreds of times before.

Brenda had met Jeri for the first time in 2001 and instantly loved her. Jeri's faith in God inspired Brenda, and her warmth and realness—the absolute absence of any type of mask—captured Brenda's heart. She admired Jeri's insistence on plowing forward, not shrinking back.

They had met many times. On some occasions, Jeri admitted that she was having a bad day or a bad season. She had no energy and she desperately wanted to have it so she could keep up with Brady and be the mother she wanted to be. Or she had spent a night in the hospital. Or she had been thinking too much of the future.

In those moments, Jeri would crawl into Brenda's lap. And to Brenda, Jeri fit perfectly—she was the size of a seventh-grader. Brenda would encourage her, comfort her, pray for her. They didn't care if anybody thought it seemed weird. They felt a human need— Brenda to hold, Jeri to be held.

This was one of those days.

Jeri rattled off all of the things that scared her—not only the complicated nature of the surgery itself, but the possibility of not being around to be Brady's mom and Daryl's wife. Tears flowed.

"What if I die?" she asked.

Brenda wanted to say, "Oh, you're not going to die." But she knew what she needed to say, so she said it: "You know where you're going if you do. You know God cares so much for Brady and would take care of him. You have to truly surrender everything you love and put it in God's hands. That's easier said than done, I know."

"I don't want to die. I don't want to leave Brady and the church. I want to be doing God's work. I love being a part of God's Kingdom, worshipping Him and loving Him."

"I know. I want that, too. But whatever happens, you will be a part of God's Kingdom forever, worshipping Him and loving Him! . . . And God will be glorified though your life."

On July 4, her small group held a going-away party for her at the home of Kip and Wendy Thomson. They hung out by the pool and then went into the family room and shared memories of their friendship, prayed over her and cried. Two days later at church, Jeri said goodbye to all of those she hadn't seen at the party.

On July 8, after she woke up and wandered to the kitchen, her first words to Carolyn were, "Well, are you ready for our Jesus adventure?"

"I am," Carolyn said. "It sure is a Jesus adventure. He'll be with us every moment."

The next day, Jeri reported to Stanford and was welcomed warmly. The biggest concern: Her bilirubin count was over 3.0, and once again they told her it needed to be under 2.8. They hinted that if it continued to be an issue, her place on the transplant list might have to be temporarily suspended.

For 11 days, Jeri mixed the business of the transplant testing with the pleasure of sightseeing in the Bay Area and catching up with Jana.

The highlight came on the final day, when Jeri, Carolyn, Brady and Jana went to Portola Valley Presbyterian Church for a yearly picnic designed to reunite heart-lung transplant recipients, many of whom arranged their annual Stanford checkup around the event.

Jeri looked around and saw a dozen people swapping stories, laughing, mingling, savoring each other's company. They weren't just alive—they were vibrantly alive. She knew she was about to enter a very small and elite fraternity. And all of them would be there for her.

She introduced herself to a woman about her height, with a "moon face"—the legacy of steroids. The woman shook her hand and said, "I'm Cindy Thilmony." As she talked, Jeri realized she was staring into a mirror.

Cindy was born on October 25, 1957, with transposition of the great vessels, meaning her heart wasn't fully developed and she had a hole between the two main chambers. Her blood did not get oxygenated as it should—part of it went from her heart to her lungs, where it stayed, and the other part went from her body to the other side of her heart. She had skin discoloration and a shortness of breath. Doctors told her parents not to expect her to come home from the hospital. Of course, she did.

In 1959, she became the third child ever to live through the Baffes procedure, which had been done successfully for the first time in 1955 and involved using a homograft to connect the inferior vena cava to the left atrium. In 1976, she had the same surgery.

By 1992, she knew her only chance of survival depended on a heart-lung transplant. Stanford accepted her as a candidate and after being allowed to stay in her Orlando, Florida, home for almost one year, she moved to California in February 1993.

After a 38-month wait, she received a new set of organs on May 8, 1995, from a 13-year-old boy in a surgery performed by Dr. Reitz. Her husband, Michael, went into her room after the surgery and immediately noticed that her right ear had taken on a soft pink hue. Then he noticed her right hand—all of the fingers were pink. He gently picked up the blankets and gazed at her toes. All pink. He broke down in tears.

Cindy didn't sugar-coat it for Jeri. The post-surgery period would be agonizing. Prednisone would cause dramatic mood swings. Cindy would tell Michael that she loved him, then within seconds tell him how much she hated him and wanted him out of her life. It would be just as the medical team said it would be—trading one set of problems for another set.

"But you will be alive," Cindy said to Jeri. "It's been a cakewalk since that first year. It's a full-time job, but we've always made it as much fun as we could."

She said that Dr. Reitz makes sure every patient's recovery period includes regular hikes on The Dish, a 3½-mile, mostly paved loop trail in the hills on the Stanford campus.

Jeri would experience an initial incline that is extremely steep and would immediately get her heart pumping. Then she would wind through gentle rolling hills, past native oaks and California buckeyes. Along the way, Jeri would pass two monstrous satellite dishes—after which the trail was named—and see ground squirrels, lizards, bullfrogs, jackrabbits, red-tailed hawks, golden eagles, herons, egrets, woodpeckers, western bluebirds. Maybe even a mountain lion. At her most glorious moment, Jeri would be able to get a breathtaking view of the Bay area—the skyline of downtown San Francisco, downtown San Jose and the Dumbarton and San Mateo bridges.

"But I didn't stop there: I walked across the Golden Gate Bridge," Cindy said. "You'll be able to do the same things!"

Cindy held Jeri's fingers, clubbed and badly discolored.

"These," she said, "will look just like mine."

Jeri gazed at Cindy's fingers, perfect and pink, and smiled. A mirror image, indeed.

The next day, Cindy and Michael visited Jeri at Jana's condo. While they talked in the living room, Brady played in the adjacent dining room. Jana noticed that he seemed down and withdrawn. She wondered if he perhaps had heard too much of the conversation, which had focused on the complications that transplant patients have to endure.

"Brady," she said, "why don't we go outside and play catch?"

As they threw a baseball, seemingly out of nowhere, Brady said, "I think my mommy may die."

The blunt comment—coming from this sweet boy—broke her heart as much as it disturbed her. What could she say in response when she knew it was a possibility? Jana didn't ask him why he would say that. She didn't want to dig into his psyche.

"How about we sit down and pray for your mom?"

And so they prayed for her healing and for God to bring her through the coming months so she'd be there for him.

Later that day, Jeri, Carolyn and Brady hopped into their rental car and drove to Bakersfield, where they stayed the night. They arrived in Las Vegas in the afternoon on July 21. Junny arrived later that day after driving Jeri's car from Katy and would fly home after a few days. Carolyn and Jeri would live in an extended-stay motel until Daryl arrived on August 1.

From the very beginning, Jeri knew something was horribly wrong. Her body immediately began to retain fluid. She felt miserable and bloated. Her swollen legs and feet prevented her from walking, so she spent most of her time in bed.

On the recommendation of her Stanford team, she went to see a cardiologist in Las Vegas, Dr. Gary Mayman. Like many doctors who crossed her path for the first time, he felt like he had stumbled upon the Patient of the Year. He wanted to fix her. But he knew he couldn't. The problem, he said, was the 2,174-foot altitude.

"The *altitude*?" Jeri and Carolyn repeated, almost in unison.

Dr. Mayman explained that a reduction in oxygen supply to the muscles and brain required her heart and lungs to work harder, which caused breathing and pulse rates to increase. Her body's attempt to cope with low oxygen resulted in changes to lung pressure, and fluid and salt balance.

After he explained that to them, her body's reaction to the altitude made sense. But why hadn't Stanford's transplant experts thought of that? They had rubber-stamped her move with no cautionary warning. This brought new meaning to the sign on the south end of the Strip: WELCOME TO FABULOUS LAS VEGAS, NEVADA.

Over the next week, Dr. Mayman called Jeri three or four times a day. Jeri cherished his dedication and love, but she started jokingly calling him "my shadow."

By the time Daryl arrived, Jeri had gained 20 pounds of fluid. Her ankles appeared to be twice their normal size and she moved gingerly, with agony. On August 3, they notified Stanford and she checked into Sunrise Hospital, where she immediately received a new medication, nesiritide, through an IV drip. After a near sleepless night spent in her room, Daryl reported to his first day of work at Pardee.

They stopped the IV after three days because it had ravaged her veins, making them red and sore. Back in their rental house on August 8, Jeri wore a tube in her nose and lugged an oxygen tank everywhere she went—something she abhorred because it restricted her activity and labeled her as handicapped.

The swelling reappeared, so Dr. Mayman suggested a procedure to stretch one of the arteries. Jeri didn't know what to do. She cried and prayed. Finally, Stanford called. The time had come to ditch the Las Vegas experience. She couldn't live there.

The message: "Don't come when you can. Come right now. Or we might remove you from the transplant list." Just as it was possible that she could be too healthy to be a transplant candidate, it also was possible that she could be too sick to be one. She had to get to Stanford by car—flying would be too dangerous.

Carolyn called Junny and said, "You need to be here." After asking God for guidance, he realized that Jayme truly needed to be in Las Vegas. Jayme had always been able to communicate with her in a way no one else could. He would have all the answers.

Junny didn't ask Jayme to come. He told him.

Jayme caught the first flight from Tampa and arrived just before midnight on August 11.

"Let's go to the Strip," Jeri said.

It seemed like an unusual request from someone who, based on his intimate knowledge of her life, appeared to be near death. But he got behind her wheelchair and guided her to the Bellagio, where they quietly watched the fountain show, mesmerized by the choreography of water, lights and music.

Brady would stay in Las Vegas with Daryl for a week while he packed up all the possessions in their house. Then Brady would fly back to Texas with Junny while Daryl and his parents drove back with a 26-foot Ryder truck and Daryl's truck on Labor Day weekend.

Daryl would have to give Pardee the bad news that his work stint was over and pray for mercy that they would allow him to transfer back to Katy and retain his job. He had left Katy with the understanding that the Las Vegas position would be temporary and that he ultimately would return to Texas, but no one expected it to be truncated quite like this.

How could things have unraveled so quickly? Hadn't God opened all the doors for this move to Las Vegas? Now those doors were being slammed shut? Why?

Jayme got behind the wheel of Jeri's car, with Jeri riding shotgun, her legs propped up on the dash. Jayme looked at her and fought off the emotions he could feel churning inside. Outwardly, he exuded cool. Inwardly, he wondered, *Will she make it?*

Jeri softly sang "Blessed Be Your Name," and when she got to the part about being "found in the desert place," she smiled at the irony.

They pressed on, stopping only for gas, food and bathroom breaks on the 545-mile journey. With the sun setting in the San Joaquin Valley in Central California, they pulled into a small service station so Jeri could use the rest room. Jayme helped her out of the car and wrapped her arm around his shoulder, helping her up the steps to the door.

Carolyn noticed a man and a woman sitting on the porch, their eyes fixed on Jeri. She wondered why they were staring. It seemed rude. She wanted to tell them that. She closed her eyes and momentarily drifted off.

When Jeri and Jayme got back to the car, Jayme said, "You know those people on the porch?"

"Yeah," Carolyn said. "I thought they were so rude."

"No. As we passed them on the way back here, they asked if they could pray for her."

They pressed on. By 10, Jeri was worn out. They briefly discussed the wisdom of just getting a hotel room, but decided to continue to Jana's condo in Fremont, arriving before midnight.

The next morning, Jayme drove right up to the entrance to the Coronary Care Unit and admitted Jeri.

After she had been examined and the test results acquired, Dr. Lynette Lissin determined that Jeri had "complex cyanotic congenital heart disease" and "massive right heart failure," with oxygen saturation of 48%. She worried that Jeri had developed progressive renal failure or a systemic infection. Dr. Lissin called Jayme out into the hallway and asked him, "How long has this been going on? She's barely hanging on."

It couldn't end like this. Not before she could get a new heart and new lungs. Not with so much more to do. Not with her friends down on their knees, begging God for mercy.

Jayme found an Internet connection and located a copy of "The Toot Song" by Herb Alpert and the Tijuana Brass that they had gyrated to as kids. He downloaded it, burned a CD, put it in his laptop and took it to her room.

Jeri had no idea what was going on until she heard the first horn blasts. She saw Jayme bending over, forcing his derriere as high as it would go and pretending to fart right at the moment the baritone sax kicked in.

CHAPTER 13

CAN YOU HEAR MY HEARTBEAT?

Dr. Wolf knocked on the door to Room 134 in the Coronary Care Unit. He didn't wait for a response. Doctors never did. The knock was just a back-handed courtesy: *We're here, and we're coming in, ready or not.*

Trailed by Kim Young, a third-year medical student, he entered to find Jeri talking on the phone.

"Brady, that's so exciting!" Jeri said. "Sounds like you had a great first day of school! I just know you'll love your teacher!"

Jeri saw them standing there, waiting. After all these years, she knew the protocol all too well. They wouldn't exit, visit their next patient and then come back later to see if Jeri was ready to be seen. It was the patient's responsibility to *become* ready.

She hung up. It killed her to be 1,900 miles away from Brady on his first day of kindergarten. This represented one of those momentous days she had always dreamed of sharing with him. She had already talked to Katie, who was hosting Brady in her house while Daryl wrapped up his stint in Vegas. She knew the day had gone well—other than some mild resistance from Brady when it came to waking up and getting dressed. Katie and Lisa had been honored to fill Jeri's spot by taking him to Fielder Elementary. He didn't cry when they left, and he appeared excited when they picked him up.

Not only had Jeri missed it, but now her precious conversation with him had been truncated. As much as she loved the staff at Stanford, she felt tempted to scream out: "Forget this transplant! I'm going home!"

Kim was at her own pivotal point. At 25, she was a third-year medical student entering a new phase. She had just finished studying for the board and had some time off, but decided to begin a clerkship to help her with her learning process. She would accompany professors on their rounds as they visited patients with unique physical conditions.

She had some doubts about being in medicine. Even though she felt God had called her to do what she was doing, she wondered if she would be able to serve the way she wanted to. She had reached the point where she was trying to reconcile her faith with what she was doing. How did it all fit together?

This awkward situation with Jeri served as the perfect example. This did not seem to be one of the strengths of hospital medicine— barging into someone's room and interrupting an intimate moment. It didn't feel right to Kim.

Jeri's mood changed from cheery to melancholy—a rare moment in her life.

Dr. Wolf and Kim proceeded to her bed and introduced themselves. Jeri was hooked up to a pulse oximeter, which monitored her oxygen saturation, and a telemetry—a heart monitor with three patches and connecting wires that were placed on Jeri's chest to transmit her heart rhythm to the nurse's station of the CCU. If an abnormal heartbeat showed up on the monitor, a nurse would come in and check her blood pressure and pulse.

He removed the patches and explained to Kim that Jeri had common ventricle, which produced a very different heartbeat. Through the stethoscope, Kim heard sounds that were nothing like what she had heard and studied for the past two years.

Kim noticed Jeri's clubbed fingers—the fingernails curved downward and the tips were bulb-shaped and flattened, making them look like tiny clubs. Dr. Wolf pointed that out, explaining that it resulted from chronic heart disease and a lack of proper oxygenation over a long period of time.

Kim also noticed the Bible verses Jeri had on the wall above her bed. On the chair next to her bed, she saw a pillow with a beige slip. She looked closer and saw that it contained various proclamations based on Bible verses, drawn with a turquoise fabric pen. One of the proclamations: *I am the body of Christ. I am redeemed from the curse, because Jesus bore my sicknesses and carried my diseases in His own body. By His stripes I am healed. I forbid any sickness or disease to operate in my body. Every organ, every tissue of my body functions in the perfection in which God created it to function. I honor God and give glory to Him in my body.*

It had a profound impact on Kim. She had been in hundreds of patients' rooms. Most of them might have a vase of flowers or some balloons, but the overriding feeling she got was that they were largely lifeless, stark, standard, staid. She had seen very few expressions of faith, other than the requisite things in a chaplain's office.

Dr. Wolf noticed, too, saying, "For some people, that's a very helpful thing. It gives them comfort."

Kim wanted very much to connect with Jeri as a sister in Christ. And yet she knew her role was to observe and learn under the supervision of a senior doctor. She didn't feel comfortable engaging Jeri in talk of faith.

When they left the room, Kim had an uneasy feeling—a feeling of something being unresolved. She had not engaged in a complete interaction. She had probed Jeri's body, but not her humanity.

A week passed. Something kept tugging on Kim's heart. *Go back. Make sure she's treated like a person.*

And so she did. Jeri's room was not part of her normal rounds. She sought Jeri out. She knew it was not something that medical students do—go back on their own time and talk with patients about life and faith. She wouldn't get herself into any trouble, but she knew it went against the assumptions and expectations of the medical field. The whole thing confused her. *Exactly what is my role?*

This time, Kim did not interrupt anything. It seemed almost as if Jeri had been waiting for her. With Jeri wearing a huge smile, Kim thanked her for allowing her to examine her the previous week.

"I appreciate you coming back," Jeri said. "I *really* do."

Kim got a chance to just sit and connect, and not be a medical observer. She heard a scaled-down version of Jeri's story. The surgery at 17 months. The carefree childhood uninhibited by worry—until the day of reckoning when she learned of her condition. The semi-rebelliousness at A&M. Dating and marrying Daryl. Finding Grace Fellowship, passionately pursuing God and the strange sensation of knowing she was regarded as a church elder—at age 34. Adopting Brady. Researching heart-lung transplants and making that decision. The nightmare in Las Vegas that had brought her to Stanford.

But Jeri didn't just talk about her life. She wanted to know about Kim's.

Kim, feeling like she had known Jeri for years, confided in her that she had been struggling with her medical condition. In college, she had suffered with an undiagnosed autoimmune condition and still labored with a lot of residual fatigue. She felt better now, but still was frequently tired.

Kim noticed that Jeri had her head cocked and never lost eye contact, absorbing everything Kim said with sympathy. But Kim's overriding feeling was that she could not—would not—feel sorry for herself when Jeri joyfully faced a monumentally life-threatening situation.

Over the next three weeks, Kim visited Jeri another four times and called her a few times after Jeri provided her cell phone number. Kim got to the point where she completely forgot that she was a nurse in the room of critically ill woman awaiting a heart-lung transplant.

It wasn't just that they shared their beliefs as Christians and how those beliefs served as the foundation of their lives. It was Jeri's *joie de vivre*. As Kim helped Jeri decorate her room with Brady's drawings, pictures of friends and Bible passages, she saw Jeri breathing life into that stark space, just willing it to be inhabited by the people who were special in her life.

If Kim hadn't listened to Jeri's heartbeat, she would have never known how sick she truly was. Jeri never acted sick. She always wore shorts and T-shirts—real clothes—even though her chest cavity sprouted tentacles like something out of a sci-fi movie. She insisted on being a real person leading life as normally as possible.

All around her, people were dying. Jeri would talk about them, mentioning them by name. That's not something Kim had witnessed very often. Most patients stayed in their room and didn't interact.

Jeri treasured her trips not just out of her ground-floor room, but outside the building. They weren't routine. Far from it. In her inimitable style, Jeri pretty much demanded that her doctors write an order allowing her to go outside. And because the staff could still see her from the CCU and pick up her heart rhythm on the portable telemetry monitor, and because she had become such a beloved fixture in the CCU, well, they let her.

With her Bible and oxygen tank, she'd sit in her wheelchair and be taken to the outdoor courtyard gardens that had been designed to take advantage of the belief that sunlight, fresh air, landscapes and tranquil settings provided therapeutic healing. Jeri loved the "garden hospital" idea. She'd sit there, amid the stunningly beautiful spread of roses and annuals, and thank God for taking her this far.

One day, she arrived to find a harpist, Barbra Telynor, setting up to play as part of the Stanford Hospital Music Program. Music, Jeri discovered, was another part of Stanford's philosophy of therapeutic healing.

Jeri struck up a conversation and learned that Barbra not only had musical ability and the compassion that comes from being an ordained minister, but also a strong connection with the patients in the hospital: She had survived a coma and had undergone a kidney transplant.

Barbra told Jeri that "a little voice" in 1998 had told her that she should "sing" to hospital patients—those both healing and dying—through her harp. She had seen the tears of patients as the stress just melted out of their bodies. And she had sat in the corner of a hospital room and played while life slipped away from a 9-year-old girl.

Jeri watched as Barbra gently stroked the harp she had affectionately named Shawna. Jeri thought, *If it can be this beautiful here, imagine what heaven is like.*

On her way back to the door, she passed a doctor who remarked, "Kind of creepy, isn't it?"

Jeri found herself in an unusual situation: momentarily speechless.

"I . . . well . . . " she stammered, then gathered herself and smiled. "I thought it was beautiful."

She realized that what she imagined heaven to be like also made this doctor uneasy. She speculated that he did not know Christ. And that saddened her.

When Kim visited later in the afternoon, Jeri asked her: "Isn't it amazing that this thing of beauty and wonder for me caused him to react in a negative way?"

They talked some more. Jeri noticed the ring on Kim's right hand and asked about it. Kim told her that she had engraved 1 Peter 1:6-7 on the inside, representing the passage: *In this you greatly rejoice, though now for a little while you may have had to suffer grief in all kinds of trials. These have come so that your faith—of greater worth than gold, which perishes even though refined by fire—may be proved genuine and may result in praise, glory and honor when Jesus Christ is revealed.*

Kim talked about the importance of her faith, her need to know the Lord, and how that works in medicine with the other doctors and nurses. They saw suffering people all the time. Kim said she felt that in her capacity as a nurse, she relied on her faith that God would ease that suffering, and she wasn't reluctant to give God glory for healing.

Jeri smiled knowingly. God had brought her through the suffering, had given her abundant life to the astonishment of more than a few cardiologists.

"Ultimately, the credit has to go to God, if there is no medical explanation for why I'm still here," she said. "I didn't just get 'lucky.' I'm not just a statistical freak."

"No," Kim said, "you're not. And after getting to know you, I know why God kept your heart beating."

Before Kim left for the day, Jeri asked one favor.

"Could you check on my car to make sure it hasn't been towed from the handicapped space?" she asked.

That's the kind of thing friends do.

They had become friends.

* * *

Natalie Standlee had reached a frightening point in her life.

Just four weeks earlier, she had earned her bachelor's degree in nursing at Cal State Bakersfield, left her family behind in Bakersfield for the first time in her life and moved to Palo Alto to start a 12-week training program in the CCU.

Shy and introverted, she didn't easily make friends. She lived in an apartment right across the street from Stanford Medical Center. She worked. She went home. She went back to work. Her work stimulated her, but sometimes it seemed that she had left her heart in Bakersfield.

Why was she at Stanford?

She was about to find out.

Her job involved taking care of two patients on each 12-hour shift. When she was with one patient, another nurse handled the other patient.

During an orientation class, she had learned about Jeri. She knew Jeri had lived her entire life with her condition, and based on what she had learned in her brief experience and what long-time medical personnel had told her, those patients typically knew how to work the system. They had spent so much time in the hospital that they knew intimately how it worked, and they knew how to work it.

Natalie knew most of those chronically ill patients did not exude vibrancy because, well, they felt miserable. There were patients who had been waiting months for a transplant and couldn't leave the hospital, patients who needed a heart transplant but couldn't have one at that time, patients who had had a transplant but their body rejected it and they were taking medication to stave off the rejection.

They frequently buzzed the nurse's station, even for something as simple as changing the channel on the TV. They seemed dependent, uncomfortable, cranky, scared—and they harbored guilt for feeling and being all of those things.

So when Natalie heard about Jeri's situation, she wondered, *Uh-oh, what's this going to be like?*

Natalie entered Room 134, along with Dr. Hugh Harris, a pulmonary specialist.

"We need to wake her up," he said.

Natalie didn't know exactly how to address her: The records said Jerami, but she had heard people calling her Jeri.

"Miss," Natalie said, standing over her bed.

Jeri emerged from her sleep. Looking at Dr. Harris, she said, "I was woken up by this pretty nurse!"

Natalie, touched by Jeri's sweetness but also embarrassed, looked at Dr. Harris and blushed.

Natalie learned very early that Jeri would be a vigilant patient. She knew her body and everything that needed to be done to it. A nurse had to earn her trust. Jeri asked questions any time anybody wanted to give her an injection. *What is this medicine? What does it do?* She made sure the needle didn't contain a single air bubble.

This could have been a daunting—perhaps even crushing— experience for a young nurse unsure of herself. But Jeri nursed 24-year-old Natalie through those awkward moments, boosting her confidence and helping to strip away any nagging insecurity or stressful feelings.

"You're a good nurse," she'd say.

Natalie wondered how Jeri could step outside of her pain and discomfort to make others feel better. She imagined that although Jeri's body had adapted over her lifetime, she still had to feel extremely anemic all the time. She wondered how Jeri could even get out of bed. She watched as Jeri took small steps and slowly made her way around.

As Natalie got to know Jeri, she concluded that Jeri was more alive than anybody she knew.

Jeri had a youthful personality—not immature, but fun-loving and driven by a hard-charging brand of enthusiasm. One of her primary goals—other than a heart-lung transplant—appeared to be setting up Jana with one of the cute doctors in the CCU.

Jeri never once said, "I'm a Christian," but she didn't need to. Natalie could sense something different.

Natalie had been forced to go to church by her father throughout her high-school years. Although she had a spiritual side, it was frequently overwhelmed by a scientific approach that manifested itself in skepticism. The faith in her heart would surface, only to be shouted down by her brain. She had never accepted Christ.

Part of that was due to her perception that some people had pushed too hard for her to do it. Jeri didn't do that. Natalie wasn't just receptive to Jeri's non-threatening approach—she was inspired.

Jeri never put her on the spot by asking specific questions about her faith. It became clear to Natalie that Jeri loved her regardless of her choices and her past. Jeri talked about the fellowship and spiritual insight she had been getting from her small group's Bible study. Natalie started asking questions. Jeri suggested that Natalie talk to Kim about her church in Palo Alto.

Not only had Jeri become Natalie's primary patient—Natalie's tag-team nurse kindly granted Natalie's request—but also a friend. Natalie didn't care about any perception that she had to maintain a distance. Why? She cared about Jeri.

She looked at it as a positive: Her friendship with Jeri made her a better nurse. She became even more aware of her nursing duties. She found herself being even more vigilant about doing the right thing—not just for Jeri, but for everyone.

Natalie's desire coming out of Cal State Bakersfield was to ultimately become a donor coordinator. Meeting Jeri, absorbing her life story, feeling her desire to find a new heart and lungs so she could continue to live boldly and passionately for her family, her church and her God, becoming a part of that story, investing in that dream—all of that inspired Natalie even more.

Wow, she thought, *this is the kind of person I would be helping.*

They could joke together: Natalie would inspire laughter with comments about Jeri's "eagle eye" presiding over the administering of medications and procedures.

They could dream together: Natalie would talk of finding hearts for dying patients, and Jeri would talk of climbing The Dish with the other transplant survivors.

They could cry together: One night, Jeri admitted her fear of not getting donor organs in time and her depression over being separated from Junny, Daryl, Brady, Jayme, Amy, and her church family.

"I miss them so much," she said. "You have no idea. They are my life. Maybe I could live without the new organs. Sometimes I think I'd rather just go home. I'm in a hospital. People in a hospital are supposed to be getting better. Being here isn't killing me physically, but sometimes it seems like it's doing that emotionally."

"You're going to get your heart and lungs," Natalie said, grasping Jeri's hand. "You have to wait, because there's no other choice."

Jeri wiped away her tears while Natalie fought back hers. They hugged.

The next time they met, Jeri's mood had brightened considerably. She called Natalie over to her bed.

"I need you, Natalie," Jeri said. "Would you be with me after I get the call about donor organs being available? Would you be in the OR for the surgery?"

"I'd be honored. That means the world to me. Of course I'll be there."

CHAPTER 14

SHE CAN'T LIVE
UNLESS SOMEONE DIES

Patience had never been Jeri's strong suit. She had been accustomed to charging head-first into whatever she set her mind and heart to. Now she was "ensconced" in a waiting game completely out of her control.

In a postcard to the church, she wrote that she wanted to "come home more than ever." She encouraged the congregation to "keep praying for those organs" and added, "All I want for Christmas is . . . a new heart and lungs!"

Of course, to get them, someone would have to die. She had a hard time reconciling that notion, but she knew it all fell under God's providence. It would be just as the authors of the Heidelberg Catechism defined providence: "His almighty and ever-present power, whereby, as with His hand, He still upholds heaven and earth and all creatures, and so governs them that leaf and blade, rain and drought, fruitful and barren years, food and drink, health and sickness, riches and poverty, indeed, all things, come not by chance but by His fatherly hand."

Not only would someone have to die, but that person would have to be roughly the same size (not just a similar weight, but more crucially, the same body-surface area in the thoracic cavity), with the same blood type (A-positive).

The good news and bad news came in equal measures.

The good news: With an A-positive blood type, she was much more likely to get organs than a person with an O type who competed with candidates in other blood groups.

The bad news: Although there weren't many competing recipients who were as petite as Jeri, there also weren't many potential donors.

The good news: Death rates on the heart waiting list for 1A candidates (the most urgent classification) had decreased sharply, going from 2,087 per 1,000 patient-years at risk in 2000 to just over 1,700 in 2002.

The bad news: She didn't need just a heart. As they had told her in the interviews in March, it was difficult to get both a heart and lung graft together, resulting in fewer than 40 heart-lung transplants every year in the United States.

Stanford—the nation's premier center for heart-lung transplants—had performed just five in 2002, the year it became the world's longest continually active team performing heart-lung transplantation.

But simply being at Stanford made her much more likely to receive one. Stanford had an association with the California Transplant Donor Network, a local organ-procurement organization that led the nation in 2002 in three critical areas: organs recovered, hearts recovered and lungs recovered per donor.

That's why wait times typically were shorter there. In 2002, 25% of the heart-lung patients listed at Stanford had received a transplant within 4.4 months of being placed on the waiting list—compared to 18.7 months for the rest of the nation. Looking at it another way, 33.3% of the patients at Stanford received a transplant within six months, compared to 11.1% for the rest of the nation. None had died while waiting in that six-month period, compared to 16.3% nationally.

Jeri had been briefed about exactly how the process would work:

The United Network for Organ Sharing (UNOS) maintains a centralized computer network linking all organ-procurement organizations and transplant centers—accessible 24/7, with organ-placement specialists available to answer questions.

Patients, after being approved by a transplant center, are placed in a national pool—and not on a ranked list. When a deceased organ donor is identified, a transplant coordinator from an organ-procurement organization accesses the UNOS computer, and each patient in the pool is matched against the donor characteristics. The computer then generates a ranked list of patients for each organ that is procured from that donor in ranked order according to organ-allocation policies. The ranking is affected by tissue match, blood type, length of time on the waiting list, immune status, the distance between the potential recipient and the donor, and the degree of medical urgency.

Organs are frequently offered first to local patients, then to a larger region, then nationally. That's done to minimize organ-preservation time, which correlates with better transplant survival. Waiting time is used to break ties between patients who are similar in other respects.

The organ then is offered to the transplant team of the first person on the list. The patient must be available, healthy enough to undergo major surgery and willing to be transplanted immediately. In some cases, a lab test is necessary to measure compatibility because patients with high antibody levels often can't receive the organ because the immune system would reject it.

A donor's smoking history can complicate the decision-making process, but many lung donors are smokers, so it is not unusual to use organs from a donor who has been a smoker. The critical thing is that the lungs must have good function—and that is tested before the organs are accepted.

In Stanford's case, if it determines that the donor organs are a suitable match for the patient, it sends its cardiothoracic team—two surgeons and a coordinator (not the same team that would perform the transplant on the recipient)—on a Leer jet to harvest the organs from the deceased. The team takes a secondary look at the organs as they are removed, and if anything unsuitable is found, the transplant can be stopped at any time.

The organs are chilled and preserved in fluids and ice in an Igloo cooler. The key is time. The team has only 4-6 hours between the time the organs are removed and the time they are reperfused in the recipient. That's why it would be very unlikely that the organs would come from a donor more than 1,500 miles away. Exceptions would be made only for pediatric donor organs, which can be kept out of the body for longer periods.

The process is magnificently choreographed, with the surgical team at Stanford starting the removal of the recipient's organs at the precise time that would allow for the donor's organs to arrive when that procedure is finished.

With all of that in mind, the goal of Jeri's team was to make sure she wasn't *too* sick to get the transplant. Organs wouldn't be risked on a candidate not likely to survive the arduous procedure.

By the end of August, Jeri would lose 20 pounds of fluid—much to the amazement of Dr. Lissin.

"I didn't think she'd live another day," she said.

Her conclusion: She didn't think it had been Jeri's time to go yet.

Her doctors stressed the importance of a no-sodium diet—much to Jeri's surprise, they told her cheese contains salt—and got more aggressive in putting her on a high-calorie diet because she had lost so much muscle tone. That meant she would be devouring bottles of BOOST nutritional energy drink, which she described as being like "baby formula on ice."

Jeri's team included a mind-boggling 50 doctors—including Dr. Reitz and Dr. Clinton Lloyd, who would be collaborating on the transplant—but there was a core of seven or eight pre-transplant specialists who were most intimately involved. Every morning, they'd huddle up like a football team near the nurse's station to brainstorm about each patient, reviewing the patient's overnight activity and outlining the game plan for that day.

Football coaches will tell you that they have to spend half of the day dissecting film because their game is a complex chess match, an intricately choreographed collision of high-speed bodies that constantly requires counter-thrusts, adjustments, deception and defiance. And it is true. But while those huddles might determine whether their seasons are terminated or extended, they don't dictate *real* life and death. Every day, Jeri's team danced with the specter of death.

Carolyn's daily routine always took her within range of the team's sphere of high-level interaction. She'd awaken in her foldout couch, freshen up and head out for a cup of coffee, always passing the huddle, always straining to overhear even the most minute tidbit about Jeri. Her harmless bit of espionage never produced anything.

Jeri's doctors were more than just doctors. They invested in her life. They treated her like she was a family member, and she did the same. She constantly asked about their personal lives—their hopes, dreams, interests, family members. When one of them came into her room, she wouldn't let him or her leave without enlightening her with at least a few personal details.

She knew that Dr. Michael Pham, a specialist in congestive heart failure, loved former Aggie All-America linebacker Dat Nguyen, who shared Dr. Pham's heritage and had become the first Vietnamese-American to play in the NFL. He'd talk about how he worked himself into a frenzy while watching Nguyen at A&M. So she arranged for Junny to find a poster of Nguyen, which she gave to Dr. Pham.

They talked of their personal lives. Jeri found out that he played the violin.

"You'll play it for me sometime, won't you?" Jeri asked excitedly. He winked.

Junny also acquired an Aggie cap from a member of the coaching staff and gave that to an intern who was preparing to leave Stanford.

Dr. Michael Fowler, who headed Jeri's team, loved Jeri so much that he brought his entire family—wife and children—into her room one day.

Other than Natalie and Kim, nobody got closer to Jeri than Dr. Jeremy Feldman. He had attended Stanford as an undergraduate student and earlier in the year returned as a pulmonary hypertension fellow. He found himself drawn in by her infectious enthusiasm for life. Like Natalie and Kim, he was fascinated that she didn't carry the baggage of a chronically ill patient who had spent her entire life closely attached to the healthcare system.

Jeri's openness about her faith did not have a discernible impact on Dr. Feldman. It didn't matter whether a patient worshipped Buddha, Yahweh or Mohammed—it was all irrelevant to Dr. Feldman, who encouraged his patients to use whatever tools helped them get through difficult times. He knew Jeri was praying for him to receive Christ. He respected the fact that Jeri's faith manifested itself in beautiful, poignant moments devoid of pushiness.

He liked her so much that he arranged for a nurse's computer—which normally would be in the hallway—to be kept in Jeri's room, so she could catch up on her e-mail and check the CaringBridge site. It was their little secret.

He usually was the first doctor to see Jeri each morning. Sometimes Carolyn would be asleep near Jeri's bed and would wake to see him talking to her. When her numbers—particularly her bilirubin—were good, he excitedly praised her. When they weren't, he comforted her.

Dr. Feldman may have had the toughest job of anyone on her pre-transplant team, for he had to balance her hemodynamics—the physical factors that govern blood flow—figuring out the precise cocktail of medications that would keep her stable and allow her to survive long enough for the transplant. With Jeri's one-chamber heart pumping blood both to her lungs and her body, he was the medical equivalent of a high-wire act.

And that list of medications was long and dizzying: Lanoxin, Lasix, atenolol, allopurinol, Aldactone, trazodone, Coumadin, Colace and K-Dur, along with iron supplements and aspirin.

On August 16, Jeri lost circulation in her left leg, which took on a warm sensation and a reddish discoloration. Her doctors determined that she had a deep-vein thrombosis—a blood clot—and ordered her to lay still. Lay still? Jeri? It turned out to be one of the longest days of her life.

As the night wore on, Junny tickled her legs and her back, gently, affectionately and patiently until she finally drifted off to sleep.

He sat in a chair at the end of her bed, allowing his mind to wander. She had always made him proud to be her dad by treating him like an exalted king and putting him as high on a pedestal as a dad could be put. In her eyes, his jokes were the best. There was nothing he couldn't fix—to the point where the rest of the family would say, "If it's broke, give it to dad. He'll go out there in the shed and mingle with the junk and make it work." The things he did were special—not goofy.

It delighted her to introduce him to her friends and fellow church members. His mind clicked back to 2001, back to a sun-splashed September day on the A&M campus. He had emerged from a morning of work at the maintenance building and noticed Jeri standing in line with over 100 others at the gate outside Kyle Field. She saw him at virtually the same moment and called out to him, "Dad!" They embraced, and she turned to a dozen friends on either side of her and said, "This is my dad!"

And what about Carolyn? On her last birthday, hadn't she awakened in a hotel room to find a note from Jeri: "You're my hero"? Did Jeri have any idea how honored she made them feel? Had they told her often enough? He tilted his head back and closed his eyes.

When he opened them, daylight had enveloped the room and seven doctors stood around Jeri in a semi-circle, discussing the options. The danger of her condition was that pieces of the clot could break off and travel through the bloodstream to the lung—a potentially fatal development. Or blood flow could be blocked to the vein, causing the blood to pool and possibly leading to permanent leg damage.

They decided to do an angiogram and thrombolytic therapy. The procedure went smoothly, but Jeri wouldn't be on her feet for a few days.

Cindy sent her an e-mail from Florida: *Remember, it will get better. I know for me, God has and continues to grace my life with so many wonderful people. Doctors, nurses, friends, family, strangers. Remember, your fellow transplant friends are here for you. We know your journey. You are a fighter, a survivor. We are fighters, survivors . . . otherwise we would not still be here. One of these days, you will walk The Dish.*

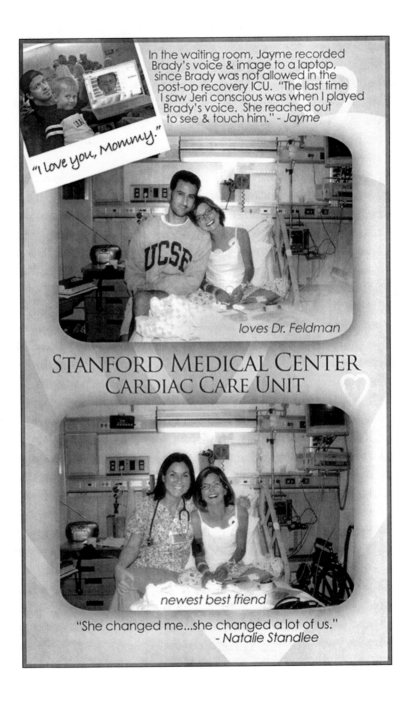

In the waiting room, Jayme recorded Brady's voice & image to a laptop, since Brady was not allowed in the post-op recovery ICU. "The last time I saw Jeri conscious was when I played Brady's voice. She reached out to see & touch him." - Jayme

"I love you, Mommy."

loves Dr. Feldman

STANFORD MEDICAL CENTER
CARDIAC CARE UNIT

newest best friend

"She changed me...she changed a lot of us."
- Natalie Standlee

And the next day, another one*: Remember to breathe. Relax. Peace be still. Try to be in the "now moment." As I waited for my transplant, a dear Christian friend shared something with me: Life is like a tapestry. Sometimes when we look up, all we see are knots (difficult times), but God is looking down and sees the whole beautiful picture.*

Jeri's immobilization didn't come at the best time—Amy had flown out to Stanford, along with 3-month-old Avery, figuring it might be the last time she'd see her sister before the transplant. Despite the fact that Jeri was bedridden, she remained in good spirits, and Amy doted on her by cutting her food, arranging flowers in vases and even—upon request—plucking Jeri's eyebrows with tweezers.

On August 27, Jeri's doctors came into her room and notified her that they had spent the early-morning hours debating what to do about the news that organs had become available. The donor was a 45-year-old smoker. Moments before she woke up, they decided that the organs would not be healthy enough for her.

Jeri, while disappointed that the organs weren't suitable, felt herself thrust onto a mountain top. She knew she had the best transplant team she possibly could have. She also knew that God would work everything out in His perfect time.

Later that day, the chaplain stopped by. Jeri told him about the prayer pager Grace Fellowship had given her, about the unbridled joy she felt when she heard it beep and knew that somebody had been praying specifically for her. The chaplain was moved to tears.

By August 29, Jeri's bilirubin stood at a very desirable 2.0 and her oxygen saturation astonishingly had vaulted to 95. When Nancy read the monitor and saw that, she hurriedly rushed out of the room to find her team nurse. Neither one could explain how it had changed so dramatically.

"Go, God!" Nancy said. "Go, God!"

Jeri continued to be a font of information for the class that regularly came into her room, giving the students fascinating tidbits of knowledge about her condition. They were witnessing things in her room that they had only read about, given the rarity of her condition and the reality that she possibly could be the oldest living American with it who had never had a transplant.

While Jeri settled into a routine at Stanford, Daryl made moves to restore stability to his life.

Trendmaker gave Daryl the news that he could return to his job in Katy, and the leasing agent in Las Vegas decided to allow them to break the lease on their rental home because she was more concerned about Jeri's health than a legal document.

On August 30, he packed a 26-foot Ryder truck along with parents, who had driven out from Texas. His dad drove the rental truck while Daryl followed behind in his work truck.

As they rolled down I-15, Daryl took a deep breath and tried to expel a dastardly combination of stress and loneliness. His son was in Texas, trying to adjust to the first structured schooling of his life. His wife lay in a bed in a California hospital, needing a death to stay alive. And he was about halfway in between, with no place to call home. Could it get any crazier?

What could be going on inside Brady's head? Did he have any comprehension?

And what of Jeri? He never heard her say, "Poor pitiful me." In her phone calls and e-mails, he noticed that she constantly praised God for everything. She had always done that, but now her journey had truly taken her to the precipice—a precipice that Daryl felt would have forced him into a me-mode if he had experienced it.

She's found a peace, he thought. *Does she know something that we don't? Has God spoken to her and told her she isn't going to make it? Has He given her a glimpse of heaven? Has He filled her with something we can't possibly understand?*

Her walk with God is so strong. She has trusted Him with every-thing. Sought Him in every decision. In everything, she has sought Him first. I don't always do that. I don't know how she does it. But it sure is neat to watch.

Daryl's mind did a lot of wandering on that 1,440-mile drive. When he reached the Dolans' house, Brady jumped into his arms, and one piece of the perplexing puzzle was fitted into place. Daryl and Brady lived in the same room, each with a twin bed.

He would spend the next three weeks looking for a house to buy, assisted by Grace Fellowship member Jay Thieme, who had helped him sell his other houses. The plan would be for Daryl and Brady to make that house their base, and they'd periodically commute to Stanford to see Jeri after her transplant. And after Jeri's 100-day recovery at Stanford, all of them would live together in that house.

Daryl intentionally chose not to ease back into the flow of Katy life. After Trendmaker's generosity in returning him seamlessly to his previous job—even if it wouldn't be in exactly the same location—he felt compelled to get right back to work.

Jeri didn't have Daryl, but her support group grew when Lisa arrived on September 1 for the start of a four-day visit.

Part of the timing stemmed from her desire to be there on Jeri's September 2 birthday. The rest was, well, a bit morbid, they'd admit. Jeri wanted very much to have close friends and family with her when she got the call that donor organs were available. But how would they know when that would happen? Well, they figured, the odds were a bit better on Labor Day weekend, with heavy traffic on the highways resulting in more fatal accidents.

Carolyn wanted Jeri and Lisa to enjoy their private time, so she left the room and moved to a nearby building with rooms usually reserved for visiting doctors. She had her own shower—meaning she no longer had to sneak into the one near the nurse's station—which made the $37-a-night fee a steal.

Lisa got the raw end of that deal. The foldout couch mysteriously disappeared from Jeri's room, leaving Lisa with a 1960s-style vinyl chair as her bed. After one night, she realized that wouldn't work, so she climbed into bed with Jeri.

When the doctors caught their first glimpse of the two of them together the next morning, they laughed heartily.

"It's a girlie thing," Jeri insisted. "You wouldn't understand. But we're snuggly and comfy, so laugh all you want."

The entire medical staff had been alerted about Jeri's birthday, so all of them visited, bringing a cake and gifts. Dr. Pham brought his violin and serenaded Jeri. Lisa decorated the room with balloons and a beautiful arrangement of flowers sent by Daryl's mom. They ate off Barbie plates, honoring Jeri's wishes. And they ate some low-sodium delicacies from P.F. Chang's Chinese Bistro, taking a brief break from her strict diet.

Before Lisa arrived, Jeri had asked about the possibility of being discharged until organs became available.

She knew that if she checked out of the hospital, she would lose 1A status because she no longer would be receiving "continuous infusion of intravenous inotropes along with continuous monitoring of left ventricular filling pressures"—unless Stanford submitted an application for 1A status to the Regional Review Board and the application was approved. She would, however, remain at the top of the normal donor list.

Dr. Lissin felt that Jeri was doing well enough to be taken off the monitor. She could be monitored closely as an outpatient and return September 10 to be examined again.

Jeri decided she'd leave. Jana offered to house Jeri, Lisa and Carolyn at her condo across the Dumbarton Bridge in Fremont. Before Jeri checked out on September 4, she gathered her flowers and gave them to a woman at the end of the hall who was too sick to get a transplant.

The next day, they went to Fisherman's Wharf in San Francisco. It became more of a high-risk adventure than either Lisa or Jeri had expected. Lisa, driving Jeri's Highlander, had some difficulty navigating the city's treacherous grid of one-way streets and notoriously hilly terrain—a polar opposite of Houston's flat-as-a-pool-table land.

At one point, Jeri screamed, "Oh my gosh, we're going to die!"

On a 70-degree, Chamber-of-Commerce day, they felt God smiling upon them. They watched the sea lions sunbathing at Pier 39, with Alcatraz serving as a majestic backdrop. They browsed in shops, trying on crazy hats. Lisa, piloting Jeri's wheelchair, pulled wild wheelies.

Goofiness and silliness prevailed. Neither of them talked about the transplant: the possibility that she wouldn't receive organs in time, or that the surgery might not be successful. They were alive, enjoying the moments they had.

Both of them decided to treat themselves to a pedicure. The technician asked them where they were from. And as she cut and filed their nails, soaked their feet, trimmed their cuticles, rubbed in moisturizer and applied the polish—pink, of course—Jeri told her story. The technician, moved by Jeri's journey, gave her a complimentary extra: flowers and sparkles over the top of her pink toenails.

Jeri never received that long-awaited phone call announcing donor organs, so Lisa flew back to Katy knowing she had probably seen Jeri for the last time before the transplant.

Back in Katy, Lisa resumed training for the Houston Marathon in January, along with Katie. They had started training in July—right after Jeri left for Las Vegas. Those sessions always powerfully incorporated Jeri, motivating them to push past the painful moments.

They thought about how hard their hearts were working, with the chambers refilling after pumping blood from the right side of the heart to the lungs. The more blood their hearts pumped, the more oxygen could be delivered to their lungs. Jeri couldn't run because her heart couldn't do that. Someday, they thought as they ran, she will be able to do it. Maybe not a marathon, but a triumphant run of any kind.

Katie couldn't get Steven Curtis Chapman's "Miracle of the Moment" out of her mind during those runs. He sings of breathing in and out and listening to the heartbeat, appreciating the beauty of being alive at this point in time: *And I don't want you to miss the miracle of the moment.*

On September 8, Jeri received an e-mail from Karen: *Sweet Jeri, you are being prayed for by the International Christian Fellowship of Balikpapan, Indonesia. I am picturing us together, holding hands and praying in the "Cry Room." "For I know the plans I have for you . . ." Thank you, Jesus, for taking care of our Jeri!*

On September 9, she came down with a 101-degree fever and sinus infection and checked back into the CCU, staying overnight. The next day, she was given a seven-day antibiotics regimen for sinusitis and released back to Jana's. She filled her days with trips to parks and gardens, just sitting in the sun and basking in its glory. She and Carolyn also frequented outdoor markets, where Jeri marveled at the dark-red plums and sumptuous peaches and berries. She had never tasted fruit quite like this.

"It makes me wonder what the Garden of Eden must have been like if California is like this," she said to Carolyn.

On September 12, Daryl and Brady arrived for the weekend. Daryl desperately needed a break, having been worn down by the triple whammy of starting a new job, taking care of Brady and trying to find a house.

They went to the beach, where they buried Brady in sand and Jeri boldly joined Brady on a carnival ride with spinning cups. On Saturday night, while Carolyn entertained Brady, they had a date night in San Francisco and stayed at the Omni.

"This has been the most perfect day," Jeri said.

The next day, before Daryl left, he could sense some trepidation in Jeri. What if the donor organs came after he left? What would it look like immediately after they received that transcendent phone call? How likely would it be that Daryl would be able to catch a flight and arrive before she went into the OR?

"I may not see you before the surgery," he said.

At the airport, Daryl held his emotions in check. He always had to be strong. He never afforded himself the chance to cry and express his fears. Brady, however, was just 5. He obviously couldn't process everything in a sophisticated fashion, but he knew something was wrong and that he would have to leave his mommy.

"Do you want mommy to go back with you and still be sick? Or do you want mommy to stay here and get well so she can run and play with you?" she asked, wiping the warm tears from his cheeks.

"Stay here," he said.

Carolyn had her own issues to work out. Her original plan had been to remain at Stanford until the organs became available. But A&M—where she worked as a senior secretary in the psychology department—notified her that she should consider returning or retiring. The new fiscal year had begun on September 1, and her family leave had run out. She had submitted her retirement papers, but they had not been filed.

She also knew she was starting to get on Jeri's nerves. As close as they were, as strongly as their souls had been aligned from birth, she imagined what it would be like to have someone hovering over her for two solid months. Did Jeri need some space?

Her answer came in a conversation with Jayme, who said, "Mom, I think you should go home for a while."

Carolyn told Jeri, "As soon as I leave, you'll probably get your organs."

"Mom, go home for a few days," Jeri said.

"OK. I'll go home for two weeks and I'll be back."

Carolyn wanted to take the train to Oakland International Airport, but Jeri insisted on driving her. At the airport, Carolyn didn't turn it into an emotional goodbye because she didn't want to trigger deep emotions in Jeri.

On the flight, something simply did not feel right to Carolyn. She had always been at Jeri's side during sickness—any kind of sickness, even the flu.

I feel selfish leaving, she thought. *I could have said, "No, I'm not leaving." But Jayme told me that I should go home, didn't he? I'm honoring her wishes, aren't I?*

On September 18, Jeri's doctors suggested that they could put her back in the hospital and administer a dopamine IV, which would make her heart pump harder and cause more blood and oxygen to reach her organs, making her healthier.

The upside? She would be back on 1A status, increasing the chance of a transplant. She liked that idea because she longed to go back to Texas, and she knew this would speed that up. The down-side? There was a chance she could suffer irregular heartbeats. She had reservations about the medication and prayed that if it was not the right thing to do, at least one of her doctors would object to the new medication.

She met with doctors the next day, and later was called and told that she could check into the hospital without going on the medica-tion. Due to her liver-function numbers, they could put her back in the CCU and back on 1A status without having any IVs.

On September 21, she suddenly felt ill. The staff discovered that she had suffered an attack of ventricular tachycardia—a potentially life-threatening arrhythmia that could lead to ventricular fibrillation and sudden death—and experienced a run of 16 VT beats. She had never had that many together. It frightened her.

Dr. Feldman said they wanted to put her on amiodarone, which is used to treat arrhythmias and to maintain a normal heart rate in patients who have not responded to other medications. He told her it is used only in life-threatening situations because it had the potential to cause side effects that could be fatal, along with possibly irreversible blue-gray skin pigmentation resulting from prolonged use or exposure to the sun without high-factor sunblock.

Jeri, distraught and uncertain about how to tell him she didn't want to take it, called Carolyn and Junny on their cell phone. Whispering so Dr. Feldman wouldn't hear her, she told them of her fears. Carolyn and Junny were on their way home from San Antonio, their favorite weekend getaway. They told Jeri they would discuss it, pray over it and call her back.

Junny veered his car off of I-35 and pulled over on the shoulder. To them, it seemed like they needed to be there. They could put their lives on hold. They had lines of credit that would allow them to afford another trip out there. They were prepared to turn the car around, go to San Antonio International Airport and catch the first flight.

When they called Jeri and told her their plans, she said, "I'm all right. You don't have to do that."

Later in the day, she called to tell them that Dr. Feldman had decided not to put her on the medication.

But all around her, she experienced more reminders of her fragile mortality. First, in a next-door room, a man died. Then, her other neighbor suffered a heart attack and could not attend his daughter's wedding. The entire wedding party visited the hospital, dressed in tuxes and wedding dresses.

Jeri came down with a bad cold and a persistent cough. Although her lungs remained clear and free of infection, she couldn't shake one thing—the thought of Daryl and Brady in Texas.

"I miss them so much that it's unbearable," she told Kim. "I really want God's will in my life more than anything, and to glorify Him. But sometimes I just want to scream, 'Hurry, God! Please!'"

When the art director visited her room later that day, Jeri had something on her heart. Three things, actually: her heart, Daryl's heart and Brady's heart. She took a sheet of paper, grabbed a crayon and drew a rectangle. Then she started forming the edges of a heart. Her heart. Then she drew two more hearts below that. Their hearts. She filled them in, then drew varying shades of blue around them.

Even before she knew of her heart condition, she had always loved hearts, one time making some out of red satin and stuffing them with cotton. It saddened Carolyn, but she never said anything.

All her life, Jeri thought Jayme and Amy had been the ones blessed with artistic talent. She had no idea she could even do what she had just done on this sheet of paper. She hung it on the wall across from her bed, so she could see it at all times, so she could bridge the daunting distance by keeping them close.

Early in the morning on September 24, she wrote an e-mail to Karen in Indonesia. She told her that her new favorite cookies, oddly enough, were from Indonesia—and that she thought of Karen every time she took a bite: *I am missing you so bad and just wish you were here to hold my hands and pray with me. I can still hear your sweet prayer voice in my head. I keep you in my prayers and pray that the Lord protects you and shows you more and more of Him. I am glad we are in this weird thing together. It helps me not feel so alone.*

Then she wrote another e-mail to her friends: *Good morning from Stanford University and beautiful California. Today it is a little overcast. I have never seen that here, so it is new. There has been a heat wave (90s) and all of the Californians are freaking out. I still don't think it feels hot here, compared to home. What a bunch of weather wimps!*

I am feeling good, getting over my respiratory infection. I have gained some water weight (due to my heart) and now have a new IV that I am getting Lasix in. I lost five pounds the day before yesterday. The medicine works fast! I am learning some new hobbies, like cross stitching. Kim came by and helped me hang up pictures in my room. Also, a couple my mom had met weeks earlier in the hospital came by. She was having surgery this morning. They lost two babies years ago from the same illness I have. They are wonderful Christians and we prayed together.

Running out of room. Thank you for all your prayers. God is in control. I trust in Him, but I do wish this could happen soon so I can get back to my wonderful Texas!!! I love you all so much.

189

What she didn't tell them was that her time was quickly running out. She had end-stage congenital heart disease and primary pulmonary hypertension, with tenuous cardiac function, extremely low oxygen-saturation levels and troubling arrhythmia issues. When she lay in bed, she'd be OK. But she had become too weak to walk much. She knew she had a week to live.

When doctors huddled that morning, they knew their best efforts soon wouldn't matter.

"She's on death's doorstep," Dr. Feldman said. "We need donor organs. Fast."

CHAPTER 15

IT'S A MATCH

Jeri was watching TV around 7:45 that night when Dr. Lloyd walked in. Jeri's mind immediately raced. Her interaction with him had been limited during her time at Stanford. He was on the transplant team, not the *pre*-transplant team. He would be the one who would assist Dr. Reitz in implanting the donor organs once they became available.

Had they become available?

"How are you feeling?" he said.

"Ready for what you're going to tell me, I think," she said, smiling.

"You're right—it's time," he said. "A 56-year-old donor has suffered brain death due to subarachnoid hemorrhage. We have the organs that match."

"I always thought I knew exactly how I'd feel when I got the news," she said, pausing to compose herself. "But . . . it's not exactly what I envisioned. I . . . I don't know if I can describe it. I'm scared . . . and excited. It's just a mess of emotions."

"I understand. I don't know exactly what you're feeling, but I've seen it in patients just like yourself. It's totally natural."

"OK, so . . . now what?"

"We're sending our team to access the organs immediately. If they're determined to be suitable, they'll notify us and we'll start prepping you for surgery."

After Dr. Lloyd left the room, Jeri grabbed her Bible and clasped it to her chest, right against the serpentine scar that signified the reason why she had come to this point. She said a silent prayer: *Lord, I know you have brought me here for this reason. I praise you for all you have done, and all that you will continue to do after this. You are amazing. But now I really need you. I'm scared. I'm excited because I know this can save my life. But I'm scared. Please take away that fear and fill me with your holy presence.*

She opened her Bible and pulled out a card from Oma that she had tucked into the back cover. Oma wrote that "the battle is the Lord's and victory is yours." She included the passage from Luke 13 in which Jesus heals the woman who had been crippled by a spirit for 18 years. She wrote, "Jeri, you have been bound these 34 years and Jesus says, 'It is time you are loose and made whole in Him to live a long, healthy, good life.' "

She ended with Malachi 4:2: *But for you who revere my name, the sun of righteousness will rise with healing in its wings.*

Jeri read that again, letting the beautiful imagery soak in.

And then she reached over to her bedside table and picked up the telephone. She had a lot of people to talk to in a short period of time.

Carolyn was asleep—and Junny was preparing to go to bed—when the phone rang.

"Hi, dad."

"Hey, Jeri. This is later than you normally call. How are you feeling?"

"Dad . . . I've got a match. What do you think?"

"I don't know. I guess you'd better go for it. What do you think?"

"I'm scared. I need you to get out here as quickly as you can."

"We will. I'll call the airlines right now."

"I love you."

"Love you, too."

Daryl was eating dinner with a friend at EinStein's Pub in Katy when his cell phone rang.

"I've got a match," Jeri said.

Daryl felt as if his vocal chords had been paralyzed. He couldn't speak. He thought he had prepared himself emotionally for this moment, but now that it had arrived, he realized there would have been no way to adequately prepare. Now, the reality truly clobbered him in the mouth: She was on the other side of the continent and he had no way to immediately get there. It had been easy to say, "I'm all for this"—until crunch time arrived.

All this time, he had masked his emotions to be strong for Jeri. Now they came flowing out. He was glad she couldn't see him now.

"Dare, you there?" she asked.

"Yeah . . . sorry."

"They have organs from a 56-year-old donor. They're flying to remove the organs and evaluate them to see if they check out OK. This is almost 100%."

"How are you holding up?"

"I'm scared. I've never done anything without . . . you know . . . you or my family. I need you. Please get here. As soon as you can . . . please. You need to get on a plane and get here as fast as you can."

"Have you talked to your parents?"

"Yeah. Give them a call. Maybe you can get on the same flight."

"I'll do that. I'm leaving soon, OK? I'll be there in the morning."

"Love you."

"Love you, too."

On the other side of the continent, at First Baptist Church of St. Petersburg, Jayme stood in the foyer, bragging to the praise band's percussion player about Jeri's courage. Band rehearsal for Sunday's worship had just wrapped up, and Jayme, the church's creative arts director, was infused with energy.

His phone rang, and he saw that it was Jeri. "You're not going to believe this! It's her!" he told the band member. Jayme ended the conversation, answered the call and walked to his truck.

"It's happening . . . finally, it's happening," Jeri said. "They found the organs. I'm going to do it now."

Ever since *Jerry Maguire* had come out in 1996, Jeri had continually told Jayme that he reminded her of the Rod Tidwell character played by Cuba Gooding Jr. because of his exuberance that sometimes went over the top. He'd say totally inappropriate things to make her laugh, get her psyched and be her unabashed cheerleader. Now she needed it more than ever.

"It's on!" he yelled. "It's going to happen! I'm pumped! This is it!"

As he barreled down I-275 at 70 mph, Jayme rolled down the window and held the phone at a distance so he wouldn't blow out her ears.

"Oh, yeah! Whoa! Whoa!" he screamed into the steamy Florida night.

Then he rolled up the window and got serious.

"I'm scared," Jeri said.

"Don't be afraid. This is the moment. You've trusted God up to this point. Keep moving ahead. It's finally here. Let's do it."

"I can't believe I'm here alone. Jayme, I need you and Amy and mom and dad and Daryl so much. I felt such a void that I asked a man who is visiting his family, 'Could you come in here and be with me?' "

"It's OK. You needed a dad figure, and you weren't embarrassed to do it."

Crying, she pleaded with Jayme, "I need you to get here right now."

"I'm on it right now."

"Love you."

"Love you, too."

Jim and Lisa had turned off the lights a few minutes earlier and were drifting off to sleep when the phone rang. They couldn't get to the phone before the answering machine picked up.

"Jim, Lisa, wake up! Wake up! This is Jeri! I need you to wake up! Wake up!"

Jeri paused, her voice breaking with emotion. "Jim and Lisa . . . This is Jeri, and I think it's going to happen. They just came and told me, so I need to talk to you."

At that instant, Jim picked up the phone. Jeri explained the scenario. She told him of her mixture of excitement and fear. She wanted him to pray not just for her, but for the family that had lost a loved one whose organs would extend her life.

And so Jim gathered himself and began.

"Before we ask you for anything, we just want to worship you for who you are. God, you're powerful. You know everything. You're present everywhere. Thank you that 100% of you is present here in the Leggett house to hear this prayer, but also that 100% of you is present in the Stanford hospital to act on behalf of this prayer. We just want to trust you with Jeri. Lord, we pray that your Kingdom come and your will be done. If you want her to go through with this surgery, will you let all those things fall into place so that she can. And Lord, if for some reason you don't want her to go through with it, would you make it not possible for her have it?

"We ask you to flood Jeri with peace that passes all under-standing. And Lord, you say that if we delight ourselves in you that you will give us the desires of our heart. Lord, I see a woman named Jeri delighting herself in you. Will you give her the desires for a new heart and new lungs that she might have pink lips and pink fingertips and pink toes so that she can live a longer life and glorify you and see her boy graduate from high school and get married and do the things that you would have for her to do? We pray for the doctors for wisdom and skill and alertness. We pray for Daryl and Brady and her parents.

"God, we don't understand how you work. You're so much bigger than us. And we trust you. So we want to trust you with this family. If there are organs, then there is a family that's hurting. So would you comfort that family right now? And Lord, somehow, allow them just a glimpse of how their loved one's death is helping somebody else."

When Jeri finished with Jim, she called Natalie, who in just a few hours would be celebrating her 25th birthday.

"I'm just calling to tell you happy birthday—"

"Well, thank you."

"—and to tell you that it's going to be my birthday, too." Natalie knew exactly what Jeri meant—that everybody who gets a heart transplant has a birthday on the day they receive it. "You're coming in to go to the OR with me, right?"

"Of course! This is great news! I'll be in as soon as I can."

Natalie immediately sat down and started writing: "Jeri, I thank God that our paths crossed, and that I have had the opportunity to know you. I've learned so much from you. Your warm smile will stay with me forever and will always be an inspiration. My prayers are with you and your family. I know, no matter what, you are taken care of. Love you, Natalie."

Carolyn, meanwhile, called Jana, reaching her while she attended a service at Embassy Christian Center in San Francisco. Jana left immediately and arrived at Jeri's room shortly after Natalie. It was a chaotic scene, with nurses and doctors probing her with IVs, measuring her heart rate, charting all of her vital signs. Jeri, charged with adrenaline and nervous energy, chatted away, alternately laughing and crying.

Dr. Lloyd came in with a waiver for her to sign, releasing the hospital of any liability should she die. It was standard operating procedure. Jeri knew she would be signing it. But in this moment, the reality of this irreversibly transcendent milestone truly registered.

Jeri looked at Jana, and Jana thought she saw fear in Jeri's eyes.

"What do you think?" Jeri said.

"Jeri, you don't have to sign it if you don't feel good about it."

It had been a source of some tension between the two. Jana had been praying and believing that God would heal Jeri, whether it was through a miracle or a transplant. But she had never truly felt comfortable with the idea of a transplant, telling Jeri that the idea of removing her heart and lungs and inserting new organs gave her a "yucky feeling" and filled her with the "heebie-jeebies."

Although she felt it was too radical for her tastes, she knew Jeri had chosen it as the route she wanted to take. Just because Jana didn't like the idea didn't mean it wasn't the right thing to do. She realized she was the healthy person, so she had tried not to insert herself too much into creating uncertainty in Jeri's mind. She hoped her comment didn't do that.

"Jana, I've prepared myself for this," Jeri said. "All the way through this process, God has opened the doors to make it happen. But it's hard to describe. Now . . . it's *here.*"

Jeri scribbled her name on the form and handed it to Dr. Lloyd.

At 12:30 a.m., Jeri called Jim back.

"They're taking me down in about one minute to the operating room."

"So it's 100% go?"

"They'll go ahead and probably put me to sleep before I'll know the final answer. So they'll take me down in a little bit, give me some drugs and then they'll make the final decision. But they think it's pretty much a green light."

"Wow."

"Yeah, if for some reason it's not, they'll just wake me up and say, 'You didn't have the surgery.' "

"Gotcha."

"Tell Lisa that Natalie is going to get to go into the operating room with me."

"Who?"

"She's the nurse that we love. Lisa knows who that is."

"Good, good."

As Jeri was wheeled out of her room and to the elevator that would take her to the second-floor OR, she was flanked by Jana, Natalie and Dr. Feldman, who had arrived while she was talking to Jim. She loved all of them and treasured the relationships she had built up with them over the previous six weeks, but they weren't the same as family.

They couldn't provide what her family could—the nurturing, all-consuming love, the unfailingly positive outlook, the rock-solid *I-believe-in-you* and *believe-pray-fight-win* mantras that had been engrained over 35 years in a life that had encompassed so many medical dramas.

What was it that Lee Iacocca said? "The only rock I know that stays steady, the only institution I know that works, is the family." So it had been for Jeri.

She lived for her family and friends. Being around them, sharing life's peaks and valleys with them, laughing with them, encouraging them, taking an interest in every mundane detail of their lives, encouraging them, praying with them—that's what truly brought joy to her life. A people person? Yes, but it went even deeper than that. She had a mild fear of being alone. When she got sick, it usually was at night, when panic sometimes set in. It always made her feel better to know someone was there with her.

And yet, Jeri could feel herself coming to an extraordinary realization: She had never been closer to God than she was right at this moment. For now it was just her and God, with her trying to deal with a complex mixture of hopes and dreams and fears and celebrations, and God delivering on His promise that He would never forsake her. She would put everything entirely on Him.

She realized that perhaps God had supernaturally orchestrated this moment. If Carolyn had been here, Jeri would have completely leaned on her, and Carolyn would have been at her side whether it was to blow her nose or help her to the bathroom. Jeri would have missed that otherworldly connection by leaning on humans. Her pipeline to God unencumbered, she closed her eyes and savored the Spirit.

They stopped at the double doors leading to the OR. This was as far as Jana could go. She grabbed Jeri's hand and prayed: "Father, we know that you will be with Jeri every step of the process. Inhabit this place and protect Jeri. It's in your hands now. Amen."

Jeri looked at Jana and said, "Remember, I laid it at the feet of Jesus."

"I love you," Jana said, "and I'll be there when you get out."

*   *   *

Back in Texas, everybody had discovered the same thing: There were no flights to California until the morning. Carolyn and Junny called Daryl a few times and managed to coordinate to be on the same flight, leaving at 6 a.m. from Bush Intercontinental in Houston. When Daryl called Jim, he found out that Jim was on the same flight. Amy and Taylor would leave from Austin because his parents lived there and would be able to drive them to the airport and then take their car home. Jayme and Stephanie would find the going much tougher: They'd have to fly from Tampa to Washington, D.C., to San Jose, arriving late Thursday night.

Daryl packed luggage for himself and Brady and drove to the home of David and Jennifer Keys, who would take them to the airport. He paced a lot, hardly even noticing what was on TV.

Carolyn and Junny left Bryan after midnight. As they headed southeast on Highway 290 and reached the outskirts of Houston an hour later, they heard the KSBJ DJ say, "We just got an urgent prayer request from the family of Jeri. She's been waiting for a heart-lung transplant at Stanford in California. The organs became available hours ago and she is in surgery. Please pray for wisdom for the surgeons and peace for the family."

"Amy called that in!" Carolyn exclaimed. "Isn't that wonderful?"

Carolyn needed that desperately. She had been beating herself up badly—questioning herself for leaving Stanford and God for allowing it. *Why did I leave her side? I could have stayed. Yes, she wanted me to take a break, but I could have insisted. God, why didn't you do something—anything—to keep me there? Why, God?*

Junny's mind was racing, too, but with different thoughts. *Carolyn will be with her every day after the transplant. How long will Jeri be in the hospital before all of us can go home together? We're going to win. We've always come out a winner. All the indicators are that we'll win again. Daryl's insurance adds Stanford as an option. His job allows them to move to Las Vegas. Jeri has a cousin she can stay with near Stanford. She has the best surgical transplant team there is. OK, so what does dad need to be doing? What time are we going to get there? Where's Jayme right now? When will he get there?*

Carolyn prayed out loud, asking God to put a hedge of protection around Jeri. She prayed Isaiah 54:17: *No weapon forged against you will prevail.* She prayed Jeremiah 29:11: *For I know the plans I have for you, declares the LORD, plans to prosper you and not to harm you, plans to give you hope and a future.*

Inside the airport, they reached the departure gate to find Jim already there, munching on an Egg McMuffin. Carolyn and Junny hadn't even known he'd be on the same flight.

"I'm so glad you're here," Carolyn said, hugging Jim tightly. She knew Daryl really needed Jim. The last time they had talked with Jeri, she said Daryl had been crying—a rare show of emotions for him.

Daryl sat next to Jim on the flight. Both of them read for a while, trying not to dwell on the transplant itself. At one point, Daryl noticed that Jim had closed his eyes and was praying. Jim's countenance made a huge impression on Daryl. He saw a peace that he wished he could also find.

He doesn't have to be here, Daryl thought. *He has a growing church to take care of—so many responsibilities and people tugging at him. And yet he's sitting next to me, an absolute rock at the time when we need him the most.*

Daryl's mind clicked back to that January morning in 1997 when he and Jeri were driving on Mason Road, en route to First Baptist. He could see the sign for Grace Fellowship. He could see himself checking his watch and noticing that the service started in 15 minutes. He could hear Jeri's voice suggesting that they make a right turn and check it out. How would their lives have changed if they hadn't made that turn? Could they have found a better pastor, a better place to call home?

Carolyn and Junny sat three rows behind them, in the aisle and middle seats. Carolyn mouthed the words to Psalm 23:4: *Even though I walk through the valley of the shadow of death, I will fear no evil, for you are with me; your rod and your staff, they comfort me.*

On the flight to Washington, D.C., Jayme had his own regret to deal with. Weeks before, he had made contact with Stanford to determine if he would be able to get a wireless laptop into Jeri's room. Apple Inc. had just come out with iChat AV Public Beta, a new version of iChat that added voice and video chat capabilities with the iSight camera. Jayme's plan was to have one in Jeri's room and one in the Dolans' house so Daryl could have a video-stream conversation with Jeri. But Jayme didn't follow through on it.

Why didn't I get that done? Jayme thought. *If I had, Jeri and Daryl would have been able to have it last night when the organs came through. What would that have meant to them? How would Daryl have felt if he had been able to solidify in his mind the last thing she said to him before she went into the OR?*

On the flight from Austin, Amy looked out the window and saw the airplane's wing cutting through puffy, billowy clouds. *That must be what it's like where Jeri is*, she thought. Then she caught herself: *No! Don't think like that! We have plans for Christmas. We'll go home together. We always go home.*

It would have helped all of them to know what Natalie knew: That Jeri had been laughing while Natalie took photos of her in the OR, surrounded by a team of nurses and a mini-city of machines, just before the anesthesia kicked in. That she had found a place where God had given her peace.

Back in Katy, word had quickly spread of the donor organs. Brenda sent out a flurry of e-mail prayer requests to the staff and the 150-person prayer team. Brenda called Dixie and said, "Jim's not here. We need to make decisions. Let's open up the sanctuary. We can have soft music playing and have a vigil, interceding for her."

Christi, who had managed to talk to Jeri before she went to the OR, got down on her knees in her kitchen and prayed with her husband, Brent, then stayed up all night, contacting others by phone, praying, e-mailing, waiting it out.

One of her e-mails went to Jeri's CaringBridge site: *If you live in the Houston area and would like to join Jeri's church family in lifting her, Daryl and Brady up in prayer, please come join us at Grace Fellowship United Methodist Church. Our sanctuary will be open all day. You are welcome. We are so excited for our sweet Jeri and can't wait to see God glorified in her!!!!*

On the other side of the world, where it was already Thursday night, Karen checked her e-mail for the final time before going to bed. She wanted so desperately to be in the sanctuary, down on her knees, just as she had been so many times with Jeri at her side. It wouldn't be possible. She sat in front of her computer screen, transfixed, praying that the typically moody Indonesian Internet connection didn't act up.

*   *   *

The Stanford donor team flew to the hospital where the donor had died in order to perform the necessary tests on the heart and lungs.

The donor had a long history of smoking, but the pulmonary function was deemed to be good. They detected some slight thickening of the left ventricle due to hypertension, but the organs had otherwise good function. The transplant was on.

CHAPTER 16

THE BIGGEST HEART
I'VE EVER SEEN

From the corner of the operating room, Natalie gazed at Jeri in wonderment.

In six weeks, they had become best friends. Natalie knew she was nothing special—Jeri had seemingly hundreds of friends just like Natalie. That was just the kind of person Jeri was. All of them felt like they were her best friend, even though they knew they couldn't be. That was Jeri's special gift.

Natalie fixed her gaze on Jeri's face—how angelic it appeared under the bright lights. Natalie felt a warmth envelope her in the chill of the sterile room. Even though it hadn't taken much effort for her to be here for Jeri, she knew Jeri treasured it as a sign of God's provision. Natalie would make this walk with Jeri, now and in the difficult months that would follow.

With Jeri hooked up to a heart-lung bypass machine—which had taken over for the heart and lungs, removing carbon dioxide from the blood and replacing it with oxygen, using a tube that had been inserted into the aorta to carry the oxygenated blood from the bypass machine to the aorta for circulation to the body—Dr. Reitz opened up the chest cavity, making a 12-inch incision with a transverse thoracotomy procedure.

He paused, stunned by what he saw.

Turning to Dr. Lloyd, he said, "It's the biggest heart I've ever seen. Very impressive."

Everyone in the room knew exactly what he meant. He hadn't been impressed in a good sense. He had been impressed in a medical sense—the condition and size of her heart were highly unusual.

He noticed dense adhesions around the left lung and in the region where Jeri had undergone the surgery at 17 months to apply the band around the pulmonary artery. The enormous mass of calcium around the artery and ductus indicated that she had had an inflammatory response to the band of material. This complicated the removal of the heart and left lung, requiring more time.

The heart-lung implantation was straightforward. They trimmed the donor heart so that it could be implanted at the exact position, then sewed it in with four connections—two for the vena cava, one each for the aorta and trachea—and implanted the lungs.

Natalie left shortly before they were finished, thinking everything was fine. She left the campus, made the short walk to her apartment and went to sleep, looking forward to seeing Jeri the next day.

Straightforward veered into serious concern. They experienced significant bleeding from the area of dissection in the left chest. The total ischemic time of the graft—the time between the interruption and re-establishment of blood supply—had been four hours and 40 minutes. Jeri's new heart was initially slow to resume contracting, but appeared to be resuscitating properly.

In the first 30 minutes after discontinuing bypass, they worked continuously to control bleeding from the left chest. They administered protamine, along with clotting factors, including fresh frozen plasma and platelets. Her blood pressure fluctuated wildly, and when the heart fibrillated, they had to reinitiate the cardiopulmonary bypass.

After going back on bypass, her heart would not contract properly. They would have to put her on the ECMO machine, which would serve as a temporary artificial lung and heart for Jeri. They closed up her chest and returned her to the ICU.

The odds that her heart would resume contractility were slim. They would have to find another set of donor organs.

Carolyn, Junny, Daryl, Brady and Jim had arrived in the waiting room shortly before Jeri had been returned to the ICU. Amy and Taylor arrived just minutes later.

Dr. Reitz would have to do something he rarely had to do—tell them the grim news. Stanford had received only five heart-lung sets in all of 2002. Now it would need to find a second set in the next 24 hours—and not just any set, but one that perfectly matched Jeri's blood type and chest cavity.

Dr. Reitz greeted the family, looking exhausted, his mask hanging from his neck. He took them into a private room adjacent to the waiting room.

"I wish I had better news to give you," he said, scanning their rapt faces. "She had the biggest heart I've ever seen—the size of a football. Taking the organs out ended up being more difficult than we anticipated, based on the tests we had run. There was a lot of scar tissue and muscle that had built up from the heart working so hard pumping all these years. Because of that, it's possible that the new organs were out of the body too long. We had success putting in the donor organs, but the new heart is not working."

Carolyn grabbed Junny's hand. Dr. Reitz paused, searching for the right words.

"The heart muscle is not working. It's getting electric impulses, but is not pumping. We have her on an ECMO machine. That's what's keeping her alive."

"Well, what are we going to do?" Junny asked. "Could her heart start beating on its own?"

"It could, but in very few instances have we seen that. We need a miracle. We need her heart to start working or we need to find a new set of organs. We don't have much time. We can't keep her on the machine for much more than a day. Every minute will provide an increased risk of complications. We've already started looking for the new organs. I can assure you we will do everything we can to get them. She's at the very top of the list."

He answered their questions for another 10 minutes. Before he left, he scanned their faces once again and said, "I'm very sorry."

Carolyn watched him as he walked down the hallway and paused in front of a door. She saw him wipe away a tear before he entered.

"This just doesn't seem possible," Daryl said. "All along, it seemed like God had opened the doors. We found out that Stanford was the only hospital that successfully does these surgeries. Then we found out that Stanford was covered on my insurance. It seemed like God was saying, 'Yes, go. This is what you're supposed to do.' Now we get this far and it's not working."

"Remember when Amy was in that bad car accident in '92 and they didn't think she'd make it?" Carolyn said. "We've heard this before with Jeri. We've heard doctors say she's not doing well. We're not going to believe it!"

A nurse came out and told them that they could go in and see Jeri—everybody but Brady, who might be overwhelmed by what his young eyes saw.

When they entered her room, they weren't prepared for what they saw. Couldn't have been prepared. Jeri was wrapped from head to toe and connected through a complex system of tubes to a variety of machines and monitors: a ventilator, consisting of a flexible breathing circuit, gas supply, heating/humidification mechanism, monitors and alarms that were regulating the volume, pressure and flow of respiration; an infusion pump that was administering fluids intravenously; a crash cart containing emergency resuscitation equipment including a defibrillator, airway intubation devices, resuscitation bag/mask and medication box; and an acute care physiologic monitoring system to measure the electrical activity of the heart via an ECG, blood pressure, body temperature, cardiac output and blood-oxygen level.

Jeri was alive, but her chest was not moving up and down. A machine was acting as her heart and lungs.

Junny placed his hand on her leg and whispered, "Hey, Pill."

Everyone formed a horseshoe shape around her bed and joined hands, with those on each open end near her head—Jim and Daryl—laying their free hand on her. Jim began praying.

"Lord, the doctor says we need a miracle. Would you show this doctor a miracle so that the eyes in this hospital would be opened to you? Lord, would you cause electrical impulses to be sent to this heart so it would start pumping? And the heart that's inside Jeri—we speak to you in the name of Jesus. We command you to pump, to beat. Do what your creator intended you to do. Beat! Pump!"

Before they left the room, Carolyn gently pulled the blankets away from Jeri's side. Pink fingertips. Jeri had pink fingertips. The machine had been pumping rich oxygenated blood in her body and for the first time since she was an infant, she had pink extremities.

"Daryl, look," Carolyn said, motioning him to her side.

"She's pink," he said.

"But we want the real thing. Not from a machine. This heart's going to start beating."

Amy leaned over and kissed Jeri's forehead.

"I love you. You're doing great."

She wanted to stay longer, but her tears and her halting voice might send the wrong message to Jeri. She didn't want to do anything that might upset this delicate balance between life and death.

Now began a waiting game. This would be much more agonizing than the one they had endured to get the first set of organs. They were acutely aware that a 24-hour timer had been set, and already an hour had elapsed.

Jim called Lisa and gave her the news, and she called Katie and repeated it. She called Christi, who was in the church sanctuary along with dozens of other prayer warriors. When she told them, they joined hands, prayed and sang "Amazing Grace."

Katie walked to her computer, went to Jeri's CaringBridge site and started typing.

Jeri's new lungs are working well. However, her new heart is not pumping on its own. Pray for her new heart, that it would start working. Pray for strength and peace for Daryl, Brady and Jeri's family as they wait with her. Jeri, I love you and know that God has this under control.

The posts flowed, one after the other—17 in all in the next five hours. They came from all over the Houston area, from all over

Texas (Austin, Temple, Waco, Bryan), from all over America (Atoka, Oklahoma, Jasper, Alabama, Baton Rouge, Louisiana).

And even from the other side of the world. Jacqueline and Mac Davies—Liz Jok's friends—wrote from Kuala Lumpur, Malaysia:

This is the beautiful thing about knowing Christ. We might never see one another but in Christ's Spirit we are there for you. We have only one faith and our trust is in HIM alone. My dear friend, be strong and have faith. Speak the Word. Say, "I am the heir of salvation. I am the heir of preservation and deliverance. In Jesus' name I believe I am healed!" Remember this: Faith sees the invisible, believes the incredible and receives the impossible!

Natalie awakened in the afternoon and called Theresa, the assistant nurse manager in the unit.

"We're not doing well, Natalie," she said. "We can't get her off bypass. The heart's not taking."

Natalie's tears fell like a soft rain. She had never expected this to not work. She thought, *This was supposed to be her birthday, and you know, nothing's supposed to go wrong. She's so young and vibrant. She has a husband and a boy. Isn't she going to wake up to see them?*

It was Natalie's real birthday. She had tickets to a Jimmy Buffett concert, but it was canceled, so she had a barbecue at her house, rather than intrude on the family's space in the waiting room. Nothing, however, could get her mind off of Jeri.

Jeri remained relatively stable on the ECMO circuit, though she continued to have severe bleeding that was simply recycled and returned to the circuit.

Her family had taken over a large section of the waiting room. Jim knew it would be critical for the family to always be there in case any news broke, so he left and brought back dinner.

On a few occasions, Junny took his cup of coffee and wandered to a large glass window that provided a brilliant view of the campus. His prayers were simple: *God, we're leaving it in your hands to do your work. This is your child, and we leave her in your hands.*

His mind also frequently lapsed into fix-it mode. Being a Maintenance Worker II at A&M—leading a crew that took care of 66 buildings—he couldn't help it. *This is broke. How are we going to fix it? What's next? What do we have to do now? We're not quitting.* He imagined the agony Dr. Reitz and Dr. Lloyd must be feeling, knowing that they couldn't fix the problem, even with their world-renowned expertise.

Carolyn thought about the surgery Jeri had at 17 months—how Dr. Johnson had decided to return Jeri to them, figuring they could spend as much time with her for as long as she lived. She thought about what a woman in the waiting room had said to them: "Just because it's raining outside doesn't mean it's raining here." Jeri didn't die then. She wouldn't die now.

Brady remained oblivious to the tension that filled the room and the spiritual warfare that was being waged. All he wanted to do was play. He started drawing pictures with his crayons of the Aggie football team.

"Papa, here's a picture of the football players," he said, looking up at Junny. "Can you take it to them?"

Junny looked at Carolyn, and she nodded.

"Brady, I'll take them to the coach. How about that?"

"Yeah!"

They had no idea that those pictures would be transferred from the football department's secretary to head coach Dennis Franchione, who would send an autographed mini-helmet along with a letter thanking him for the pictures and finishing with, "I hope you enjoy the gift." All they knew was that Brady didn't understand that his mother was hanging by a thread in a room just down the hall. And perhaps that was a blessing.

God didn't answer everyone's prayer. Well, at least not in the way that they were praying it. Instead, He did something that no one honestly could have expected.

Shortly after 6 p.m., Dr. Reitz walked into the waiting room and announced that another set of donor organs had become available. The donor's story was remarkably similar to that of the first donor: 51 years old, with a hypertensive and smoking history.

"We have to act immediately," he said. "We are approaching the end of our window. This is the only shot we have. But this is great news."

Some people wait two years to get one set of heart and lungs. In just over 24 hours, Jeri had received *two*.

The room filled with cries of celebration, tight hugs, tears of joy. Carolyn got down on her knees and cried, "Thank you, God, for this miracle!"

They felt so thankful, so grateful. And yet the family had been waiting for something like this to happen. Deep down, they expected a miracle of some sort. Miracles had been pretty common in Jeri's life. The family had never become blasé about them—they always classified them as miracles. But they had been normal for Jeri. As someone once told her, "Miracles follow you around."

"This is another one of those things from God that was supposed to happen," Daryl said.

He felt a sudden pang of guilt that he had questioned God earlier and had even felt overcome with some anger. Somewhere deep inside of his psyche, he didn't think Jeri had a chance of being saved with another set of organs. The tide had turned in miraculous fashion. She would be healed. This would work.

Everybody went back into the private room and prayed. They knew Jeri's body was in shock after one major operation and now would be shocked again with another one, so they prayed for healing. They knew the doctors and nurses were exhausted from an already long shift and facing a second day without sleep, so they prayed for strength and steadiness.

At 8:08 p.m., Rob Emmick—whose wife roomed with Jeri in Dallas before Daryl moved there—posted on CaringBridge:

My brother works as a nurse on the transplant floor of Baylor Hospital in Dallas. When he heard that they had found a second donor, his response was that this, in itself, is a miracle. He has never, NEVER heard of such a thing happening. Let us not lose hope. We are watching the Lord do for Jeri what doesn't happen for others.

Three hours later—just after Dr. Reitz and Dr. Lloyd began the second transplant—Norene Gonsiewski posted. Her daughter, Amelia, had corresponded for weeks with Jeri earlier in the year when Jeri attempted to be accepted by Stanford. If anyone knew what the family was going through, it was her. Amelia had been in a coma for three weeks, had undergone two additional operations and was near death.

With the healing power of Jesus, she recovered fully and is in Portland tonight, praying for Jeri with every breath. Jeri can make it through these huge complications and with all of our prayers, she will. Let us give some of those prayers up to Him for her mom, who brought Jeri into this world and tonight has to face some very scary places. My prayer, Lord, is that while you are there holding Jeri fast and strong through her second surgery, you will look also upon her lovely mother who trusts you so fiercely. Send her your love, your courage, your peace and your faith.

Jayme and Stephanie arrived an hour after the second transplant had begun. He was struck by the ragged appearance of everybody in the room and the low energy level they seemed to be exhibiting. They wore the trauma of this experience—for some, two days without sleep, along with a constant emotional tug-of-war. The only exception was Brady, whose hyperkinetic energy belied the seriousness of the vigil.

Jayme could see in their eyes a what's-going-to-happen look. At the same time, everybody emanated a we-believe optimism. He imagined that somebody from the outside might say, "That's pretty much denial. They went through one transplant that didn't work and now they're saying, 'Wow, what a crazy plan God has. Now there's another, better part.'"

Dr. Reitz came into the waiting room just before 4 a.m., wearing a professional—but obviously relieved—countenance that hid his own ecstasy.

"We were successful—her heart is beating on its own," he said.

More cries of celebration, more tight hugs, more tears of joy.

"She's doing well," he continued. "We're not out of the woods yet. Her body has undergone severe trauma and she's been under anesthesia for a long time. A lot could happen. But it's a match, and it worked."

Dr. Reitz ushered them into her room, Daryl first, followed by Carolyn, Junny and Jim. He told them Jeri likely would have no recognition of their presence.

Having gone through this once before, Daryl was prepared for what he would see, even though there was a new twist this time—many of the tubes leading from her chest cavity were filled with blood.

He couldn't see much of her face because of the mass of tubes, but he could see enough to know that the bluish tint in her lips had been replaced by pink. Her lips were cracked and dry because her mouth had been open for so long, but they were pink.

Jim gently pulled back the covers on the side of the bed, exposing her left hand. She had gorgeous, luminous, perfectly pink fingertips, and her fingers were not marred by the clubbing she previously had.

"Isn't it a beautiful sight?" Carolyn said.

"Finally, she has what she wanted," Daryl said. "And it's from her own heart—not a machine."

He gently touched her hand, placing four fingers in her palm and his thumb on top of her fingers. "You look great," he said. "I love you. You'll be out soon."

Jeri's eyes opened. He could feel her fingers curl around his index finger, and he could see her mouthing out the words, "I love you."

Carolyn leaned over and whispered in her ear, "Jeri, you have pink lips and fingertips." It's hard to smile when you have a massive tube in your mouth, but that's exactly what Carolyn thought she saw Jeri doing. When Jeri tried to rise from the bed, Carolyn said, "Honey, that's OK. You can see them later."

Carolyn could imagine Jeri was thinking, *They're here. And I'm here. I've made it.*

Jeri closed her eyes. Jim wiped away his tears, placed his hand on Jeri and began praying.

"God, we're going to bless you whether things are great or not going well. And Lord, things are going great right now. We thank you. We thank you for this miracle that we never could have thought up on our own. We were thinking, 'Get this first heart working,' and you gave us a second heart. Thank you. Your ways are higher than our ways. Blessed be your name. Please heal her. Sustain her organs. Heal the parts of her body that have been bruised through this surgery."

Carolyn had decided that they wouldn't give Jeri even the remotest sense that this might not work out. They would do what they had always done. They would encourage her that everything would be OK. *We can beat this. We can do this.*

And so they joined hands and sang "Blessed Be Your Name"— the most joyous, emotional version they had ever sung.

After Katie posted the news on CaringBridge, the site was filled with 17 posts in a four-hour span. Christi wrote:

All Jeri wants is for God to be glorified! Go share this miraculous news with everyone you meet today! Tell them how good our God is and how much he loves them! Jesus, I pray that each and every person touched by Jeri's story would be drawn to you, that their own heart would be transplanted with a heart that loves you and accepts you like never before!

Pink seemed to pop up everywhere.

Grace Fellowship member Barbara Oswalt finished reading the e-mails and started getting ready for work. Then she glanced into her backyard and noticed all of her pink roses blooming. She went out, cut several of them and took them to work in honor of Jeri's pink lips and fingertips.

A co-worker, after hearing Jeri's story, said: "So when you look at these roses today, think of Jeri and praise God for his miracles."

Later in the morning, Barbara noticed the roses had blossomed even wider. She thought of God working in Jeri, strengthening her, building her up, sustaining her pink lips and fingertips.

Back in the waiting room, Jim had a lot of work to do in preparation for Sunday's sermon. Before he left for Stanford, he had submitted his sermon notes to Brenda so they could be typed and given to the congregation. But that would be only half of the sermon. The other half would be flushing out all the words, including the introduction.

Jim was in the middle of a sermon series, "The Main Thing is to Make the Main Thing the Main Thing." That week's sermon would be, "The Main Thing in Marriage."

Jim thought, *Jeri's story should be the introduction. I'm going to tell everybody about some intimacy I saw between a husband and a wife on a death bed.*

And so he began writing: "I watched a husband almost lose his wife this week." He went through the story of how Jeri called with news of the donor organs and took the congregation all the way through the second surgery.

He ended the introduction: "I watched a man get his wife back. And I can't think of any better time to ask you, Grace Fellowship: How much do you appreciate your wife? How much do you appreciate your husband? Do you know why you're married? Do you know the purpose of your marriage?"

CHAPTER 17

BLESSED BE YOUR NAME

Jayme's fertile mind started hatching its own plan. If Brady couldn't go in to see his mommy, perhaps they could make a reasonable facsimile and take that in. He figured that it was hard to know exactly how much Jeri was processing, so it was important to be positive and tell her things she couldn't see with her eyes shut. He wanted her to *feel* Brady's presence.

Jayme retrieved his 17-inch Apple PowerBook, found a picture he had taken of Brady at Jeri's house before she left for Las Vegas — a goofy shot with his eyes wide open and his mouth agape, exposing the back of his throat — and started playing around with it in Photoshop. He made it full screen in the PowerPoint-hitting presentation.

Then he ushered Brady out of the waiting room and into a quiet area in the hallway. Using a software program called Sound Record with a two-track recorder, he said to Brady, "Speak into this mic. Say a little something to your mommy."

Brady thought for a moment.

"Hi, mommy. I love you, mommy. . . . Hi, mommy, I love you."

Jayme took that audio clip and normalized it, making every sound wave as loud as it possibly could be. Then he attached it to the PowerPoint slide so that when the slide came up, Brady's voice would play.

Jayme carried the laptop into Jeri's room and held it over her stomach, angling the screen so that Jeri's face reflected in the screen on top of Brady's life-size facial image. Stephanie pressed the play button.

"Hi, mommy. I love you, mommy. . . . Hi, mommy, I love you."

Jeri's eyes burst open and she struggled to grab the sides of the bed in an attempt to raise herself up.

"Whoa!" Jayme yelled. "That's wild!"

He speculated that since she was almost legally blind without her glasses or contacts, she must have seen Brady's face and not the computer, and thought he was sitting on her tummy.

"I probably didn't think this through enough. I never planned to do something that might not be healthy for her—something that would use her energy."

He looked at Jeri. She seemed OK. He looked over at the nurse. She hadn't even noticed. Whew! They slithered out of the room, stunned at what they had just seen but feeling quite certain that Jeri was very much alive.

Natalie, who had called that morning and been told of the success of the second transplant, arrived and visited Jeri. She gave Daryl an album full of the photos that had been taken in Jeri's room after news of the donor-organ availability and then in the OR in the moments before the surgery.

They talked briefly, but Natalie felt herself overcome with emotion. She didn't feel she should intrude on their time, so she kept the visit brief.

After everyone had visited Jeri, the medical staff stressed that she needed rest to deal with this critical part of her recovery. Three hours passed. Eleven more people posted on CaringBridge after Katie's message describing how Jeri had recognized her family. It became obvious that God had turned it into a story that went far beyond Jeri's new heart and lungs.

In a post at 11:14 a.m., Katie wrote: *A group of Jeri's friends were praying last night and someone asked if we were organ donors. Now is a great time to be sure that those close to you know your wishes. Two strangers did that for Jeri and we are all forever grateful for their unselfish acts. There are so many people as precious as Jeri waiting for transplants. Talk about it today. I am writing "organ donor" on the back of my Texas drivers' license in permanent marker. (Not sure if I'm allowed to do that!)*

Around 1:15 p.m., Dr. Reitz gave them news of a serious setback: Jeri had continued bleeding and had become hemodynamically unstable, with worsening lung function, and an X-ray revealed a large collection of blood in her left chest. Another operation would be required so that her lungs could expand and allow proper breathing.

Dr. Reitz evacuated the left and right cavities of all clot, washed out all three chest drains, irrigated the closed surfaces and mediastinal cavity and re-expanded the lungs. They closed up her chest. She still required an FIO2 (the fraction of inspired oxygen in a gas mixture) of 100%—as opposed to the 21% that's in the air we normally breathe—but Dr. Reitz considered her hemodynamic condition to be much improved.

Carolyn and Junny, waiting in the hall for the doctors to come out of the OR, saw Dr. Reitz. When he noticed them, he gave the thumbs-up sign. Then he returned to the waiting room to brief them.

"You've got yourselves a miracle here," he told the family.

Coming from a man who had pioneered heart-lung transplantation and had seen everything—all possible scenarios, all possible outcomes—it resonated remarkably. But was there more? Was there a spiritual angle? Daryl had come to the conclusion that many of the doctors on the team didn't believe in the healing power of Jesus, based on Jeri's continued efforts to minister to them. Maybe Dr. Reitz had changed his mind. Maybe there was more meaning behind his statement than simply, "You've got yourselves a miracle here."

Everyone who had ever known Jeri certainly knew where she stood. They knew what she had overcome and to whom she attributed it.

"We all know she's strong enough to get through," Carolyn said. "That's her personality. That's who she is. She's a fighter. God gave her a fighting spirit."

"Tell me about it," Junny said. "She's lived through this her entire life. She could have gotten down about her situation, but she didn't."

"A weaker person wouldn't even had made it this far," Amy said. "I think a person has to *want* to live to endure one of these surgeries, much less two. She has the desire to live. I think that's kept her alive."

Shortly after 6 p.m., they got word that Jeri's kidneys were not functioning properly—probably the result of the stress of three surgeries in such a short period of time. Dr. Reitz said that the encouraging thing was that her body had become tough over the years by adjusting to her increasingly low oxygen-saturation levels. If her kidneys did not improve by the morning, she would be placed on dialysis.

In the next few hours, her condition stabilized but no visitation was allowed. Carolyn paced the waiting room, occasionally venturing out into the hall. From that spot, she periodically would see nurses go in and out of the area near Jeri's room. One time she saw a nurse emerge in tears.

Why is she crying? Carolyn thought. *Maybe it's because of the way Jeri looks with all the machines and tubes. . . . No, that's silly. This is what she does. She sees this all the time. Is this worse than they're telling us?* Carolyn didn't tell anyone what she saw.

Daryl, battling sinus problems and exhaustion, thought this would be an opportune time to use the hotel room that they hadn't visited since they had arrived. Jayme and Stephanie would room with him, with Amy and Taylor in an adjacent room.

"We're home free," Jayme said. "No need to stay here and sit in a waiting room."

At 3:38 a.m., the phone rang. Daryl fumbled in the darkness to find it.

"Mr. Paholek?" the ICU nurse said.

"Yeah."

"You need to come to the hospital."

"What's happening?"

"We just need you to come back up here now."

The phone call jolted Jayme out of a dream. A bad dream. A dream about Jeri dying. His heart racing wildly, he admonished himself: *What was that? Get rid of the negativity! How did I have those thoughts? Move on! She's fine!*

But when Daryl told him what the nurse had said, he knew she wasn't fine. She couldn't be fine. Not with a plaintive plea in the pitch black of night. Jayme, racked by guilt and disgust with himself, didn't mention his dream to anybody.

They went next door and awakened Amy and Taylor. By the time they got to the waiting room, Carolyn, Junny, Jim and Daryl's parents, Bobby and Margaret, had been rounded up and briefed.

"Jeri's blood pressure is dropping and she's retaining fluid," Carolyn told them. "Her kidneys aren't functioning. Her body's shutting down."

For the next two hours, while Jeri's family called out to God, the medical staff applied venovenous hemofiltration to stave off renal failure, trying desperately to remove small and medium-sized molecules and replace electrolytes.

Progressive pulmonary edema had ravaged her body. Her heart no longer could remove fluid from the lung circulation. The increased pressure in the blood vessels in her lungs had forced fluid through the air sacs, preventing them from absorbing oxygen. Her veins had deteriorated so badly over the course of her life and were so overworked that they couldn't stop bleeding.

Just after 7 a.m., a nurse approached Junny, put her hand on his shoulder and said, "Y'all say your goodbyes." She searched Junny's eyes for a few seconds, started crying, turned and slowly walked back into Jeri's room.

The family followed her into the room and circled the bed, with Daryl next to Dr. Lloyd.

Dr. Lloyd put his hand on Daryl's shoulder and whispered in his ear, "We've done all we can do."

Daryl collapsed to the edge of the bed on his knees, weeping softly. He looked up and cried out, "What's happening, Jayme? What's happening?"

Jayme reached across the bed, locked hands with Daryl and pulled him up. They squeezed their hands tighter, like they were holding onto something, like they were bracing themselves for a big dip off a roller coaster and about to squeeze the bar in half.

Everyone laid hands on Jeri and prayed for her, prayed like they had never prayed before, pleaded with her and with God.

"C'mon, Jeri, c'mon!"

"You can beat this!"

"Live, Jeri, live!"

"Your little boy, Brady, needs you!"

"Jesus, breathe life into Jeri! Jesus, bring Jeri's blood pressure up!"

"Live, Jeri, live!"

"C'mon, girl, c'mon!"

Jim lifted the blanket that covered her body. The pink coloring in her fingertips had vanished.

"This can't be!" he wailed. "It wasn't supposed to happen this way! She's supposed to see her boy graduate from high school! She's supposed to see her grandchildren! No, Lord, no! It can't be this way! Oh, God, it can't be! Can't be!"

They stood and watched as the activity on the monitors gradually slowed, then finally flatlined. Jayme haltingly reached over and closed Jeri's eyes, his tear glancing off the sheets. Junny kissed her on the forehead. Carolyn ran out into the hall, collapsed on her knees and threw her arms into the air, pleading, "God, let her live!"

Jim went over to Jeri's side. He knew that in Scripture, Jesus had raised people from the dead. The son of the widow from Nain. The daughter of Jairus, the synagogue ruler. And, of course, Lazarus, who had been dead for four days.

Jim was prepared to exhaust every resource he knew of. So he leaned down and whispered in Jeri's ear, "In Jesus' name, live. Get up."

* * *

Back in Katy, care pastor Cindi Lomax sat in her car, watching her daughter, Laura, as she slept.

Jeri had been Laura's impact leader during the Sunday night youth-group gatherings. Both of them adored Jeri—Laura because Jeri had been the greatest influence in her decision to accept Christ, and Cindi because she had counseled Jeri many times about the transplant and treasured Jeri's impact in Laura's life.

They had spent all night praying for Jeri. Preferring to do it in a private manner, they had driven to Jeri and Daryl's house and parked in front by the curb, summoning God to save Jeri. Then they went to Lisa and Jim's house and continued praying in their car. They made a series of phone calls to Stanford and knew Jeri's life hung in the balance.

Now, as darkness gave way to light, Cindi watched as the sky turned a bright, hot pink. A nature enthusiast and sunrise aficionado, Cindi had never seen anything like it in Katy.

She woke Laura and said, "My goodness. You have to see the sun. It is hot pink. It is bright pink. It is sparkling pink, Laura. Not orange-pink. The whole sky is on fire pink."

They looked at each other and nodded. They sensed that Jeri was gone, and that hot-pink sunrise crystallized everything: It was Jeri's reflection.

*   *   *

For over an hour, they sat in her room, crying, hugging her, stroking her hair, holding her and rubbing her feet.

Then Jim opened his Bible. He could feel God leading him to specific passages. He began praying Scripture to God.

First, from Psalm 22: "My God, my God, why have you forsaken us? Why are you so far from saving us, so far from the words of our groaning? Oh, my God, we cry out by day, but you do not answer. We cry out by night. Yet you are enthroned as the Holy One."

Jim flipped over to Psalm 10 and prayed it to God: "Why, O LORD, why? Why do you stand far off? Why do you hide yourself in times of trouble?"

Then to Psalm 13: "How long, O LORD? Will you forget us forever? How long will you hide your face from us? How long must we wrestle with our hearts? How long will the enemy of death triumph over us? Look on us, God, and answer, O LORD, my God. Give light to our eyes or we'll sleep in death. Our enemy will say, 'We've overcome him.' So we trust in your unfailing love, and our heart rejoices in your salvation. We'll sing to the Lord, for you've been good to us."

Then he flipped to Job 1:21 and prayed to the Lord on behalf of everyone in the room: "Naked, Jeri came from her mother's womb and naked she would depart. The Lord gave and the Lord has taken away. Blessed be the name of the Lord."

The room was silent for awhile. Then, one faint voice sang, "Blessed be the name of the Lord. Blessed be your glorious name." Others joined in, lifting their voices, gaining strength, offering up the song that had defined Jeri's last three months. The song faded out and the room went silent.

Jim turned to John 11:25: "And Jesus said, 'I am the resurrection and the life. He who believes in me will live, even though he dies. And whoever lives and believes in me will never die.' "

Then II Corinthians 5: "Now we know that if the earthly tent that we live in is destroyed, we have a building from God, an eternal house in heaven, not built by human hands. Meanwhile, here on earth, we groan with the longing to be clothed with our heavenly dwelling, because when we are clothed, we will not be found naked. For while we are in this earthly tent, we groan, and are burdened because we do not wish to be unclothed but to be clothed with our heavenly dwelling, so that what is mortal may be swallowed up by life. Now it is God who has made us for this very purpose. And He's given us His Holy Spirit while we're on planet earth as a deposit, guaranteeing what's to come in heaven. Therefore we are always confident and know that as long as we are at home in this earthly body, then we're away from the Lord. We live by faith, not by sight. We are confident, I say, and we would prefer to be away from the earthly body and be at home with the Lord."

Then to II Timothy 4:6: "The time has come for my departure. Jeri fought the good fight. Jeri finished the race. Jeri has kept the faith. Now there is in store for Jeri the crown of righteousness, which the Lord, the righteous Judge, will award to me on that day—and not only to me, but also to all who have longed for His appearing."

Finally, Jim went to the last two chapters in the Bible.

To Revelation 21:4: "He will wipe away every tear from their eyes in heaven. There will be no more death in heaven. There'll be no mourning in heaven. There'll be no crying in heaven. There'll be no pain in heaven. For the old order of things has passed away."

Then to 22:3: "No longer will there be any curse. The throne of God and of the Lamb will be in the city—heaven—and His servants will serve Him. They will see His face, and His name will be on their foreheads. There will be no more night. They will not need the light of a lamp or the light of the sun, for the Lord God will give them light. And they will reign for ever and ever."

Jim closed his Bible and softly repeated, "They will see His face."

Jayme realized at that instant that he had dreamed everything he had just seen. *Everything.*

"I've seen this already," he said to Stephanie.

"What do you mean?"

"When the phone call came, I was dreaming that we were standing over Jeri's body, singing 'Blessed Be Your Name.' Everything that happened, everything that we did and said, I had already dreamed."

"Really?"

"Yeah. It's really freaking me out. What does it mean?"

"I don't know."

"Is it some kind of connection you can't explain? They talk about twins having that connection. Did I just think through the realm of possibilities and put that together coincidentally? Is it a spiritual thing, God's way of saying, 'I'm in control, and this is my plan?' How else could another person have seen the script exactly? After I realized it, it was like déjà vu that wouldn't end."

Later, in the hallway, Jayme approached Jim and told him.

"I think it's really neat that you have that connection," Jim said.

Jayme thought, *Every time you tell this story, you're going to look more crazy. This is too much.*

Jim and Daryl went to the waiting room, found Brady and took him to the private meeting room. The next step in this process could come only from Daryl. And it would have to come right now—before Brady saw everybody crying.

But *how*? How does a man tell his 5-year-old son, who has already lost his biological mother, that he now has lost his adoptive mother? Could the heartache get any worse?

Daryl looked straight into Brady's blue eyes.

"You know we were trying to get a new heart to make mommy better, right?"

He nodded.

"Mommy didn't make it. She died. She went up to heaven to be with Jesus."

"Oh."

Daryl had been concerned about what Brady's reaction might be, but obviously there was no comprehension. No tears. No emotion at all. While Daryl might have wanted to agonize over the loss of Jeri, Brady just wanted to find a ball and play.

Jim slipped out of the room. Now he had his own moment of agony. He would have to tell Lisa and the entire church family that Jeri was gone. He had held everything together in the family's time of need, but now he could barely get out the words as the tears came in a torrent.

"She died?" Lisa asked.

"Yes."

"She died? . . . She died?"

Lisa kept repeating that phrase, disbelief washing over her. She looked at Katie, who was standing in the kitchen after their training run. How could this be? They had just used their precious thoughts of Jeri as inspiration to get them through another grueling session. Jeri's heart was beating just as their hearts were beating, finally, just as she always dreamed. And now her heart wasn't beating at all?

Jim comforted Lisa with some of the same passages he had shared with Jeri's family. He said he couldn't wait to get home and be with her. He would be there in about 10 hours.

When Jim originally booked his flight to California, he arranged for an early Saturday afternoon return because there was nobody else who could be prepared to preach on Sunday. He hated to leave the family, but there was nothing he could do. He hustled to San Jose International Airport, barely catching his flight.

He wanted to tilt his seat back, close his eyes and let his aching body drift off to sleep, but something kept nagging at him.

I can't do a sermon on marriage tomorrow, he thought. *A congregational death has just occurred. Not every death is body-wide, but this one is. She was known by two-thirds of the church and regarded as a cherished elder. This is Grace Fellowship's personal 9/11. The only appropriate thing is to address it. Even somebody who never met Jeri will be ministered to when they hear this story. Fourteen hours from now, I will be standing in front of 600 people. God, how do I lead them through this?*

He prayed and turned it over to God. Then he pulled his sermon notes from his briefcase and slashed a large X over them. He would tell Jeri's story, from birth to death, with all the glory in between.

It would be called, "The Main Thing In Death." He would write it out word for word in outline form, with a bullet preceding every item. He wouldn't have to read it verbatim because the first line of the bullet would remind him of what the section was about. Writing it out would help him choose the words so that when he spoke, many of the words would come back to him.

When he landed in Houston, he would call A.J. and request that he play "Blessed Be Your Name" and MercyMe's "I Can Only Imagine." And when he got home, he would collapse in Lisa's arms, fatigue and heartache overcoming him.

Carolyn and Junny sat in the waiting room, wondering when the nightmare would end, wondering when someone would come out and say, "Come quickly! Her heart started beating!" No one came.

Carolyn broke the silence.

"I feel her heart may still be working," she said to Junny. "I'm going back in."

When she walked into Jeri's room, they had already put her body in a bag. Carolyn placed her hand on the bag, tracing it to the area where she thought Jeri's heart would be. She thought she could feel a faint heartbeat. She kept her hand there. No, there was no heartbeat. Her mind had played tricks on her. Sobbing, she turned toward the door and saw a nurse entering.

"I'm so sorry," the nurse said. "I . . . I thought you were finished."

Carolyn went back to the waiting room, where everybody was milling around, hugging, commiserating. What would they do now? What do you when you lose your daughter, your sister, your wife, your mom? They didn't know.

But they knew one thing: The time had come to leave the waiting room for good. It had the smell of death.

Taylor went out to the parking lot and was maneuvering the rental car toward the pickup area when he nearly ran into Dr. Lloyd, who was walking across the driveway, his head down, oblivious to his surroundings. Taylor pulled up and rolled down his window.

"On behalf of the family, I want to say thanks," Taylor said. "You guys put your heart and soul into this."

"We hated desperately to lose Jeri," Dr. Lloyd said. "She was a wonderful person. She endured so much to get to this point, and we wanted very much to give her a new life. We did everything humanly possible."

"Well, sometimes that's enough. God's in control and this is the way it was meant to be."

Taylor searched Dr. Lloyd's bloodshot eyes. For the first time, he understood this wasn't just about somebody having a procedure. It had gone much deeper than that. The human side had connected far beyond the clinical. The surgeon Dr. Lloyd had moved to the man Dr. Lloyd. This thing had stripped him to the core.

Taylor hadn't gotten the reaction he had expected. He had expected Dr. Lloyd to say, "Man, I haven't slept in two days. I can't wait to collapse in my own bed." Instead, he had given a soft, heartfelt response.

Taylor thanked Dr. Lloyd once more and watched him walk slowly into the parking lot. Taylor sensed he was looking at a man who had something left in the tank, a man who wanted to try one more thing to save Jeri.

Natalie and Kim both learned of Jeri's death that afternoon.

Nurse Theresa called Natalie to tell her the news. Natalie cradled a picture of Jeri, her hands trembling. Her notion of transplants as the cure-all had been radically shattered. Now she knew they weren't always successful. She could feel some blame seeping in.

How could I let myself get close to a patient? How could I not have been realistic about her situation?

But then she realized something else: Her friendship with Jeri was a gift that would live on for many years as she explored the God that Jeri had worshipped and wanted her to know.

Kim went into the hospital and didn't see Jeri's name on the board. She asked where Jeri was and a nurse solemnly showed her a line saying she had expired. On the way out to the parking garage, Kim called her father. Then she sat in her car for an hour, crying and searching the Bible for comfort. She went to Psalm 30:5: *For His anger lasts only a moment, but His favor lasts a lifetime; weeping may remain for a night, but rejoicing comes in the morning.*

She looked forward to the morning, when she could rejoice, when she could truly be grateful to God for placing Jeri in her path.

Carolyn and Junny drove back to the hotel, but they quickly realized they couldn't spend the rest of the day there, feeling the walls closing in on them. They decided to go for a drive.

As Junny started backing the car out of the parking space, Carolyn stopped him.

"Wait," she said, "I forgot my cell phone."

Junny put it in park and shut down the engine. As Carolyn's mind started processing what she had just said, she broke down. She knew she wouldn't need that cell phone.

"Jeri's . . . not going to call me," she said.

They didn't know where they were going. Not on this night. Not in the future. They ended up at Wal-Mart, searching for a blanket for the plane ride home. It occurred to Carolyn that it was in a Wal-Mart in Grand Prairie, Texas, almost 34 years ago, that she had taken Jeri for what she thought might be the last picture taken of her. Now they were in a Wal-Mart in Palo Alto, and there would be no more pictures.

In the housewares department, they ran into the head nurse from Jeri's floor in the CCU. When she saw Carolyn and Junny, her eyes welled up and the tears started flowing.

"They called me and told me about Jeri," she said. "Jeri talked about you a lot. She was a wonderful lady. We loved her."

"And she loved you," Carolyn said. "We know she was more than a patient to all of the nurses and doctors."

"Thank you for serving our daughter," Junny said.

They hugged.

"I'm so sorry," the nurse said.

Later that night, Carolyn asked Junny to drive to the funeral home. She just wanted to be close to Jeri. After 35 years, she couldn't just permanently turn off her "mom" switch—not after everything they had endured together, not after so many mountain-top triumphs that drowned out the agonizing heartaches, not after two-a-day phone conversations, not after a husband and an adopted boy and two hearts that had become hers. Not after pink lips and fingertips.

They found the front door to the funeral home locked, so they walked all the way around the building, knocking on doors and windows. Finally, the director heard them and opened a door. They asked when her body would be flown back to Houston, and he said it would be on a Continental flight at midnight on Sunday.

"We're going back on that plane with her," Carolyn said to Junny. "I've never let her do anything without me. That's the least I can do—go back with her."

Daryl made plans to fly to Austin-Bergstrom International Airport with Brady the next morning at 6:30, using the tickets his parents had given to him when they offered to drive the Highlander back to Texas.

Emotionally, he had shut down. He didn't want to deal with it. Simple as that. He had a 5-year-old boy who thought life would go on as normal, and for the rest of the night, Daryl had to continually shift out of the debilitating numbness he felt in order to deal with Brady and be the father he knew Brady needed.

Back at Grace Fellowship, the news had spread through e-mails and phone calls. Brenda opened up the sanctuary for prayer, and dozens of congregation members filed solemnly into the dimly lit room, getting down on their knees at the altar or finding a private spot to meet with God.

Brenda requested to prayer-team members that they ask God to raise her up.

"God is the ultimate decision-maker," she said. "He said that Scripturally, it's true—that not only will they lay hands on the sick to recover, but they are able to raise up from the dead. It's way out of our comfort zone—beyond any scope of ministry we have ever done. But let's ask."

And so they did, with broken hearts but also with the knowledge that God's way are so much higher than our ways.

A congregation member later called Brenda with an idea: What if they could put pink bows on all of the trees on Mason Road leading to the building? And why stop there? Why not make a small pink bow for everyone who would attend the Sunday services?

A small army of women spread out all over Katy, raiding the fabric stores for every inch of pink ribbon they could scrounge up. Deep into the night, they shaped that pink ribbon into 1,000 bows, each with its own safety pin, each in loving memory of Jeri.

CHAPTER 18

POWER IN PINK

Reaching in the darkness, Jim fumbled around in search of the ringing alarm clock. He tried to focus his eyes on the illuminated green numbers. 4:45? Had he even fallen asleep? It seemed like his head had just hit the pillow.

He swept his legs to the side of the bed and slowly sat up. He had pulled a few all-nighters in college, but never had he felt like this.

His eyes scanned the room, locking in on a pink dress shirt draped over the hanger near his closet. Brenda had bought and delivered it to Lisa on Friday, when Jeri appeared to have survived the second transplant. The idea was for the entire church to wear pink in her honor. Now they would wear it in her memory.

Jim did everything he normally did on a Sunday. He prayed, showered, ate a full breakfast by himself, arrived at church at 5:55, met with A.J. at 6 for an hour of prayer and worship, then went to his prayer closet to pray and talk the message out. On his desk was a file, put there by Brenda while he had been away. The file was labeled, "Jeri Paholek, For The Year 2050." Later that day, he would have to do what he never wanted to do—orchestrate Jeri's wishes in death.

Before the service, he went to the altar, knelt and began praying. One by one, congregation members left their seats and joined him at the altar, dozens of them huddling in a tight semi-circle, laying hands on him or on those who had laid hands on him, pushing in just a bit closer.

In that instant, Jim had become a representation of Jesus as Shepherd. The Body of Christ desperately desired to be around him and find comfort in his presence. It was their outward expression of their heartfelt inward need for their shepherd, and Jim was in that place of shepherding them.

Jim finished praying and took his seat. From her seat nearby, counseling pastor Ruby Renz contemplated the congregational prayer she had been asked to give.

Oh, Lord. What do you say to the congregation when someone dies? Even if everyone didn't know Jeri personally, they all knew her story and were praying fervently for her to live. How do you address that?

She assumed the pulpit and led the congregation through the same story that had immediately come to Jim's mind after he met with Jeri to plan her funeral—the story from Daniel 3, where Shadrach, Meshach and Abednego refused to serve the god of King Nebuchadnezzar.

"They said, 'We don't need to defend ourselves—our God is able to save us from your fiery furnace. And our God will save us. And even if He doesn't, we won't worship anybody but Him.' Our God was able to save Jeri, and we believed He would. And even though He didn't, we're not going to let the enemy in. We would still worship no one other than our God. God doesn't necessarily give us what we fervently ask for, but He gives us what His good and perfect will says."

Jim followed Ruby. Looking out into the congregation, it seemed to him that at least half were wearing pink. It served as a powerful testament to Jeri's impact on the church, this mighty little woman who couldn't get enough of God's presence and couldn't stand the idea of people wandering through life without knowing Him.

"You can save your sermon notes for next Sunday," Jim said. "We'll hit the marriage topic next week. If you brought a Bible with you, please turn to Psalm 22. You might grab a blank sheet of paper and jot down some of the Scripture we look at together this morning.

"Yesterday, a wonderful 35-year-old member of our congregation died after having two heart-lung transplants. Her name was Jeri Paholek. If you'll excuse me, I'm going to sit down during our time together."

He turned to his right and sat down in a chair. He would tell a story, not preach a sermon, and he would do it in a warm, conversational style, with heart-rending eloquence that belied the difficulty he had endured and the preparation he hadn't been able to do.

He described how Jeri had been born with a heart defect and given a medical death sentence, how she kept exceeding the doctors' predictions and ended up going to A&M, marrying Daryl and adopting Brady.

"Jeri Paholek lived life to the fullest. She loved her husband. She loved her boy, Brady. She loved her church. She loved her friends. She loved her home group. Jeri was a prayer warrior. She would pray all the time with everybody. In the last five years, she prayed with me—every single Sunday morning, practically."

He talked of her discolored extremities, of her desire to have pink lips and fingertips, of the worsening of her condition to the point where only a transplant could save her, of her acceptance by Stanford at the same time the congregation had been studying the book of Joel.

"So she became a living picture for all of us," he said. "When God says to Joel, 'Rend your heart,' that means, 'Rip your hearts open to me.' And Jeri . . . what Jeri was being brave enough to do became a picture for us. That's what God wants every single one of us to have—a heart-lung transplant. In the emotional and spiritual realm, He wants us to rip open our chest cavity and take out our old heart and our old lungs and trust Him to put a new heart and new lungs inside of us."

He described how Jeri had come to him to plan her funeral, and he encouraged those in attendance to do the same.

"I think every single person on planet earth should plan their funeral while they're young," he said. "It gives you a heart of wisdom. Nothing gives you or I more perspective than thinking about how short our life is, and planning our funeral. So I double-dog dare you to plan your funeral now."

Then he told the rest of her story—how they moved to Las Vegas, how she was forced to go to Stanford, how Jeri and Lisa slept in the same bed together ("Guys, we'd never get away with that!") and spent "lots of money" in San Francisco, how the call came with the news of the donor organs, and how the new heart did not work.

"And so, we prayed like crazy," he said, "and you prayed like crazy, and the whole . . . people all over the U.S. and the world were praying like crazy. We prayed for a miracle. You prayed for a miracle."

And it happened, but not in the way they had prayed. And then there were complications. And so they prayed some more, and sang "Blessed Be Your Name." He described the song and the way it had captured Jeri's heart.

He bowed his head briefly, allowing silence to fill the sanctuary. Softly, he began singing, *Blessed be the name of the Lord, blessed be your name. Blessed be the name of the Lord, blessed be your glorious name.* Some began singing with him, helping him finish.

He described how they had to operate to drain the blood in her chest cavity, how her kidneys began failing, how Daryl got the mid-morning phone call, how they surrounded her bed and cheered her on, how they caressed her body after her soul had left it, how they sang "Blessed Be Your Name" one more time.

"Want to know what the main thing is in death?" he said. "It's the glory of God in the face of Jesus. And Jeri Paholek can see the face of God."

And as Jim stood up and walked down the steps, A.J. and the praise band sang her song, one more time. And the women of her small group—all dressed in pink—knelt at the altar, put their arms around each other and let the tears flow.

After the service, Waldo and Dixie were approached by a friend who had just attended his first service at Grace Fellowship.

"I've never seen that much love in a church," he said.

They nodded and thanked him. Jeri would've loved to have heard that comment. That's the way she always wanted Grace Fellowship to be.

Daryl's flight arrived in Austin shortly after noon, and he and Brady drove to Katy in his parents' car. Christi and Katie worked furiously to clean Katie's house and set up the food table as guests arrived to welcome Daryl.

When he got to the front door, Christi could see the countenance of a man who had lost his wife. She hugged him and said hello to Brady.

"Miss Christi," Brady said, "my mom's in heaven."

"I know," Christi said, trying with all her might to fortify the dam that was holding back the flow of tears. "I'm so happy for her."

* * *

Carolyn and Junny stood in the midst of incomparable beauty— smack-dab in what *Conde Nast Traveler* would later describe as the "Number 1 Best Ambiance City" in America.

Carmel was a place where residents had rejected the idea of house-to-house mail delivery in favor of a central post office, where there were no physical addresses, street lights or parking meters, and no sidewalks outside of the downtown commercial area. It was a spectacular beachfront community favored by honeymooners and romantic souls, an enchanting mix of rustic cottages and Frank Lloyd Wright organic architecture.

They stood at a striking scenic lookout, but they might as well have been at an inner-city bus stop, choked by exhaust fumes. They weren't even looking out at the majestic waves breaking off the shore—not directly, anyway, not with any kind of recognition of the beauty, only with glazed eyes filled with sadness. They were just killing time until they needed to be at the airport.

Back at the hotel, Carolyn sifted slowly through Jeri's CaringBridge site, savoring and treasuring the outpouring of posts in response to the news that Jeri had passed.

One of the messages was from Carrie Estrada, a California resident the family had befriended during the interminable hours in the waiting room. She had been there — passing time until she could visit her mother in a neighboring ICU room — and had heard the family singing "Blessed Be Your Name."

I will never forget the sounds of them singing praises to God as Jeri moved into God's presence. I am a Christian, but I have never witnessed such faith in the face of such heartache. I did pick up some pictures that Brady had been drawing and left in the waiting room. I have placed them in my Bible. Beautiful airplanes. The family blessed us all and increased my Christian walk. To Jeri's mom: God bless you, my sister. I am sorry for your suffering and hold you close in my heart.

Another message was from a Houston woman named Michelle Rathmell, who had never met Jeri and only knew of her because a Grace Fellowship member shared her story in a Bible study the day before Jeri died. Eight years ago, she underwent a heart transplant and spent some time asking God, "Why me?" She had taken her life for granted since the transplant, but she wouldn't any longer.

Life is fast, furious and oh, so precious. Your story is going to change me! I am committed to slow down and smell the roses, sit on the floor with my kids and play a game, take a bike ride with my family, even if I just took a shower. Just simple things you can never get back. Your story will touch many forever and bring a lot of us back down to earth. You will always be in my heart.

Cindy Thilmony wrote from Florida:

I know Jeri is in a better place and is free to run to her heart's delight. But my heart grieves for our loss. It grieves for her family, who also fought so hard with her. I did not have the privilege of knowing Jeri as long as many of her friends, but she certainly touched my life . . . and has left her footprints on my soul.

And this from "anonymous":

I am deeply touched and greatly saddened by Jeri's passing. Although I didn't know Jeri that well, she has impacted my life. I don't sweat the petty problems that arise daily. These are the days when you smile a little more, watch the sunset or maybe tell your family how much you love them. We do this because we have seen the grace, courage and faith God can give a person. Jeri's impact on believers and non-believers is truly God's miracle. This miracle will last an eternity!!!

That night, Carolyn and Junny packed and headed for San Francisco International Airport. At 7 a.m., they arrived in Houston. As they disembarked and walked to the gate, they saw a container being unloaded from the plane.

"I just wanted to make sure she got here," Carolyn said. "That's all."

She held Junny's hand and watched until it disappeared from view.

*   *   *

On the other side of the world, Karen mourned the loss of her friend and prayer partner.

Darkness had fallen in Indonesia on Saturday when she received an e-mail from Brenda notifying her that Jeri had passed. Danny had been sent to the U.S. a day earlier on a business trip. Her children—Daniel, Katie and Kimberly—watched as she fell apart.

Daniel walked up behind her as she sat in front of the computer screen, placed his hand on her shoulder and said, "Jeri loved you and you loved her. I'm sorry, mom."

None of it made any sense to her human brain. God had directed Jeri on the entire process. Karen had observed the whole thing, prayed with Jeri and felt the Holy Spirit's guidance.

She tossed and turned throughout the night, but managed to drift off. As she awakened, she had a vision: Jeri was standing next to Jesus, animatedly talking and gesturing.

"Karen! It's Jesus! It's Jesus!"

Karen could see that Jeri had a firm grasp of Jesus' arm, overwhelmed with His presence. Karen couldn't see Jesus' face, but she just knew He was looking at her with pleasure and love.

She has Him, Karen thought. *She was in a non-stop, chasing-Jesus lifestyle, and now she's caught Him. She's fine.*

Karen smiled. She still longed to be back at Grace Fellowship, where she could fall into the arms of those who could comfort her, and she in turn could comfort them, but God had given her a most generous gift. And another one arrived soon after.

The doorbell rang. She answered it to find a friend, Janet Westcott, standing there with two gardeners. In the bed of their pickup truck stood a seven-foot tree in a beautiful clay pot.

"My heart is breaking for your heart," she said, "so I bought this tree and I want it to be in her memory."

Karen took it to her backyard patio and put a sign in the pot. At the top she wrote the words, JERI'S TREE. Below that, "He will wipe every tear from your eyes. There will be no more death or mourning, or crying, or pain, for the old order of things has passed away."

Karen knelt on the pavement and said goodbye to Jeri in her own private memorial service, thanking God again for the vision and pledging to trust Him for what he was doing: "OK, this is what you've done. I accept it. Not that I have a choice, but I need to do this in my heart. Please comfort Daryl, Brady and her family. I love you, Lord."

*   *   *

From that day in 1997 when Jim showed up on their doorstep to deliver the small-group lesson, Daryl knew Jim was more than just a pastor—he was a solid-as-a-rock, considerate, gentle, humble servant. He always knew he could count on him. He just had no idea he would need him as badly as he did now.

Early on Monday morning, Jim dropped by the Dolans' house and picked up Daryl and Jayme for a day they dreaded. They would have to subvert their emotions and shift into get-down-to-business mode, for this was details day.

They drove 95 miles to Bryan and visited Rest-Ever Memorial Park & Mausoleum. It seemed to be just what Jeri wanted—not just a mausoleum, but one near her beloved A&M campus. But Daryl didn't just pay for spots for Jeri and himself—he bought two spots right next to theirs for Carolyn and Junny.

Then they went to Schmidt Funeral Home in Katy and picked out a casket.

Then they went to a florist and settled on the flowers.

Daryl—still numb, still angry, still trying to figure out why God had allowed this thing to go so horribly wrong after all the doors had opened and they felt they had followed God's will—got through this day only because of Jim. He knew exactly what to do, but better yet, he did it with such a soothing presence.

You know the old Footprints story? A man has a dream in which he's walking on the beach with the Lord and he gets a vision with scenes from his life, featuring two sets of footprints in the sand—one his, the other the Lord's. He sees the final scene and notices that during some difficult times in his life, there is only one set of footprints. He questions why the Lord abandoned him during his despair, and the Lord whispers in his ear: "My son, my precious child, I love you and I would never leave you. During your times of trial and suffering, when you see only one set of footprints, it was then that I carried you."

Daryl felt like Jim had put him on his back—just as Daryl had for Jeri during the times when she gasped for air and couldn't walk another step—and carried him through this nightmare.

Daryl, in addition to being an introvert, had shut down emotionally. He knew he had to be at the viewing Tuesday night and the memorial service and funeral Wednesday, but he rebelled against the idea—not out of disrespect for Jeri, but the notion that dozens of people would want to talk to him. Drained and disillusioned, he didn't want to converse and ruminate.

Schmidt's funeral director did just as the family wished: He dressed Jeri in a long-sleeve pink top, Capri pants and pink flip-flops, and—meeting a request he had never heard before—he kept the casket completely open so everybody could see her feet, including the flowers and sparkles that the pedicurist had put over the top of her pink toenails on that glorious day with Lisa in San Francisco.

Jeri had been proud of her feet. As a child, she always wanted to go barefoot, even when Carolyn insisted she wear shoes. "My beautiful feet are my best feature," she'd say. "Why would I cover them up?"

As an adult, she still thought she had pretty feet, and even contemplated entering a "Pretty Feet" contest advertised by the

Houston Chronicle. At one point, she even told Jayme, "I should've been a foot model." And she wasn't kidding.

But there was profound symbolism at work. "Pretty feet" had a double meaning because Jeri loved to share her faith. One of her favorite passages was Romans 10:13-15: *Everyone who calls on the name of the Lord will be saved. How, then, can they call on the One they have not believed in? And how can they believe in the One of whom they have not heard? And how can they hear without someone preaching to them? And how can they preach unless they are sent? As it is written, "How beautiful are the feet of those who bring good news!"*

Spiritually speaking, Jeri had beautiful feet because she loved to tell other people about Jesus.

*　*　*

They called it a "memorial service." But it would be just as Jeri wanted it to be—a service of praise, a celebration of her life, an invitation to those who did not know Christ to gain a glimpse of what Jeri knew.

It began with Nicole Nordeman's "Legacy," a song about avoiding the workaholic, materialistic view of the world and instead forming relationships that will live forever: *I want to leave a legacy. How will they remember me? Did I choose to love?* The song played out against a backdrop of pictures from Jeri's life, ending with the "I feel free!" shot from Half Moon Bay.

The song faded softly to silence and Linda Alexander, the church's pastor emeritus of care, began.

"Jeri Ivison Paholek, we love you. We come today for healing and to celebrate the life of Jeri Ivison Paholek. Jeri . . . wife, mother, sister, daughter, daughter- in-law, friend, beloved child of God.

"Oh, Lord, we come this morning, bodies bent before the throne of grace. Oh, Lord, this morning, we bend our hearts beneath our knees. We come this morning like empty pitchers to a full fountain, with no merit of our own. Oh, Lord, open up the window of heaven and pour down your spirit upon this place. Lord, without you, we are nothing. Let your Holy Spirit take over and fill this place with your power. Lord, let healing happen here. Hold up each person here as we mourn, as we celebrate, as we share our great love for your child, our sister, Jeri.

"Oh, Lord, you are the rock of our salvation. We come into your presence with praise and wonder, our hearts filled with awe and with love. You are a great God, king above all. We come before you and bow down. We kneel before our maker. You are our God and we are your people. And we are glad that *you . . . are . . . God.* Hold us up. Let us mourn together, let us celebrate together. Only you can bring that mourning into dancing. Listen to our hearts. Come, Holy Spirit. Come. In Jesus' name, amen."

Jim began with the story of how Jeri came to his office July 2 to plan ahead, but he agreed to do it only if he could label it for 2050. This, he said, would be *her* service.

"Better get comfortable, because there is a lot of stuff she wanted us to do," he said. "We're going to be here for a while. It's going to be good. She wanted her service to be a service of praise and worship, so we're going to be doing lots of singing. There will be an open microphone later to share your memory of how she touched your life. Inside of the bulletin is a blank sheet of pink paper, MY NOTES TO THE FAMILY. Jot down some notes you'd like to pass on to the family. There are pink baskets on your way out.

"It's OK to grieve. God is the One who created us in the first place, and He made us with emotions. He made us to be sad when sad things happen, so it's OK to be sad, to mourn, to cry and to grieve. We who know Jesus Christ will grieve differently than people who don't know Jesus Christ. Because we know that Jeri invited Jesus Christ into her life when she was 14 years old, Jeri has been forgiven of all her sins and that she is spending eternity right now with God in heaven.

"When she met with me to plan her funeral service, she wanted it to be a praise and worship service. He is worthy of our worship when things are going great and He is worthy of worship when things are not going great. Matter of fact, that's the message of Jeri's favorite praise and worship song. I want these words to soak into your soul so that when you sing them, they have meaning to you."

A.J. and the praise band sang "Amazing Grace," "What a Good God," "God of Wonders," "Blessed Be Your Name," and "One of These Days."

Jayme went up and sang "The One." Jim played the answering-machine message she left the night the organs became available, saying he believed it represented the last recording of her voice. Then he began a loving and truly lovely eulogy, tying together everything he knew about her and things her family had told him the night before. To do it, he organized it into a PINK acrostic, speaking for over 10 minutes on each of the four letters.

"P," for PEOPLE LOVER. He told stories of her ability in high school to be a part of every crowd, of her sacrificial love, of the way she transformed the hospital staff at Stanford, of her joy for Amy after she became a mother for the first time, of her excitement in playing Jayme's CDs for friends and saying, "That's my brother!"

"Jeri loved people with that big ol' heart the size of a football," Jim said.

"I," for INTERCESSOR. He told stories of how she stood in the gap on behalf of others in prayer, of how people were amazed that she would invest so much time in praying for them when they should have been praying over her, of how her story had multiplied intercession by mobilizing people from all over the world to pray.

"Jeri, you taught us how to pray!" he said. "Thank you!"

"N," for NO TIME TO WASTE. He told stories of how she had been told continually that she should not be alive and yet had lived life to the fullest, of how she threw a spur-of-the-moment party for Taylor after he called her and said he was on the way to propose to Amy, of how she loved to drive really fast and wrecked a new silver Ford Tempo by running into the rear end of a car driven by Fairfield High's most popular kid, of how she energetically attacked her years at A&M.

"Jeri was adventuresome," he said.

"K," for KNOWS JESUS. He told stories of how she sometimes doubted and got mad at God and nobody judged her because those are the kind of emotions you experience when you have a real relationship with someone, of how her faith was authentic, of how she knew God personally by faith living in her body on earth but now knows God face to face.

"Jeri knew Jesus," he said, "and Jeri knows Jesus."

Jim opened up the microphone for thoughts, memories and tributes. Jayme went first.

"Jeri and I shared a passion to be genuine and real when we talked, and not shape our words and speak properly, but tell it like it is. Speak at heart and be authentic. Out of that, I want to share some things with you. Love says to somebody that you would take their place and carry their burdens. That's love. Many of you here today know the extreme highs and lows of our journey. To live out all the miracles that all of us can testify to would require some courageous love, and that radical, risky love was instilled by God and Carolyn and us. It was acted out for 35 years in tangible ways. And it is so evident even today.

"She literally showed us how to roll up our sleeves, stay awake for days on end and get wiped out in tireless prayer. She showed us how to love with all of our heart. We forged on in the midst of terrifying news, over and over. God formed a rock. Myself and others stood on that rock and fought for her life over and over since 1968.

"I remember being 7 years old, and my dad took me with my little tiny guitar and little amp to a Methodist church prayer group in south Fort Worth. I grabbed the door knob and he turned to me and said, 'Be sure to go in there and ask those guys to pray for your sister.' I remember going, 'I don't know how to talk to men and ask them to pray.' But he set the path and the pace. My sister Amy and I grew up around machines and waiting rooms and the serious talks we had to have. We grew up in the hospital. My dad gave us the confidence and that capacity to do whatever it takes, and that we'd be able to love somebody with all of our heart and never hold back. He's been my personal champion.

"These people were the pioneers that shaped and showed us how. My grandmother, uncle and cousins did this all of our lives. They showed us how to love with risky and reckless abandon—the same way that Jeri loved us. I finished this next song last night so we could all cry out together.

"The verses of the song represent how torn we are in our shattered emotions. It's written in first person, and I want it to be your lyrics. The chorus of the song represents what we did, from Carolyn's faith-filled walk and Jeri's steady, faithful walk, and the amazing saints of the church. We've given Jeri the gift of encouraging and helping to strengthen the relationship with the One she now lives with. Don't take it lightly that you gave it to her. We definitely were the receivers in the relationship but we gave that—you gave that—to her. Each of us can only hope to know our Creator that closely. This song celebrates the fruit of Jeri's life, her unabashed proclamation that God is to be glorified in all things."

He sang "With All Your Heart":

If you'll stay with me
I would bleed for you
If you'll walk beside me
I will breathe for you

All the pain, now lovely
All the love, now painful
And I long to be with you

If you'll speak my name again
I would speak a trillion prayers
If you'll just say, "won't you rub my feet?"
I live always on these prayerful knees
To our God sent you, I will be indebted
For you
For all my days—always

And we learned . . .

Only think on hope
Only walk by faith
Only trust
Only truth
Only risk to love with all your heart

And learned . . .
And she showed us all to sing . . .

To God be all the glory
To God be all the glory
To God be all the glory
Forever and ever

After Jayme finished, Carolyn took the mic.

"I am the most honored woman on earth to be Jeri's mom. She strengthened me. She honored me and I honored Jeri. I am so grateful. We wouldn't be who we are if we didn't have Jeri."

Then Amy.

"I knew I copied Jeri with all the major decisions in life. She would get mad and say, 'Would you get your own ideas and stop copying me?' But today, God really showed me and reminded me that I wanted to have that relationship. I grew up in the church and learned about God. She joined a church on her own while we stayed in the church we grew up in. I wanted to have what she had. I wanted that thirst for life. I wanted that joy. And copying her again, I went to church camp with her. I remember the invitation that happened. I wanted it so bad. I wanted to have what she had. God welcomed me and opened the door. I said the prayer to accept Jesus in my life. I was 13 and had Jeri in church camp with me. Jeri was so excited for me. I remember running through the dorm all night and being so excited to have God in my life."

Then Grace Fellowship member Nancy Peroyea.

"Her heart's desire was that everyone know God. This is for Daryl. Jeri had a close friend named Karen Coolidge, who is in Indonesia. This is a note from her: 'We talked a lot the last few months about Jeri's heart, her weak, fragile heart, a heart that would not allow her to climb stairs or do much of anything those of us with so-called healthy hearts take for granted. But in reality, the part of her body that was considered the most fragile was actually the strongest. Think about Jeri's heart. Have you ever seen so much love come out of one little person? Whenever I would tell her that, she would just laugh and say, "Oh, please," because her heart was humbled. But I meant it and she knew I meant it. In my eyes, her heart was practically perfect. It was always mine that needed fixing. Jeri's heart exuded strength, beauty and love. Out of her imperfect heart flowed perfect love. Now Jeri will fuss at me when I get to heaven if I don't tell you the source of that love is Jesus Christ. Jeri was a self-proclaimed Jesus freak. And her favorite place to be was at His feet, soaking in His presence and His love. Then she got on her feet and shared that love with everyone she came into contact with. Thank you, Jeri, for modeling for me what it means to love the Lord God with all your heart, soul, and strength, and to love your neighbor as yourself. You're the real deal, Jeri, and when I grow up, I want to be just like you. I miss you, love you and will see you again soon.' "

Then Christi.

"Jeri was my soul friend. I had the privilege and honor of loving Jesus with her. I know the one thing she always said was, 'I want God to be glorified.' So I challenge each and every one of you to take that and glorify God in all you do."

Then Dixie.

"Well, it's all been said. I heard her say a number of times that Daryl was the perfect husband, that he was God's gift. She felt the same way about all her family friends and church family. I want to lift up her grateful heart. She was so thankful for her family, and to know Christ, and that He had taken the nails in His hands for her personally. Over and over, she'd say, 'I understand that every heartbeat and every breath I take is a gift of God's grace,' and she never stopped being grateful and thankful. A lot of us loved to pray for her, and she would stop us and say, 'All right, I want y'all to remember this is not about me. It's all about God.' We talk about running that race a lot with perseverance. And she did. She's run her race. And she's passing the torch off for us to remember: It's not about us. It's about God."

As everyone filed out of the sanctuary—hundreds dressed in pink, wearing pink ribbons, walking past arrangements of pink flowers—they heard the praise band sing those familiar words: *Blessed be the name of the Lord, blessed be your glorious name* . . .

One more time. For Jeri.

CHAPTER 19

THE THEOLOGICAL DEBATE

W hy did Jeri die?
How could it be that Stanford, the transplant center best equipped to deal with Jeri's advanced condition, isn't contracted with Daryl's insurance company, and then suddenly, just weeks after Jeri starts researching transplants, becomes a place where she can go? How could it be that, with a week to live, she receives a transplant? And when that one doesn't work, with 24 hours to live, donor organs become available? How could it be that instead of triumphantly hiking The Dish with the other transplant survivors, she ends up in an airline container on a Continental plane flying almost directly over that spot?

As it turns out, Jeri received two of the three heart-lung transplants performed at Stanford in 2003, two of six in Region 5 (California, Nevada, Utah, New Mexico and Arizona) and two of 29 in the entire nation.

Two sets of organs in less than 24 hours. Same blood type. Same chest cavity size. Both deaths probably occurring on the West Coast.

How does this not end in victory—or at least what everyone perceived victory would look like?

In the days after her death, Jim went to great lengths to reassure everyone that they had done nothing wrong. No one failed to pray the correct formula of prayer. No one failed to exhibit the requisite faith. No one blew it by sinning. No one made a wrong decision that cost Jeri her life.

Why did he say that? Because the Bible says so in John 9: *As Jesus went along, he saw a man blind from birth. His disciples asked him, "Rabbi, who sinned, this man or his parents, that he was born blind?" "Neither this man nor his parents sinned," said Jesus, "but this happened so that the work of God might be displayed in his life. As long as it is day, we must do the work of him who sent me. Night is coming, when no one can work. While I am in the world, I am the light of the world."*

Many struggled to come to an understanding of what had happened. Amy found herself asking, *Why do we even pray? Why do I ask God to watch over my children? He's going to do whatever He wants to do anyway.*

Jim told everyone that it was OK to question God, to feel anger, to cry out, "Why?" The reason? Because in Matthew 27, Jesus himself did that while hanging on the cross: *My God, my God, why have you forsaken me?* And in Psalm 10, King David cries out: *Why, O LORD, do you stand far off? Why do you hide yourself in times of trouble?* If Jesus and King David could pray like that, so could we.

Jim made sure that even though many could not comprehend why God didn't heal Jeri in the way they were praying for Him to, he could declare with certainty that God is good. He directed them to many passages, including Psalm 34: *Taste and see that the LORD is good; blessed is the man who takes refuge in Him.*

As for the resurrection attempt that did not work, Jim said that it only takes the faith of a mustard seed. But in 1 John 5:14-15, it says: *If we ask anything according to His will, He hears us. And if we know that He hears us—whatever we ask—we know that we have what we asked of Him.* So Jim concluded it wasn't God's will for her to come back to life. And that's OK, because God is bigger than all of us. He's God.

Although Jim told them he had questioned God's timing, he was certain that when he got to heaven, he would stand in front of God in wonder, amazement and awe and say, "Oh, *that's* why you allowed Jeri to come to heaven in 2003. You *do* know what you're doing. God, you are so good. I couldn't see it then, but I see it now."

Why did Jeri die?

He could cite the Bible's explanation: She died because Adam and Eve sinned.

When God created Adam and Eve in Genesis 1 and 2, He created them perfectly and, in Jim's understanding, in a manner that they would never die. They were without sin. He set them up in paradise in the Garden of Eden in a perfect relationship with Him. He put only one boundary on them: Don't eat from the tree of the knowledge of good and evil. They chose to disobey God and eat from the tree, and when they did, sin and death entered the world.

God warned them ahead of time: If you disobey me, then death will enter the world—and as an extension, sickness, illness, cancer, pimples, mosquitoes and fire ants. Everything, Jim believes, ultimately can be traced back to that event.

God then set up a solution, which would be the sacrifice of His son. He announced it in Genesis 3:15, talking about the seed of the woman that will crush Satan. That's the first glimpse of God's permanent solution. That solution isn't an instantaneous one—it comes over time. A few thousand years pass before Christ comes onto the scene. But Christ's dying on the cross and then rising from the dead was God's solution to sin and death.

But then God doesn't close the door just yet. He's waiting to close the door until every group of people has had the chance to hear about the solution.

So why do bad things happen? Because the door hasn't been closed yet. Jim believes we won't go back to perfection until Christ comes again, takes us to heaven and the doors are closed. Then we will be in paradise: no sickness, no death, no cancer, no pimples, no mosquitoes, no fire ants.

But He waits to close that door. He's patient. From 2 Peter 3:9: *The Lord is not slow in keeping His promise, as some understand slowness. He is patient with you, not wanting anyone to perish, but everyone to come to repentance.* Later in that chapter, it says that the reason He waits is to give those who haven't heard about Christ to do so, because when He comes back and fully closes the door to death and sin, then time is up, and all who haven't received Christ will not be with God. So He continues to allow temporary suffering so more and more can have eternity in heaven with Him.

Why did Jeri die?

Because she lived in a time period between Genesis 3 and Revelation 19. Until the door is closed and we're into Revelation 21, cancer is going to happen, genetic defects will be produced in the birth process and hearts and lungs will fail.

"Oh, Lord, take all of that away," we say.

"I'm going to one day," He says. "I'm waiting because people you know have not received me yet. You want no more death, no more sickness? Because the second I make it that way, those people you know have no opportunity to come to heaven."

But if God is capable of doing supernatural things by intervening in this sin-filled world to perform miracles—and that's all over the Bible and in modern-day testimony—and if He was capable of giving her a new heart and new lungs and helping her body accept the heart and lungs that were transplanted in her, why didn't He do that?

We don't know. Jim cites Isaiah 55:8: *For my thoughts are not your thoughts, neither are your ways my ways.* God can see things we can't and is working on a bigger picture. God thinks in terms of billions of years, while we think in terms of immediate comfort. He's working out a billion-year plan, while we focus on days, weeks, months and years.

As Jim told the congregation in a sermon three years after her death, "Always trust in God for a miracle. But God, in His sovereignty and perfect wisdom, might not deliver a miracle."

Why did Jeri die?

In the weeks after her death, Jim never ventured into a theoretical theology room because it would have been insensitive to her family members and friends.

But now, five years down the healing road, he can do that. Putting aside the reality that we are finite creatures while God is an infinite creature—meaning anything we say can be overly simplistic—he can wonder: What if Jeri's death impacted a hundred other people who weren't going to heaven and now are going to heaven because somehow they were touched by her story?

The way he sees it, that math equation works. Some suffering among family members—losing a wife, a mother, a daughter—is nothing compared to a hundred people who were going to spend eternity in hell and are now spending it in heaven. He sees some evidence in Scripture.

2 Corinthians 4: 16-18: *Therefore we do not lose heart. Though outwardly we are wasting away, yet inwardly we are being renewed day by day. For our light and momentary troubles are achieving for us an eternal glory that far outweighs them all. So we fix our eyes not on what is seen, but on what is unseen. For what is seen is temporary, but what is unseen is eternal.*

Romans 8:18: *I consider that our present sufferings are not worth comparing with the glory that will be revealed in us.*

He believes that if we have all the answers to all the questions about suffering, then we're getting to see it all. If we have all the answers, we actually aren't hoping, because we have the complete picture. God is taking the suffering in any given situation and bringing ultimate good out of it for believers. That's part of our sanctification. It's making us more like Christ now. And it's also our glorification in heaven.

How many people have accepted Christ as a result of Jeri's story?

Jim presented the gospel very clearly at Jeri's memorial service, but didn't ask anyone to come to the altar or fill out a card, so only eternity will tell that story. And maybe it's best that way.

But we get poignant glimpses of the wondrous Kingdom that Jeri, in death, has added to.

When Brian left Grace Fellowship in December 2001, he moved to Christ United Methodist in College Station to serve as director of youth ministry. The day after she died, he gave his testimony to about 100 kids, none of whom knew Jeri, some of whom didn't have a personal relationship with Christ.

He started out by talking about the juxtaposition of life and death, of this life and the life to come, how the earth is moaning and groaning, wanting to be with the Father, how we go through these pains, how so many times we see only the earthly. Then he told Jeri's story, from birth to her final moments just 36 hours earlier.

"See, people with conditions like Jeri had see eternity in a much different perspective," he said. "They appreciate life so much more, but they have the opportunity every day to deal with mortality and the struggle between life and death. They have the opportunity to just live each day to the fullest and be right with God. I'm not saying she was perfect, but she was always striving to seek God in *every* situation and circumstance.

"You've heard me tell you that we take for granted our tomorrows. But this is a situation where we face death every day. It's around every corner. Several times I talked with Jeri about John 10:10—that the thief comes to kill and destroy, but Jesus came to give life to the fullest. Over and over, that was a recurring thought for her. She was in a battle with the devil for her life, and she did not want the devil to win and steal her joy—steal every moment that the Lord had planned for her."

He paused, searching their eyes, some filled with tears. He could see that the chord had been struck.

"So . . . how will you choose to live your life?"

Moments later, he had an altar call and six teens came forward and gave their lives to Jesus Christ. They will tell others of that night on September 28, 2003. They will tell others of Jeri's story and how it impacted them. And maybe those they tell will come to the same defining moment in their own lives.

Why did Jeri die?

To break down strongholds. Her death inspired many congregation members to smash down the walls that had hindered them. They felt total freedom. No longer would they be hesitant to tell others about Christ. They didn't fear the potential rejection and skepticism.

And maybe we have it all wrong. Maybe we're asking the wrong question. Maybe the question isn't, "Why did Jeri die?"

Maybe the question is, "Why did God remove Jeri's medical death sentence and keep her alive as long as He did?"

Living 35 years with common ventricle and primary pulmonary hypertension was far more improbable than dying after two heart-lung transplants.

She almost died after the surgery at 17 months—surgery that was not designed to repair the defect, but simply to keep her alive until technology caught up. She wasn't supposed to celebrate any birthdays beyond her 12th. What about the coma five years later? And how about all the trips to the emergency room where they measured her oxygen saturation and wondered why she wasn't already dead, or at least in ICU? Even the renowned staff at Stanford couldn't come up with one instance of an older living person with her condition who had never had a heart-lung transplant.

How many cardiologists and doctors and nurses have altered their thinking, abandoning a purely clinical view of medicine?

What about everybody in her path? What about the kids on her flag corps? What stories do they have to tell about this frail, pale, terminally ill classmate who marched just like they did? What about the teens she worked with at Grace Fellowship? What about all the people she prayed with at the altar? What about an entire floor of Stanford medical personnel who fell in love with her? How was it that they could leave Jeri in the hospital each day but carry her so powerfully in their hearts?

How many e-mails are scattered all over the world—e-mails from people who didn't even know her, e-mails people are still ruminating over?

She lived a life of faith, not just with her words but with her actions. And she did it while suffering *every day*. Everybody focused on what was wrong with her heart, when in reality her heart was beautiful. Her message to the church and to everyone who came into contact with her was, "I'm sick, but I still pray with all of my heart, and I still trust God with every aspect of my life." People saw how God used a broken body that could not be fixed by our human hands.

How much do we complain about the temporary annoyances in our life? Jim thinks about his family vacations to Colorado. He thinks about how he reacts to reduced oxygen at high altitude, where his saturation level goes from 99% to maybe 89%. He'll get headaches and think, *I don't want to hurt.* And then he thinks of near-death levels that were normal for Jeri, and how she still lived a joyful life of faith. *Quit your bellyaching, Jim, and buck up and live,* he'll tell himself.

In *It's Not About Me*, Max Lucado describes a friend battling cancer: "Seeing his sickness in the scope of God's sovereign plan gave his condition a sense of dignity. He accepted his cancer as an assignment from heaven: a missionary to the cancer ward." He quotes his friend as saying, "I reflected God."

And that's the way it was with Jeri. She accepted her terminal heart condition as an assignment from heaven. She was a missionary. She reflected God.

Why did God remove Jeri's medical death sentence and keep her alive as long as He did?

So she could stumble upon a start-up church called Grace Fellowship and turn to Daryl and say, "Let's go try it." So she could help to make a close, loving church even closer and more loving.

Jim and Brenda both believe that the period leading up to the transplants, then her death and the immediate aftermath was, in many ways, the greatest in Grace Fellowship's history. And still is.

As Brenda cried out to God after Jeri's death, she felt Him speaking to her.

In your oneness, I am glorified.

And so she wrote a letter in which she said she felt God "reassuring me that He has been, is being, and will be glorified in our unity. If unity equals glorifying God and Christ (John 17), then our prayers have been answered. Just like our sweet Jeri, we can only be where Jesus is if we accept this gift of eternal life. And that in our oneness, in our unity, the world can see and know. God's splendor has been on display for the world to see by the Body of Christ (us) in one voice, praying, seeking, asking, and . . . trusting. Jeri's prayer and Jesus' prayer was to bring God glory and for God to glorify His son. This is done by our unity. And our unity witnesses to the world Christ's gift of love."

Maybe the message God wanted to send was, *You can come together and talk to me.* We can get lazy and set in our ways after awhile. We can pray and go to church and worship, but during the week, it's same old, same old. Jeri's life—particularly the final nine months—served as a wakeup call.

Here's a sampling of exactly what Jeri meant to Grace Fellowship—some comments written to the family on pink paper and placed in a pink basket:

Jim:

God has deeply impacted my life through Jeri. I will never be the same. Through Jeri, God has taught me how to trust Him, authentically and real; how to drive into the hurricane; how to live today to the fullest as though it is the only day I have left; how to have a spiritual heart and lung transplant; how to really care; how to feel again—grieving Jeri with you has opened up tear ducts that have been closed for too long.

Pat McAnear:

Jeri made such a huge difference in my girls' Christian lives. I'll have to wait to thank her personally when I see her in heaven. I will be eternally grateful to God for having brought Jeri into our lives. She taught all of us what a real Christian should be. And she will continue to inspire me for the rest of my life. I rededicated my life to Christ today because of Jeri.

Emma Kirchhofer:

My favorite quote from her is, "I just love prayer." I don't think I had ever thought of prayer that way. She has changed my focus of praying FOREVER!

Amy Fuqua:

What a beautiful young woman—her life touched everyone. I will remember her in my heart forever. She knew and taught the meaning of life.

Rob Matchett:

I can't help but think that your love and faith have given this church a heart transplant. Your story has changed our church for so many years, but especially this last year. We have been "revived" through your courage and faith. We now know the purpose is to glorify God in everything.

Jayne Couch:

I have realized that I must get up and really start living for God—doing God's will, winning others to Christ. I would always look at her and say, "I want to be like that." I'm ready to just quit talking about God and start acting out God.

Crystal Smith:

My favorite memory of her was at a women's retreat. She and I were praying for Brady. We were crying, praying and hugging. Then, as we walked back to the dorm, she held my hand. I don't know why, but God brought that memory to me last night, and how special she made me feel, holding my hand all the way back to the dorm. I felt like we were sisters, and I have had a special place in my heart for her ever since.

Brettne Shootman:

Jeri was the first person I knew at this church, and it was a fluke. She sat next to me in church on the day she got up to talk to the congregation (three years ago) about her condition and how God had been such a constant in her life. I joined her small group the next day, not even realizing that she was the leader. She was the first person I ever prayed out loud with. I feel that I was touched by an angel in that I knew her, even if it was for a brief time. The impact will last my entire life.

Why did God remove Jeri's medical death sentence and keep her alive as long as He did?

So she could impact the world for Christ until God called her home.

Daryl couldn't help but question why God had called her home. He reached his lowest point about six weeks after she died. He'd cry himself to sleep, beating on his bed with his fists, asking God, *Why? Why did you take me through this just to leave me alone?*

Over time, Daryl came to understand that we are all aliens here in this world. We're supposed to be strangers. We're not supposed to make ourselves *too* comfortable and make this our home, because our real home is in heaven.

Jim directed him to Revelation 22:3-5: *No longer will there be any curse. The throne of God and of the Lamb will be in the city, and His servants will serve him. They will see His face, and His name will be on their foreheads. There will be no more night. They will not need the light of a lamp or the light of the sun, for the Lord God will give them light. And they will reign for ever and ever.*

And Daryl began to imagine what that moment was like for Jeri when she hung in that suspended place between life and death.

He imagined that on one side, she had the people she loved the most saying, "C'mon, Jeri, live! Don't leave us Jeri! Live! We need you! We love you, Jeri! Live!"

And on the other side was the most beautiful and marvelous face anybody's ever seen—the face of her Creator, her Savior, her Lord. Jesus was extending His hand to her. And Daryl could imagine that it was just like 2 Corinthians 5:8 said: *We are confident, I say, and would prefer to be away from the body and at home with the Lord.* And so Jeri left her body and went home to be with the Lord.

Last year, Daryl read *90 Minutes in Heaven,* a true story about ordained minister Don Piper, who was pronounced dead by EMTs after a car accident, but came back to life 90 minutes later. He returned with vivid visions of loved ones and friends he had met in heaven, a feeling of pure peace and sounds of glorious music echoing in his ears—along with the nagging mystery of why God had put him back on earth to face a grueling recovery.

Daryl had always believed that things like that happened, but it further cemented in his soul the feeling that once you experience the glory of God, nothing else would matter. Life on earth wouldn't make sense and you would think, "Well, I don't want to go back to pain and suffering when I can have this."

He's certain that Jeri wouldn't regret being there. Not for a second. Not after always being ready for Jesus' return. Not after suffering the way she did. He believes she would have answered God's call immediately.

We'll all be lucky if we know God the way she knew God at the time of her passage. We'll be lucky if we're *that* ready, if we have been talking to God *that* often and with *that* much conviction, if our relationship with Him is *that* well-nurtured.

CHAPTER 20

PINK PARTY

J eri is everywhere.

She is in a candle-lit arena in Aggieland. She is in a stately Texas Red Oak tree rising out of the hard, uncompromising soil on a 700-acre ranch. She is in a famous song. She is in the hearts of heart surgeons. She is in the prayer room at Grace Fellowship. She is in pink parking passes. She is in Scripture-filled balloons released to the heavens.

This side of heaven, those whose lives she touched cannot know exactly what she's up to. So they're making their own heaven here on earth, carrying her in their hearts and treasuring the incomparable beauty in what she left behind.

They're holding a pink party. You're invited.

* * *

On April 21, 2004, Jeri's family and friends attended Aggie Muster, A&M's annual tradition of honoring current and former students who died during the previous year. With 12,500 filling Reed Arena, Jeri and 138 others were remembered.

Muster had been officially held since 1922 as "a time to look to the past, present and future . . . not only to grieve but to reflect and to celebrate the lives that connect us to one another. A gesture so simple in nature yet so lasting in spirit, Muster is the lasting impression every Aggie leaves with us; it reminds us of the greatness that lies within these walls, of the loyalty we possess, of the connection that binds us, and of the idea that every Aggie has a place of importance—whether they are present in flesh or spirit."

The most poignant portion of the night came when the arena was darkened for the "Roll Call for the Absent." Poems were read. Then the names of the 139 were given.

When the speaker said, "Jerami Ayn Paholek," Daryl rose and answered, "Here"—along with Jayme, who had surprised the family by flying in from Florida—as a candle was lit in her remembrance. Following the honor guard's 21-gun salute, buglers played Silver Taps, one of the most revered traditions at A&M.

A new display called Reflections gave others a glimpse into Jeri's life. Carolyn submitted pictures depicting her years at A&M—at graduation, with Reveille, A&M's official mascot, and at the Bonfire cut—and also ones of her with Daryl and Brady and at her wedding. Jeri's section also included her Bonfire ashes from 1990 and her maroon boots that have A&M written on them.

And one more thing: a newspaper clip from *The Battalion*, the school's daily, in which Carolyn was quoted, "Her last written words were, 'God's grace is perfect for me.'"

* * *

Delinda Sterling and her family met Jeri and Daryl at Crier Creek's family camp and just happened to have scheduled another trip there on the weekend Jeri received the call notifying her of the donor organs.

After learning of the first operation, Delinda and another family purchased a Texas Red Oak sapling and received permission from Crier Creek to plant it near the Whitetail Lodge porch in honor of Jeri's new heart. They called it "Jeri's Tree."

The idea was that as it grew stronger, so would Jeri. She would be alive to see it turn into a massive shade tree in 10 years and a forest giant in 25.

They planted it on Saturday morning, right around the time Daryl was telling Brady that his mommy had gone to heaven. So "Jeri's Tree" would take on a new significance. It would be a visual reminder of Jeri's life that would allow future families to learn about her and her love for the Lord.

But the story doesn't end there.

In the summer of 2006, Crier Creek asked Jim to speak twice a day for a week at family camp. Jim didn't know it at the time, but he had been assigned to the Week #2 family camp—the same one Jeri and Daryl had attended, featuring many of the same families she had met in 2003. "Not a coincidence," Astare would say, "but a God incidence."

Around the second day, all of the families realized that Jim was the pastor of Jeri's church. And the stories flowed.

Jim felt God leading him to scrap one of his planned lessons and tell Jeri's story in detail, so he asked Brenda to fax him the notes from his Sunday morning sermon after her death.

"It was very, very powerful," Jim says, "because some had grown very close to Jeri, but they lived in Dallas or San Antonio and didn't have any way of processing it. It was a really cool God thing that He had us there for that week."

One morning, Lisa and her son, John David, knelt at the tree, examining some painted rocks. A woman approached them and asked, "Did you know Jeri?"

"Did I know Jeri? She was one of my best friends."

And the stories flowed.

"Jeri's Tree" is now 15 feet tall. In his reflective moments, Astare looks at it and feels the warmth he first felt when he met Jeri and Daryl. He loves to tell others why "Jeri's Tree" is there.

"To me, planting a tree is similar to what they did in the Old Testament—putting a rock on the ground and saying, 'This is to remember how God has worked here,'" he says. "Like the Ebenezer stone, this tree was planted in remembrance of her and also the uniqueness and excitement that is life. The tree grows and develops.

My mind thought at one point, *The tree didn't need organs to be alive, but it was still a life. God sustained the tree.* It's cool. It reminds me of her."

*　　*　　*

On the first anniversary of Jeri's death, right after the first of Grace Fellowship's two Sunday morning services, the pink-adorned women of her small group piled into Peggy Howard's Suburban and headed to Rest-Ever Memorial Park. They put in a tape of the sermon Jim gave the day after Jeri's passing, and for most of the 90-minute ride, not much was said.

As they approached Bryan, they started talking about "Blessed Be Your Name."

"You know," said Cindy Smith, "I've always had a hard time with the part about, *You give and take away.* I know we're supposed to understand that, but it's hard. But I'm going to mean it when we sing, *My heart will choose to say. . . .* I'm going to choose to say, 'Blessed be your name.' "

The somber mood gave way to levity when they reached the mausoleum and saw that Jeri's site was lavishly adorned with plaques, plants, flowers—even a George Bush bumper sticker hyping his re-election bid—while the adjacent sites were barren, nothing but the name.

"She's even popular at the cemetery!" Lisa said.

And they all cracked up. They had always joked that she was popular wherever she went.

They placed pink roses on the concrete border, sang Jeri's song, shared memories of her and prayed.

They thanked God for her life, for being allowed to be a part of her life. They prayed that her death wouldn't be the end of her story, that they would carry on her faith and her we-have-to-tell-people-about-Jesus fervor. They prayed for Brady, Daryl, her parents, Jayme, Amy.

In their pain and their tears, they worshipped Him, knowing that in the midst of all of it, He was still God. They didn't like it, didn't get it, and wanted it to be different, but they would trust Him anyway.

Some of them ran in the Houston Marathon the following January, wearing a T-shirt with FOR JERI on the back.

The following year, their tribute to Jeri was wiped out by the mayhem created by Hurricane Rita.

In 2006, they wanted to do something typically Jeri, so they decided to make a pilgrimage to Escalante's. Katie prepared a CD of songs Jeri liked, ones that reminded her of Jeri or ones she thought Jeri would love if she were alive. They listened to that at Katie's house as they painted their nails various shades of pink. They took 50 pink balloons into the restaurant and partied in her name.

They'd laugh wildly, then get sentimental and quiet, sometimes just nodding, thinking, smiling. Memories tossed about in their minds like tumbleweed on a Texas prairie. They had a great time, but the dinner had a foundation of melancholy. They didn't have to express what they were really thinking: *Jeri should be here with us.*

On the ride back to Katy, they drove into a canopy of gun-metal-gray clouds. A storm had battered Katy and was heading east, tossing out bolts of lightning. Katie couldn't help but wonder if this wasn't Jeri saying, *Hey, I'm really not gone.*

Back at Katie's house, they devoured massive bowls of ice cream, sacrificing in Jeri's honor.

* * *

Matt and Beth Redman wrote "Blessed Be Your Name" a few weeks after 9/11. It has nothing to do with that day, but they admit that it was birthed from the spiritual awakening that developed out of that dark time and the realization that "we will all face seasons of pain or unease."

In their book, *Blessed Be Your Name: Worshipping God on the Road Marked with Suffering,* they explained that the world needs its songs of lament, and much of the Psalms are filled with intense cries to God.

"Songs of lament are a very biblical thing to sing in worship. Yet they are also a relevant thing to sing, for we live in a world full of anguish and heartache. As Christians, yes we live in victory, but in paradox we also exist as strangers in a foreign land, aching for home, and knowing deep within us that the world we see is not as it should be. So the question is this: if songs of lament are firstly thoroughly biblical, and secondly extremely relevant, then why on earth are there not more songs to help us voice these heart-cries? As Frederich W. Schmidt Jr. writes, these Psalms do three things: 'They give us permission to ask our own questions about suffering. They model the capacity to ask questions we might otherwise suppress, but can never escape. And they model how those questions might be asked without fear of compromising our relationship with God or with other people.' "

Jeri never got to read the Redmans' book, which came out in 2005, but she would have understood with perfect clarity what they were saying.

She also would have celebrated the song's ascension.

KSBJ first played Matt Redman's version of the song in July 2002, and that was the one Jeri adopted in her heart. But in mid-January 2004, KSBJ started playing Tree63's version, which ended up in the No. 1 spot on the national Christian music charts. More than five years later, the song remains one of the 20 most popular songs KSBJ plays, according to a poll of the station's listeners.

It churns up complex emotions for everyone who knew Jeri and how much she embraced it. While many of her friends cherish hearing it, Daryl struggles on those occasions when it's played.

Until almost a year after Jeri's death, A.J. would call Daryl and say, "Just giving you a heads-up. We're going to be playing 'Blessed Be Your Name' this Sunday at church, in case you want to miss worship and come in late." And Daryl would do just that. He'd also turn off the radio or switch stations if he heard it.

Over time, he has felt God speaking to him and telling him he needs to hear the song.

Last year, he was at an arts and crafts show in Alvin, 30 miles south of Houston. As he strolled the grounds, he passed a stage where a group was playing a variety of secular songs. A few minutes later, he could hear the opening notes to "Blessed Be Your Name." What was the chance of that?

And Daryl began to think, *God wants me to hear this song. Yes, He takes away, but He also gives back. He's saying to me, "It's OK to listen to. I'm here. I'm in control. You can't run from it forever."*

And so, while Daryl does not voluntarily play the song, he doesn't shut it out completely.

*   *   *

Dr. Lloyd moved on from Stanford, taking a job at Derriford Hospital in Plymouth, England, specializing in heart-failure surgery and aortic and mitral-valve repair.

Something about Jeri continues to tug on his heart. In an e-mail, he wrote:

I have many memories of Jeri and her life and death at Stanford that are of enormous significance to me. Among the most important to me is the deep feeling of regret that we/I could not help her through the operations she waited so long for. I am sure I could fill fifty pages of thoughts and feelings around the time of her surgery in a moment, as they are all so crystal in my mind. I cannot begin to go through the many emotions I felt the time of her death, and they will have to stay personal to me. . . . Jeri was a wonderful person and I hope your book succeeds in sharing that.

Dr. Reitz still leads Stanford's team of cardiac surgeons. He says that getting involved emotionally with patients is "not something I want to do, and I don't think many surgeons do. It's not really feasible to do that, just because of the number of patients you have with compelling situations. People don't undergo this type of thing unless they have complicated histories."

And yet, when asked about the family's memories of the tears they saw him crying, he says, "Their observations about what happened are real."

He says he spends about 5% of his time studying ways to make heart-lung transplants better and more reliable, primarily through the use of drugs in combinations that are more effective.

Five months after Jeri died, Stanford formed the Stanford Cardiovascular Institute, a research center focusing on the prevention, treatment and ultimate elimination of cardiovascular diseases.

Things they learned from Jeri's complicated and highly unusual case will save other lives in the future. That is another compelling component of her legacy.

* * *

Who died? How did they die? How did they live? Why did they want their organs to go to someone in need? What were their stories? What should Jeri's family know about them? Much of the story may forever remain shrouded in mystery.

Carolyn wrote an anonymous letter to the families of the two donors whose organs ended up in Jeri's body.

We are very grateful to your donor for helping to fulfill the dream our daughter had of having a heart and lung transplant! Her goal was to be well and get to be an active mommy for her little boy and to see him grow up. Even though that was her earthly goal, her life goal was to please God and for His will to be done in her.

Your donor also was an answer to many, many prayers for this transplant! We had no idea that God's plan was to take her home to be with Him that week after the transplant, but we know that He is in control and knew what was best for her.

One family responded to Carolyn's letter of thanks: the daughter of the second donor.

Here is part of her letter:

My mother was the most kind and loving person I have ever known. My mother grew up on the East Coast, yet spent half of it on the West, in California. She was highly moral and was raised Catholic. Her younger sister was her closest friend and they shared a deep love and connection.

My mother loved adventure and traveled to all corners of the globe. Her career as a flight attendant was filled with many friends and happy stories. When she was thirty, she had the first of three children. They were her truest love. My mother was very creative, graceful and loving.

* * *

No place at Grace Fellowship was as sacred to Jeri as the prayer room. That room doesn't exist anymore. But when the church finished its expansion in 2007, it built a much larger room in The Mansion, which houses the offices and meeting rooms.

On one of the walls is a plaque that Carolyn and Junny donated in her memory. It contains the passage from Isaiah 52:7 about beautiful feet. Below that, the words, IN MEMORY OF OUR PRECIOUS JERI PAHOLEK. 9/2/68 TO 9/27/03. SHE LOVED JESUS AND BROUGHT US JOY.

She lives on in the parking lot, too. Those who have mobility issues that prevent them from walking long distances receive a "Paholek Pink Parking Pass"—a long, slender, pink-leather strip— that allows them to park in the Special Care spots. Along with it, they get a letter with this short message: "In honor of Jeri Paholek, you have been bestowed a pink parking pass. Please hang it on your visor for the parking attendants to see. Think and pray for Jeri, her family and Brady."

But there's so much more—so much that goes beyond plaques and parking spaces, so much in their hearts that the passage of time can't erase or even dull.

"We all have something we gleaned from Jeri that was formed by having a relationship with her," Brenda says. "We may not verbalize it, articulate it or share it a lot with one another, but it's there. There's so much. Jeri wasn't a surfacey type of friend. She really let you into the raw stuff of life.

"Thinking about her is joyful. Even now, I can't help but smile when I think about her. We laughed a lot, we smiled a lot, we cried a lot, we prayed a lot."

Karen, Danny and their kids moved back to Katy on July 3, 2006, and resumed their worship at Grace Fellowship. But it's just not the same without Jeri.

"What I carry most from Jeri is the way she pursued the Lord wholeheartedly," Karen says. "She loved being in the presence of Jesus, and she was happiest when she was there. I've realized that Jeri's death sparked a prayer movement. It sparked people to fall to their knees and in that, relationships with the Lord were formed and strengthened.

"Jeri was the bravest person I've ever met. She trusted Him. The way she described her heart and what was wrong with it, it seemed that every day she woke up and breathed, it was a miracle. It was like God healed her heart every single night while she slept. And he did that every night for 35 years."

Christi's mind clicks back to Jeri's final Sunday at church before leaving for Las Vegas. A.J. played "Blessed Be Your Name," and after the service, Christi and Jeri hugged tightly and absorbed each other's tears.

"I need you more than you need me," Christi said.

"No, that's not true," Jeri said.

Christi never saw Jeri again. The day Jeri died, she spent the entire day at Lisa's house. Around 10 p.m., they prayed for Brady and Daryl, then Lisa drove Christi home. When Christi started to put her key in the door lock, she noticed a praying mantis perched peacefully on the frame.

"We'd lived there for eight years, and I'd never seen one," Christi says. "I know God put that there. It was a little gift from God. Then we went to Crier Creek a month after she died. I saw one on the cabin door. I've never seen one since. It almost seemed that every time I thought of her when I was outside, a butterfly came around. I think that was God's gift to me, because butterflies are a beautiful example of His power and redeeming love.

"It's also interesting that after she died, pink became very popular. And flip-flops became so fashionable—on necklaces, bracelets, earrings. I just feel like that was God's little affirmation that she's OK, although we didn't need to know that."

Katie's mind goes back to that profound connection she immediately felt with Jeri because of the medical dramas they had endured— Jeri with her heart, Katie with Emily's disabilities and heartbreaking death. They needed each other, understood each other perfectly.

"I feel like even though there's tragedy, there's always a blessing," she says. "Emily's short life was a blessing. The fact that Jeri lived to be 35 was a blessing. I remember her 30th birthday. Most people turn 30 and are like, 'Oh, I'm getting older. What am I doing with my life?' For us, it was, 'Jeri's turning 30 and we're going out to celebrate!' She had been a miracle 100 times over."

Her memories are a patchwork of fun times, hanging out as girl-friends. She can picture Jeri's determination in spreading the gospel, the way she'd say, "I don't care if they think I'm a Jesus Freak. I'm going to do what my heart tells me needs to be done." She can picture Jeri dragging that bulky Grayco stroller out of the trunk and wrestling with it like it was an alligator. And Katie would joke, "Get an umbrella stroller!"

And she can picture Jeri talking about her days on the flag corps. It wasn't until after Jeri died that she found out from Jayme that Jeri had been hauled off the field more than once in an ambulance.

"Jeri," Katie says, eyes lifted heavenward, "you didn't tell us *that* part!"

*   *   *

Jayme admits that he's having a hard time moving through the stages of grief after losing Jeri. He'd give anything to spend another uncomfortable, sleepless night in a hospital waiting room. He'd give anything to sit on her bed, playing Go Fish and Hearts while they waited for the latest lab report. He'd give anything to put on Herb Alpert and the Tijuana Brass and play "The Toot Song" for her.

He misses his biggest fan. Nobody will ever be bigger. A hundred times, she introduced him to her friends by saying, "This is my brother! He's a musician!" And a hundred times, he could feel that warm sensation spread throughout his body, just knowing the depth of her love without any quantification or explanation.

Did she know that he felt the same way about her? Did she know that he told her story to anyone who would listen? Yes, she did. He knows that.

"Life's been a lot harder, because I've had to do all this stuff without her," he says. "For me, there's this big void. Now I don't have this huge source of belief and this huge power of confidence behind me, that big wind blowing me wherever I go. Now I've got to believe in myself."

Jayme hasn't performed "With All Your Heart" since her memorial service. That song was for that one moment, and the moment is gone.

He wrote a song called "Dreaming Memory," which was recorded by his group, Ivison, on its 2006 EP, *Convergence*. It's about making new memories when he dreams. He is hanging out with Jeri. They can do supernatural things together, like flying through the air a la Superman. And then the dream ends.

Amy thinks back to her agony in the hours after Jeri's death. Back at the hotel, standing by the door of a vacant room that was being renovated, she closed her eyes and said, "C'mon, Jeri, c'mon! Come back!" Part of her believed God could still heal Jeri.

And now? She believes God healed her as soon as she crossed over. It wasn't the kind of healing everybody wanted, but she has been healed.

"She's with the saints, cheering us on," Amy says. "We have good memories. Avery out of the blue will say, 'Aunt Jeri's in heaven, right? When do I get to see her?' When we talk about heaven, they know that they will get to see Aunt Jeri. I tell the kids about her. When Sawyer was born, I told Avery about my sister. I told her, 'A sister is your best friend, and you can tell everything to her. When you get bigger, you'll be so glad you have a sister.'

"I tell them, 'She was mommy's good friend, mommy loved her very much and she got sick. It was time for her to be with God in heaven.' They say, 'She got sick and went to heaven?' I say, 'God made her heart different than ours. It didn't work like ours, and doctors tried to fix it, and it wasn't God's plan for it to be fixed.' They really understand it. We've talked about dying and death with Avery since she was little. We would rather explain it thoroughly than have someone else say something that's not true."

*　*　*

Carolyn and Junny live at the end of a lazy cul-de-sac in a two-story, country-style home on 3.9 acres of heavily wooded property, adjacent to a pasture where cows graze and deer roam. They have two goats, which they use to clear the land near their backyard, and two dogs: Lacy, a miniature Schnauzer/Pomeranian, and Gizmo, one of her puppies.

It's classic country living—bucolic, relaxed, unstressed. They're close enough to College Station to feel the buzz and far enough to have their own piece of placidity.

Junny uses the detached garage for his mechanical shop, and he also built a wood shop where he putters around. He's an avid gardener, tending to his patches of strawberries, tomatoes, cucumbers, beans and squash.

Carolyn works at A&M, cooks and dotes on her grandchildren, including Brady. She selflessly serves others and is especially adept at delivering birthday surprises.

Occasionally she'll go into the CaringBridge site—which has lived on—and see if anyone posted. Carolyn made many posts in the first three years following Jeri's death, but she hasn't posted in almost three years.

Jayme worried initially that the family might lose Carolyn shortly after Jeri's death, either from a physical death or a psychological death where she just shut down internally. He figured that the part of her that didn't die along with Jeri would be overpowered by the part of her that did.

It never happened. She's still here, and she's still as engaged as ever in life, which Jayme attributes to God's supernatural work and Carolyn's survivor traits.

"It's just the grace of God that I'm where I am," she says. "I didn't think I could live if she died. All of those years, I had suffered with her and taken care of her. It's hard to believe I could have a life without her. But it's totally from God. It's not me.

"I felt it pretty much immediately. I stood up at her service. I just felt, 'This is what she'd want. Not make a scene crying and moaning.' I miss her. I wish I could talk to her. I think, *I wish I could ask Jeri this. I wish Jeri could be here to see this.* Then I think, *What she's seeing is a lot more beautiful than what I'm seeing.* It's incredible to know she's face to face, experiencing that glory. That's kind of what she wanted."

"She got to do so much," Junny says. "We weren't parents who had a child who got on a motorcycle one morning and was gone from an accident. We were the parents of a child who woke up with a cloud over her head every day, took the best she could out of life and got to do everything she wanted to do."

Carolyn picks up a Willow Tree figurine of an angel with her arms spread wide. It's called "Happiness." The inscription says, "Free to sing, laugh, dance . . . create!" Amy gave it to them because she said it reminded her of Jeri in that "I feel free!" picture.

There are many other things that keep Jeri close. A framed picture of the three-hearts drawing by Jeri hangs on the wall. A candleholder from Daryl that says, "Perhaps they are not stars in the sky but rather openings where our loved ones shine down to let us know they're happy." Little hot-pink glass flip-flops that hang on their wall, and somewhere in the homes of 10 of Jeri's closest friends—gifts from Carolyn and Junny.

At Christmas, all of the family members hang an ornament on the tree that includes this inscription: "I'm spending Christmas with Jesus this year."

Every year on her birthday, they buy pink balloons and fill them with messages. One year, Jayme wrote, "Jeri lived life to the fullest, loved her family more than herself, gave herself tirelessly to others in prayer and support and loved God with her life. She showed us how to be alive and changed us forever. On this earth from 1968 to 2003 but alive forever. Oh, how we miss her, love her and thank her for giving us herself—always and forever."

Then they find a scenic spot and release the balloons, watching them until they soar out of sight.

Someone will find one of those balloons and realize the depth of their love and the meaning of Jeri's life.

*   *   *

We make the 25-minute drive to Rest-Ever Memorial Park, turn into the driveway, pass a row of majestic Live Oaks and stop at the Shrine of Love Mausoleum. The late-afternoon shadows cast an intriguing light on this glorious, 73-degree mid-November day.

Carolyn and Junny walk up to the 75-foot by 25-foot granite structure and stop at Jeri's corner, on the southern side of the west end, just as they have so many times before. There's an Aggie wind chime, an artificial tree with Aggie maroon and green leaves and an Aggie flag stuck in the tile base, a solar lamp that keeps the spot lit at night—just as Jeri wanted it during her life—and the last words she uttered: "Remember, I laid it at the feet of Jesus." On top of the solar base are two crosses, one made from nails at a youth camp Jayme attended.

In the spring, they'll add some potted plants. In December, something with a Christmas feel.

Planted in the grass near the cement is a sandstone block with some of the lyrics to "With All Your Heart." Inside the shape of a heart, they wrote these words: "We will miss you, Jeri." In the grass nearby, they planted a Live Oak on the second anniversary of her death. As it grows, the foliage will shade the wall of the mausoleum. And in April, the tree is surrounded by breathtaking bluebonnets planted by Junny a few years ago.

In this place, there's a whole lot of love.

"We didn't want it to just be a burial spot," Carolyn says. "If somebody came into town and wanted to see her gravesite, we wanted them to see the site was not being neglected."

On the morning after Jeri's service, Carolyn was here at dawn. And in the months that followed, she came here as often as three times a week. She'd sit on the bench nearby, sometimes calling a prayer friend to talk.

She doesn't do that anymore.

"I do miss her a lot, but I just don't cry," she says. "Sometimes I wish I could. Not that I'm trying *not* to."

"Carolyn was such a servant to her," Junny says, "and all at once, it was gone. That servant part of a mother never goes away."

"One thing that really helped was that Amy was here a lot, so we talked a lot," Carolyn says. "Jayme missed that. He was in Florida, mourning by himself. I think it is really healing to talk a lot. And laugh. And say, 'Wouldn't Jeri have laughed at that?' "

"Jeri would call and she had a special little tone in her voice, and she would say, 'Hi, daaaaad,' " Junny says. "It was like, 'It's Jeri, and I'm welcoming our conversation.' *Hi, daaaaad.*"

They go quiet. The only sounds are of chirping birds and the distant hum of cars moving down Highway 6.

"I'm really glad Daryl chose this place," Carolyn says. "I think she would like it. It's out here by itself. You can see the sky and the stars."

* * *

For the first two months after Jeri's death, Daryl couldn't summon up the strength to take off his wedding ring. And living in the new house—what was supposed to be *their* new house—only compounded the pain.

But as the holidays approached, he started thinking about the way Jeri had implored him to go on with his life and re-marry, and in fact had even prayed for him to find a woman who would treat him as good as he had treated her. So he went out on a few dates and found that it was good to have somebody to talk to.

He started asking friends, "If I told you I was dating somebody, what would you say?" Everybody said it wouldn't mean that he was failing to honor Jeri's memory, that he shouldn't worry about anybody harshly judging him. That removed the pressure he had been feeling.

What he didn't know was that somebody he vaguely knew already felt like she would be his next wife.

Charmel Turner had divorced in March 2001 and started attending Grace Fellowship later that year. She had taught Brady's Sunday school class, but when Daryl dropped him off and picked him up, they shared nothing but "Hi" and "Bye."

Charmel had followed Jeri's story, heard the phone call to Jim that was piped into the PA system during service, even followed the e-mails on the CaringBridge site. The day Jeri died, Charmel's tears moistened the keyboard of her computer.

The next night, she could feel God saying, *He's for you.* And she thought, *What? He's for me?* She felt horrible. Wracked by searing guilt, she couldn't believe the thought had even entered her mind. But the feeling stayed in her heart: *He's for you.*

Jim and Lisa apparently had the same feeling. Charmel had taught their son, Smith, in fifth grade at Fielder Elementary, and they admired the way she was raising two young children as a single mom. So one day, as they walked down a hallway at Fielder, Jim mentioned to Charmel that they had been talking about her the previous night.

Lisa pulled her aside and said, "We were wondering if you'd be interested in meeting Daryl Paholek."

Charmel, knowing her track record of dating after her divorce, said, "It makes me nervous because if we do go out, I wouldn't want to be the one who hurt him." Nevertheless, she couldn't squelch the excitement she felt. Lisa said she would tell Daryl about her. Nothing like an endorsement from the pastor's wife, huh?

He never called, and Lisa never said anything more about him. Charmel started plotting how she could break the ice. The next time Daryl dropped off Brady at church, she would ask him his plans for spring break.

He didn't attend church that Sunday, so she switched to Plan B: The following Sunday, she would ask him how spring break went. He didn't show again.

They finally ended up talking at Fielder one day, and Charmel could tell that Lisa had been talking to him about her. They talked on the phone a few times and he asked her out. Their first date would be over dinner at Carmelo's Italian Restaurant.

From the very beginning, they were very open with each other. Charmel, sensing no walls and feeling emboldened by her penchant for saying what was on her mind, asked about Jeri. Daryl immediately liked her sense of humor and the absence of uncomfortable dead spots in their conversation.

As the year wore on and their relationship strengthened, Charmel could tell that Daryl didn't want to forget Jeri—he was just looking to be happy again. Charmel never got even the slightest feeling that Jeri's friends were judging Daryl's new relationship.

Still, she sometimes felt like she couldn't possibly measure up to Jeri. She thought, *Jeri was a saint with no negative qualities. And here I come, a divorced woman with some very apparent ones. I don't have the faith she had. She brought people to Christ. I tend to judge first. How can I compare to someone who was so respected that Jim abandoned his sermon to offer a tribute to her? There would never be that many people who cared about me if I died tomorrow. I haven't done anything in my life that anybody would notice. What if I don't meet the standards she set?*

Daryl, patient and understanding, helped her to realize that he didn't view it as Jeri vs. Charmel. He loved her for who she was.

On her birthday, October 16, 2004, Daryl took her to Vic and Anthony's Steakhouse in downtown Houston. What she didn't know was that he had contacted management and arranged for an engagement ring to be put in the bread basket the waiter brought to their table. When she reached for the bread, she found the ring. Daryl got down on one knee and asked her to marry him. When she said yes, a large group of people eating at a neighboring table cheered wildly and sent them a bottle of champagne.

They were married on February 12, 2005, in the sanctuary at Grace Fellowship in front of 350 friends and guests. Jim presided over the ceremony and A.J. sang. They had a cake-and-punch reception in the foyer after the ceremony.

Over the years, Charmel has displayed uncommon selflessness and grace in dealing with Jeri's memory. She could have wilted under the pressure of living up to Jeri, but instead she has shined.

"She has always made it safe in our home to keep Jeri's memory alive for me and Brady," Daryl says. "Sometimes it might be hard and uncomfortable, but she has embraced it 100%. She even talks to Brady about it and helps him when he has questions. She's given me reassurances that it's OK to remember and talk about her if I need to."

"It's important for Brady," she says. "When I look at Brady and I think of my children, I think, 'If I were to die tomorrow, what is it I would want them to have?' I would want them to move on and have a mom and live a 'normal life.' I wouldn't want them to dwell on my memory. But I would want them to have the knowledge that I didn't run off on them but I died, and I loved them tremendously.

"I'm not going to deny it's hard. I can tell Daryl that he's the love of my life, but I don't know that he honestly can return that and say that. Maybe he's had two loves. So it's hard at times."

One night, her son, Kyle, asked her, "If Jeri came back to life, would Daryl leave you and go back to Jeri?"

"That's hard to answer," she told him, "because first of all, she's not, so it's not something I have to contemplate. Do I think Daryl still loves her? Of course I do, and I don't think he will ever stop. But I also think his heart is big enough that he can love both of us just like I can love you and Kelli exactly the same. I couldn't close Jeri out of his life even if I wanted to, and I don't. And I can't close Brady out of Jeri's family's life. They don't have her, but they do have him, and they know how much she loved him."

This is how much Charmel embraces her life as the wife of Jeri's husband and the stepmother of her son: A few years ago, she approached Jeri's friends and asked them to contribute to her project to keep Jeri alive in Brady's heart. Would they write a letter explaining the things that made Jeri special, the things they cherished, the things Brady should know?

"It all came out of the fact that I was thinking about Brady and about what I'd want for my child as a mom," she says. "After a few years, people's memories start to fade and they might not remember those events. I wanted him to remember. I wanted him to know, 'This is what people thought about your mom. This is what I know about your mom that nobody else knows.' "

* * *

Brady is sitting on the end of Daryl and Charmel's bed, his legs crossed, his blue eyes fixed on Charmel's. She is triggering thoughts and memories and impressions of Jeri by asking him questions that allow his imagination to run wild.

And it is good. It is good for a boy to crystallize those memories into snapshots and videos that will be there anytime he wants them, summoned from a file he can call, THE BEST MOM EVER. It is good, especially when that boy does not prolifically express his inner-most feelings.

"What are your best memories of your mom?" she asks.

"I remember going to the beach with her. And we went to pick up seashells."

"What else? What was the weather like? The sky?"

"It was cold—not in the summer. The water was cold. The sun was out, but it was cool. I think it was at sunset. The wind was blowing a lot and there were a lot of waves, and they were going in the same direction as the wind. It would have been fun to be out there on a boogie board. Like if you went out there during a hurricane. That would be really cool. I have some seashells in my room and I think it has the date on them."

He runs to his room and comes back with a bottle, but the inscription says "St. Petersburg" and the year was 2000. His beach memory is actually a collage of memories. He says Daryl was at work, but that was the day they drove into Tropical Storm Fay at Galveston.

He doesn't *specifically* remember the Fay day at Galveston, but he remembers people telling him about it. And for a 5-year-old, that was a very exciting thing. The boat and the waves in Galveston and the shells in St. Pete—that's what sticks with him.

It's similar to Jeri's death. As people remind him, he can remember Daryl taking him into a private room and telling him that his mom had died, but he doesn't remember what it meant.

"Do you remember where you were when your dad told you?" Charmel asks.

"In a room at the hospital. I remember being sad."

"You know more now that you're 11, right? Do you think you really understood what it meant then?"

"No."

"When you were 5, did you realize her heart needed to be fixed?"

"Yes, my mom had problems with her heart. I remember her getting sick a lot."

"Did you think at the time that it was serious or something like a cold?"

"I think I thought it was a cold."

"Did you know what was happening when you moved to Las Vegas?"

"Yes, I got a choice in deciding if we moved."

"What do you mean?"

"I got to decide if we should move so she could get better or if we should stay here."

"Well, what was your vote?"

"Go where she could get better."

"You don't feel like it's your fault, right? You know they were trying to make her better?"

"Yes."

"Were you worried about it at all?"

"I was worried she might die, but I really thought she'd be better."

"Close your eyes and see if you can picture her."

"Pretty."

"Can you describe anything else?"

"Pretty."

"OK, what color was her hair?"

"Blond."

"Long or short?"

"Short."

"What kind of things did you enjoy doing with her?"

"I liked going to the Fun Plex. She would ride the Ferris wheel with me and we'd play Putt-Putt. Nana was there, too. Mom won sometimes, but I won the most. I got excited at the top of the Ferris wheel. She loved to be at the top of the Ferris wheel. She would look down and wave. I remember feeling really good about being there. I remember that she was always smiling."

"What did you eat?"

"Popcorn."

"Did mom eat it with you?"

"No. She got a salad. Nana and mom got a salad."

"What kind of games did you play with her?"

"Candyland and Chutes and Ladders. Sometime she'd win and sometimes I'd win."

"Do you remember accepting Christ and how excited she was?"

"Every night, I would kneel at my bed and pray. One night, I asked God into my heart during that prayer time."

"How important is Christ in your life now?"

"Very important."

"Why is He very important?"

"Well, because my mom died and went to heaven, and God is with her. I know that He is protecting mom and watching over our family."

Yes, Brady, she went to heaven, and God is with her, and He is protecting her and watching over you.

She is running, jumping, dancing, doing things she never got to do. She is taking in deep, glorious breaths and exhaling with no struggle. She is basking in the glow of the face of God.

She is doing all of that.

With pink lips and fingertips.

ACKNOWLEDGMENTS

God is always at work.
Do you doubt that? You shouldn't.

This book is the result of one seemingly insignificant conversation in the kitchen of Nita Taberner's home in Katy, Texas, in December 2005. Nobody can remember the exact date of the gathering, or why we were even gathering—only that it birthed something that took over my heart and soul.

As the afternoon wore on and we polished off Nita's eggplant parmigiana and chicken drumstick, the conversation turned to my writing. I told Ruby Renz, counseling pastor at Grace Fellowship United Methodist Church, that two potential book projects had fallen through, but I still hoped to write a biography.

"What about Jeri Paholek?" Ruby asked. "You'd be able to go really deep into her story because she's from our church and it's all so fresh. One of our congregation members came up to me and said, 'Somebody needs to write a book on her.' When you said 'biography,' I thought, *You need to write a book about this. You're a writer, and you like biographies, and this is THE story.*"

"I don't know," I said. "My sense is that it doesn't work unless the person is already famous."

"What about Joni Eareckson Tada?" she said. "Nobody ever heard of her before a diving accident left her a quadriplegic. She learned how to paint with a brush between her teeth and turned that into a ministry. She wrote her autobiography, and then they turned it into a movie."

"Yeah, but . . . "

"Do it! Do it!"

I planted Ruby's seed in some pretty barren land—might as well have been Death Valley—as I went about the daily routine of mundane tasks that I thought were more important. What I couldn't see was that God had constructed a rather extensive irrigation system below the surface. He started watering, then He started working on my heart as I went to Him in prayer about His wishes.

I found myself gazing at a sheet of paper taped to the wall above my desk. Written in blue ink were five goals, the last of which read, WRITE A BOOK BY AGE 50.

What are you waiting for? I could hear God saying to me.

On May 9, 2006, I called pastor Jim Leggett.

"She's got an awesome story," he said. "I would love for the world to hear it. I think it's very exciting."

He suggested that I keep her husband, Daryl, and her parents, Junny and Carolyn Ivison, in mind as I approached the project. He said "going down this road could be healing for them or disturbing for them." His sense was that it would be healing, but he encouraged me to approach them with sensitivity.

I contacted Daryl. He prayed about it and gave me his blessing. Then he posed the idea to her parents, and they gave me their blessing.

And then some amazing things happened that could have been orchestrated only by God.

On July 23—the morning after I had met Carolyn and Junny for the first time and had been warmly welcomed into their Bryan home for an entire day—I walked into the sanctuary at Grace Fellowship and took my seat. As I scanned the bulletin, I could not believe what I saw. The very first song by the praise band would be "Blessed Be Your Name"—the song that had spoken so powerfully to Jeri and defined her life leading up to the transplants at Stanford, the song that had galvanized an entire congregation.

On July 28—just minutes after talking to her brother, Jayme, for the first time by phone—I fired up my backyard grill, went to the refrigerator and grabbed a pack of swordfish. When I removed the cover, I once again could not believe what I saw: Two steaks, each shaped like a heart.

God, I thought, *you are not kidding around.*

In the early stages of this project, when the enormity of the endeavor became more obvious and my research didn't produce tangible results, I came under attack. I could feel Satan saying, *This is too difficult. This is too risky. This isn't worth it.*

God always came through, giving me exactly the encouragement I needed, at the times I needed it most.

One day, it came from a Fellowship of Christian Athletes devotional that arrived in my e-mail inbox. Jere Johnson—an FCA staff member who had helped me with a story on an NFL player for the FCA's *Sharing the Victory* magazine—titled it "Use Your Gift." He wrote that not a week went by that Satan didn't attack him and tell him to stop writing because no one cared. "And it is usually at those moments when I will get an e-mail or phone call. Those are God's way of reassuring me that my gift is being used for Him."

One day, it came through the daily devotional from a calendar, Joyce Meyer's *Battlefield of the Mind*—given to me at Christmas by my sister, Shirley Siegrist. The devotional cited Romans 4:20-21 and described how Abraham remained strong and grew in his faith: "God wouldn't expect us to do something and not give us the ability to believe that we can do it. Satan knows how dangerous we will be with a heart full of faith, so he attacks us with doubt and unbelief."

Another day, five months later, a similar message: "If you know God has asked you to do something, don't back down just because it gets hard. When things get hard, spend more time with Him, lean more on Him, and receive more grace from Him. . . . Beware of 'I can't do this; it's just too hard.' "

And now it is done.

I want most of all to thank God for rescuing me from the darkness in 1999, pulling me out of the wreckage that my life had become, dusting me off and whispering gently into my ear, "I will take care of you." I don't know where I would be without Him. I don't even want to think about it. I'm just so grateful that God gave me the ability to write, that I could use that ability to glorify Him, and that He entrusted me with this project, as small as it might be in the overall scheme of His Kingdom.

Ruby would tell you that she was just a conduit that day at Nita's house, that the main reason she blurted out her suggestion/order was because talking is her forte and I just happened to be in the way. The truth is, she didn't have to honor God, but she did. In a big way.

My parents, Dick and Vi, gave me an ideal and idyllic childhood, stoking my dreams, believing in me, never harping on my mistakes, allowing me to grow. They didn't laugh at me when I sat in the basement, watching an NBA game on TV and then hacking out a crude game story, hunt-and-peck style, on an Underwood typewriter. When I wanted to investigate the journalism schools at the University of Tennessee and the University of South Carolina, they rented a Winnebago and made it a road trip. And when I started this book, they constantly reminded me of the joy they would experience on the day it appeared in a bookstore and could serve as an inspiration to believers to take their walk with Christ to a new level and unbelievers to accept Christ.

My son, Austin, has been riding shotgun with me on this journey—not just the book, but my entire life. When he was born, I cried tears of joy, basking in the magnificence and innocence of a new life, but never did I picture that it would be *this* good, that he would so powerfully show me the beauty of viewing life through the eyes of an imaginative boy. How could I know that he would invite me into his bedroom, collect my imaginary ticket at the door, rip off his warm-up suit to reveal his two-sizes-too-small Katy Youth Basketball uniform and then play an entire game on the Huffy hoop mounted to his door, with a request that I handle the game clock? And then play out an entire 21-game season, keeping stats for high scorers and rebounders? How could I know that both of us would take this journey together after being diagnosed with Tourette Syndrome, and gain strength from each other's determination to rise above it? Do I really deserve a kid like this? Thank you, God.

My sister, Shirley, has been one of the key encouragers in my life. We survived some intense childhood battles for control of the channel knob of the TV—she wanted *That Girl* and I wanted that Lakers game—but we emerged relatively unscathed and moved into a beautiful adulthood relationship of mutual respect. She consoled me after I was dumped by my first love and then after my marriage broke down, always with gentleness and compassion. And how cool was it that I was able to call her at about 5 a.m. on her 40th birthday and tell her that her nephew had just been born?

All the way through this project, Jeri's precious parents humbly poured out their hearts, offering thanks and continually saying how honored they felt. This is just a small part of one of many e-mails Carolyn sent me: *Thanks again and again for all you are doing for Jeri and the book about her life!!! You amaze us with your love for Jeri and your dedication to see this book published for God's glory!!!* They opened up their home to me and made me feel like a trusted friend, not a journalist wondering how deeply to dig. Jeri was indeed very fortunate to have such loving parents.

Daryl was incredibly patient and understanding when I peppered him with questions, trying to elicit microscopic details about events I would have barely remembered if they had happened a year before, let alone 10 years. He entrusted me with Jeri's passionate, prayerful journals—a remarkable gesture that made this book come alive by allowing the reader to be taken straight into her heart. His wife, Charmel, exuded an extraordinary comfort level with my interrogations, never once making me feel like this project was an intrusion on their marriage.

Jeri's brother, Jayme, and sister, Amy, gave me so many evocative snapshots of her life. Jayme is the family's deep thinker, always able to eloquently describe not just the scenes that played out, but what they meant in the grand scheme. Amy's love for Jeri could never have been more poignant than when she pulled out the photo of her wedding, noting that Jeri's head was cocked in wonderment as she gazed at Amy in her gown.

Jeri's cousin, Jana James, and aunt, Oma James, provided me with a window into Jeri's soul—Oma with Jeri's early life and Jana with the last few months.

Grace Fellowship is incredibly blessed to be led by Jim and Lisa Leggett. When they started the church to be a "House of Prayer for All Nations," they created a place that doesn't just talk about prayer, but a place that passionately lives it out. In this place, Jeri was able to do what she most loved—talk to God, feel His presence, know Him intimately. Jeri loved Jim and Lisa with all her heart, and they loved her with theirs.

Thanks to those at Grace Fellowship who contributed in the interview process, offered stories about Jeri or provided encouragement: Katie Dolan, Christi Corbin, Brenda Martin, Karen Coolidge, Linda Piazza, Jane Wiley, Dixie and Waldo Leggett, Linda Alexander, Yvonne Chumchal, Cindi Lomax, Liz Jok, Deb Hubble, Brian Smith, A.J. Bass, Martha MacRae, Mitch Peairson, Rob Matchett, Morgan Pylant, Cindy Smith, Penny Nelson, Boyd Baker, Kathy Smit, Brenda Gerland, Russell Edwards, Tammy Hughey, Gloria Vela, Brian Wilkin and Wayne Kerr.

To other friends of Jeri's: Jana Terry, Suzanne Milligan Sansom and Sam Holm.

To the doctors, nurses and staff members at Stanford and Texas Children's Hospital, some of whom have since moved to other positions: Natalie Standlee, Kim Young, Dr. Bruce Reitz, Dr. Clinton Lloyd, Dr. Jeremy Feldman, Marguerite Brown and Dr. Ronald Grifka.

To Maryann Kovalewski, a fellow graduate of the great Penn State who offered numerous suggestions on how to reach people with this book and encouraged me not just to finish it, but to start another one.

To Michael Thilmony, who gave me insight into his beloved Cindy's relationship with Jeri after Cindy passed away on November 17, 2007.

To Jerry Jenkins and the fabulous authors and guest speakers at the Writing for the Soul Conference who stoked my imagination and gave me the tools to navigate the maze of book writing and publishing.

To Judy Lockhart, for tirelessly transcribing recordings of interviews.

To KSBJ music director Jim Beeler for historical information on "Blessed Be Your Name" and DJs Susan O'Donnell, Mike Kankelfritz, Liz Jordan and Joey K for positively influencing my walk with Christ, directly impacting this book.

To Xulon Press and Judy Gibbons, Jeff Fitzgerald and Karla Castellon, for enduring my obsession for doing things thoroughly.

And finally, to those who contributed financially to help make this book possible: Grace Fellowship, Brenda Gerland and Austin Bauer, Maryann Kovalewski and Julie Simpson.

All my love to everybody.

Printed in the United States
149544LV00004B/2/P